A Season of Renewal

A Season of Renewal

*The Columbian Exposition
and Victorian America*

DENNIS B. DOWNEY

Westport, Connecticut
London

Library of Congress Cataloging-in-Publication Data

Downey, Dennis B., 1952–
 A season of renewal : the Columbian Exposition and Victorian America / Dennis B.
Downey.
  p. cm.
 Includes bibliographical references and index.
 ISBN 0–275–97186–4 (alk. paper)
 1. United States—Civilization—1865–1918. 2. United States—Social life and
customs—1865–1918. 3. World's Columbian Exposition (1893 : Chicago, Ill.)—
Influence. 4. Technological innovations—Social aspects—United States—History—
19th century. 5. Social change—United States—History—19th century. 6. National
characteristics, American—History—19th century. I. Title.
 E169.1 .D695 2002
 973.8—dc21   2001021669

British Library Cataloguing in Publication Data is available.

Library of Congress Catalog Card Number: 2001021669
ISBN: 0–275–97186–4

First published in 2002

Praeger Publishers, 88 Post Road West, Westport, CT 06881
An imprint of Greenwood Publishing Group, Inc.
www.praeger.com

Printed in the United States of America

The paper used in this book complies with the
Permanent Paper Standard issued by the National
Information Standards Organization (Z39.48-1984).

10 9 8 7 6 5 4 3 2 1

to
Jean Ann and Bernard Louis Downey
and to
the memory of their parents

Contents

Photographic essay follows chapter three.

Acknowledgments

I began thinking and writing about the World's Columbian Exposition more than two decades ago. In the intervening years other scholarly projects have been engaged and completed. Though they have had their therapeutic benefits, it is nice to bring closure to this enterprise. Over the years I have accumulated a large number of debts. Numerous friends and fellow historians have helped to shape my thinking on Chicago's fair and its relationship to the cultural landscape of the 1890s, and I am pleased to be able to acknowledge their assistance.

Like all of my teaching and writing, this manuscript reflects the abiding influence of the late William D. Miller. Bill taught me by example to respect "the ways of long ago" and be skeptical of academic fads. Together with his wife Rhea and their children, he offered hospitality, community, and friendship. My only regret is that he did not live to see this study to publication.

Several friends have been important sounding boards. William A. Kerr, now a college president, is a valued friend and critic, a fellow traveler in pursuit of what Bill Miller called "clarification." Similarly, Dick Crepeau is much appreciated for his dry wit and unpretentious manner and for his comments on Henry Adams. Donald Yacovone, Frank Bremer, and James Jolly are good friends and good scholars, and I appreciate how they have indulged my ramblings about cultural history. Roger and Holly Webster are treasured friends who offered important words of encouragement in times of need. Jack Fischel has been a cooperative department chair, a friend whose intelligence and humor have helped to keep me on track. Michael Phayer, Karel Bicha, and especially Robert Hay provided valuable comments on an early version of this manuscript. At Praeger, Heather Staines, Jennifer Debo, and Linda

Robinson have been exceptionally patient and understanding. I thank them for their good judgment and kind attention to this work. I wish to acknowledge the perceptive comments of an anonymous reviewer for the press, whose discerning observations were extremely beneficial.

The Chicago Historical Society has been a gracious host for intermittent research sojourns over two decades. At every turn the staff has been generous and helpful. The Newberry Library, the Special Collections Division of the Chicago Public Library, and the Daniel Burnham Library of the Chicago Art Institute provided a welcoming spirit and valuable assistance in their collections. In this and other projects the research staff at the Library of Congress has been extremely cooperative. I would like to thank John Zukowsky, Susan Prendergast Schoelwer, and Archie Motley for their early encouragement. Marquette University and Millersville University provided financial assistance at various stages, and the latter provided released-time from an otherwise heavy teaching schedule. Millersville's Faculty Grants Committee has been generous in its support, as has the Ganser Library's library loan services.

On a more personal note, I thank my wife Traci for all that she is and all that she does. Traci is intelligent, generous, and unconditional in her love and encouragement. Together we have learned to appreciate what Clara Claiborne Park calls the "precious ordinariness" of everyday life. She is my true north, and everything that I am and that I believe is in relation to her. I thank Bernie, Maggie, Kara, Thomas, and Anna for the patience they have shown a father sometimes stuck in a previous century, and for their reminder to keep first things first. Finally, I dedicate this book to my parents (and their parents) as a small gesture toward the immeasurable debt I owe them.

Introduction

In Marietta Holley's *Samantha at the World's Fair*, one of several novels written about a visit to the 1893 Chicago world's fair, the precocious Samantha observed on her entrance to the magisterial Court of Honor, "Never agin'—never agin' will such a seen [*sic*] glow and grow before mine eyes, till the streets of the New Jerusalem open up before my vision." Sister Arvilly Lanfear of the same novel found this "marvelous City of Magic" "full and overflowin' of object lessons a teachin' of the greatness and the glory of the Lord of Heaven, and the might and power of the human intellect."[1]

The fictional Samantha and her companions were not alone in appropriating biblical imagery to give meaning and form to the World's Columbian Exposition. If Samantha could find the mirror image of the New Jerusalem—the "holy city coming down out of the heaven from God" in the words of *Revelation*—others likened the Chicago fair to the City Beautiful, or the more ethereal Celestial City of John Bunyan's *Pilgrim's Progress*. Commentators frequently used religious terms in describing this great world's fair, freely mixing sacred and secular imagery to define the most spectacular cultural event in Victorian America.

Over a six-month season beginning in May and ending in October 1893, Chicagoans hosted an international exhibition to commemorate Christopher Columbus's encounter with the New World and, in their words, to celebrate four centuries of human progress. A sweeping panorama of buildings and statuary built on six hundred acres of reclaimed swampland along the lake shore, the World's Columbian Exposition was a commercial enterprise of extraordinary cultural significance.

In many respects, the fair brought the world to America, and America to the world. More than any other world's fair to date, the Columbian Exposition brought international exhibitors to America to compete with the homegrown producers in a consumptive feast of unparalleled diversity. But the "encounters" sponsored by this Columbian exhibition were more than commercial. The fair also brought millions of international visitors to the United States and to Chicago for an unprecedented intermingling of peoples and cultures. The confluence of human activities along the fair's crowded corridors, and especially along the Midway Plaisance, added an important human dimension to the oft-told story of towering buildings and glistening exhibits.

Masculine and feminine images—Columbus and Columbia—mixed freely in the poetry and descriptive prose, as they did in the Exposition's central artistic feature, the Court of Honor.[2] Columbus was the personification of masculine vigilance and fortitude, and Columbia embodied feminine virtue and maternal strength—attributes that paralleled cultural understandings of gender roles in the era.

But actually, the thread of Columbus (and Columbia) as it ran through the season of days, tended to be overshadowed by a larger drama that was unfolding. From the opening day ceremonies to the season finale, the World's Columbian Exposition became a grand allegorical setting for a more nationalistic celebration of American institutions and ideas. In the words of its benefactors, the Chicago world's fair was a catalog of the intellectual, material, and artistic progress of the United States. Keeping with the religious spirit, the Exposition was said to be a "revelation" of Divine favor and human possibilities enshrined on the lakeshore of America's most rapidly industrializing city. Coming as it did during a period of unprecedented social reorganization in American life and in the midst of enormous economic upheaval weighted the Columbian Exposition with considerable cultural baggage.

The American historian Henry Adams provided the most telling observation on the Chicago fair when he wrote, "Chicago asked in 1893 for the first time the question of whether the American people knew where they were driving." Claiming uncertainty for himself, Adams professed in his autobiography that at Chicago his personal *education* began anew.[3] But Adams was not alone in associating the fair with the present state of American national development and with the larger workings of history. If Henry Adams found metaphysical meaning in the technological exhibits, other visitors were inspired by the Nubian dancers of the Streets of Cairo concession on the Midway Plaisance, where the anatomical gyrations of exotic young girls seemed to defy the laws of physics and Victorian propriety. In the minds of most visitors, the Columbian Exposition offered new and novel opportunities for education and for entertainment, and few persons were disappointed in their visit to Jackson Park.

A mood of festive celebration informed the Columbian Exposition, and the celebratory rhetoric reflected a self-conscious pride that was not uncommon for great fairs in the late nineteenth century. In its exhibits and programs—in its form and spirit—the fair combined elements of retrospection and speculation with a decidedly American emphasis. Historical displays mingled with the latest mechanical devices, emblems of a receding past and a future coming into clearer focus. At Chicago in 1893 the past was venerated, but only as a preamble to future progress.

The same year that Chicago hosted the Columbian Exposition, Josiah Strong published a work of social criticism, which he entitled *The New Era; Or the Coming Kingdom*. In a critique laden with assumptions about the present aspect of American life, Strong said that America had come to an end and a beginning in its national development.[4] With words that foreshadowed Frederick Jackson Turner's "frontier thesis," which would be delivered in July to the Exposition's Congress of Historians, Strong claimed that America was poised at the dawn of a "new era" of history unlike any that had preceded it. Combining a supernatural faith with a faith in human progress, Strong wrote of the nineteenth century as a "time of preparation" for the "new era" of order and beneficence that would unfold in the twentieth century. "Everywhere the old order is changing and giving way to the new," he declared in an apocalyptic tone. Science, which Strong judged "as truly a revelation from God and of God as the Scriptures," and the "march of democracy" had cooperated to "remove an immense amount of rubble which lay in the path of progress."[5] The new century would be the American Century, a time in which the greatness and goodness of America would unfold in a glorious realization of national destiny and providential design.

Josiah Strong's faith in a "new era" incorporated elements of Christian evangelism and nineteenth-century liberalism to buttress what might be thought of as the "religion of American progress." For a generation enamored of natural evolution and notions of social hierarchy, Strong's invocation of Science as a complement to Scripture provided a powerful rationale for the status quo in American life. In a manner reminiscent of an enduring millennial impulse in American social thought, Strong's *The New Era* followed a jeremiad tradition with its promise of a new beginning filled with sacramental meaning. Furthermore, Strong refashioned sentiments of exceptionalism and national destiny to help his generation interpret the revolutionary changes of their own time.[6] But unlike Edward Bellamy's *Looking Backward* (1888) and Frank Baum's *The Wonderful Wizard of Oz* (1900), Strong gave a literal meaning to biblical allusions to a "new heaven and a new earth."

The Chicago world's fair was consciously identified with this notion of a "new era," a belief that America in the 1890s had come to an end and a beginning in its national development. In a manner similar to Josiah Strong's polemic, as well as Frederick Jackson Turner's "frontier thesis," the Exposition embodied what John Higham has called the "myth of American newness." For all of its importance as an international exhibition, the rhetoric that defined the fair to a national audience had a decided "American-centeredness."[7]

From the opening ceremonies through the closing events six months later, the Exposition was likened to the handmaiden of progress, ushering in a new and unprecedented phase of human history. And like Josiah Strong, the fair's champions informed their self-congratulatory rhetoric with powerful religious allusions. This deliberate and repeated appropriation of sacred imagery to give meaning to a commercial enterprise is an important reminder of the place of religion in the public culture of late nineteenth-century America.

One finds in the Columbian Exposition elements of American civil religion, what Robert Bellah describes as "that religious dimension . . . through which it [a people] interprets its historical experience in the light of transcendent reality."[8] This "civic faith," to borrow Martin Marty's expression, reflected a commonplace tendency to appropriate religious signs and sentiments—to blend history and theology—to give meaning to public ceremonies.[9] This willingness to associate American national development with a transcendent authority had deep cultural roots and reverberated throughout the Exposition season and the cultural landscape in 1893. The "continuing biblical and republican traditions" that Bellah places at the heart of public discourse in American life were repeatedly and deliberately invoked in the popular commentary to provide meaning for the Columbian Exposition and its efforts to define the contours of a national society in the 1890s.[10] As Victorian America's preeminent civic pageant, the Chicago world's fair was seen as a veritable "sacramental season," which combined the themes of Protestantism and Nationalism in a benediction of triumphant democracy and American exceptionalism.[11]

In one of the era's supreme ironies, Chicago's festival to American progress opened the very week that instability in the national trading markets gave notice of a coming economic depression, the Panic of 1893. And in this sense, the timing of this world's fair could not have been more significant. For Chicagoans and other Americans, the 1880s was perhaps the most tumultuous decade of social and economic change in the nation's brief history. Rapid industrialization and urbanization, accompanied by the quickening pace of foreign immigration by decade's end, contributed to an accelerated reordering of modes of production that influenced a broad spectrum of social relations. A rising level of labor conflict in the northern states and pervasive racial violence in the old Confederacy lent greater weight to the discontents that surfaced during years of economic decline.

With memories of the 1886 Haymarket tragedy still fresh in residents' minds, Chicago moved to secure the right to host an international exhibition to commemorate four centuries of American progress. And as management settled on the issue of an appropriate site in late 1890, the western Indian wars were brought to an unceremonial conclusion at Wounded Knee.

It seemed that ancient antagonisms and new causes of dissension were threatening the fragile equilibrium of a nation less than a generation removed from its own Civil War. Champions of the Exposition were not unaware of these tensions, but they did address them from a particular cultural perspective, which came to inform the enterprise.

My reading of the Columbian Exposition is similar to what Robert Bellah describes in a different context as a "representative character," or what late-century observers called an "object lesson." I conceive of the Columbian Exposition as a civic ritual invested with great cultural meaning, a representative event or "kind of symbol . . . by which we can bring together in one concentrated image the way people in a given social environment organize and give meaning and direction to their lives."[12] I am aware that this approach to culture studies has fallen out of favor with some scholars. But, I would suggest that it has a meaning and utility in trying to come to terms with so diverse an enterprise as the Columbian Exposition.

I do not conceive of "culture" in a formal anthropological or linguistic sense, although any theory of culture per se involves a "view of man" in a social environment. Nor do I embrace completely a theory of cultural hegemony that has come to inform so much of recent writings in cultural history, as well as scholarly judgments on the Columbian Exposition. Like the Columbian Encounter itself, the Exposition literature can be read to reveal as much about historical understandings as present-day discontents. Readers interested in the historiographical and ideological debate surrounding world's fairs may wish to consult the critical biographical essay at the end of this volume.

With respect to the study at hand, I imagine the contours of culture in a broader, literary sense, which finds common ground with what some ethnohistorians have said about the process of cultural exchange.[13] "Among other things," Sacvan Bercovitch has suggested in a way that makes sense to me, "culture is how people interpret and what they believe." I think of culture as a creative conversation, what R. W. B. Lewis described as "a protracted and broadly ranging conversation: at best a dialogue" on the salient issues that every historical generation faces. "So long as it is vital," Robert Bellah has written in a similar vein, "the cultural tradition of a people is always an argument about the meaning of the destiny its members share. Cultures are dramatic conversations about things that matter to their participants, and American culture is no exception."[14]

Cultural conversations are composed of different and diverse and conflicting voices—some would say "official" and "vernacular"—that nonetheless share similar preoccupations and interests.[15] Such conversations not only engage the dominant voices of a generation, they also reveal the voices of dissent, the proverbial "other" on the margins of institutional power. As viewed in public ceremonies like the Columbian Exposition, such conversations may also incorporate elements of retrospection or remembrance with speculation about future developments. Lawrence Levine has written persuasively of the tendency to remember coupled with a willingness to prophesy as the "central paradox of American history," and I believe the Columbian Exposition is a case in point.[16] One finds in the Chicago world's fair elements of retrospection or nostalgia, coexisting with themes of progress and speculation about the future. I would add that this tendency to remembrance, at least as embodied in the fair, was shaped in large part by the sustaining influence of religious signs and symbols as an ordering point in public discourse and private belief.

Where these dialogues—these communities of discourse—converge in their interests, one finds the basis of a common culture. If grounded in the social realities of the times, such an approach to culture studies will allow us to recover the notion that there are shared assumptions and preoccupations that inform every historical generation. It is worth noting that these tenets do not necessarily derive from a shared historical experience on the part of all participants. (Immigrants, for example, often lived quite comfortably in a world of dual allegiances as they negotiated the boundaries of their ethnic community and mainstream society.) It is possible to speak of and write about a common foundation for social life, while allowing for the sharp contrasts and conflicting tendencies evident in every historical period. Subversive voices engage dominant voices, and together they negotiate contested cultural terrain in a process of "brokering," which apostles of rigid cultural hierarchy have not always recognized.

"Culture as conversation," which has important implications in world's fair studies, makes it possible to accommodate forms of expression that do not fall neatly into the categories of "highbrow," "middlebrow," and "lowbrow," the bifurcation between consensus and conflict schools, or the debate over Modernist and Antimodernist sensibilities.[17] One can thus imagine architects and artists, social reformers and entrepreneurs, feminists and housewives, laborers and managers, and scientists and philosophers, as well as common folk and the custodians of high culture, engaging in a loosely organized but substantive dialogue on the salient issues of the day. Such an approach gives to culture a dynamic quality and provides a more inclusive and elastic framework that is respectful of historical realities.

In the wealth of popular commentary, in the richness of recollections and remembrances of visits to Jackson Park in 1893, it is possible to discern the features of a creative conversation (or parallel conversations). This conversation had as its chief object of concern the merits and meaning of the Columbian Exposition; it also had a broader intention. The Chicago fair became the focal point for a consideration of the present aspect of American national development at the end of the nineteenth century. In an age of fundamental transformation and reorganization, an age of turmoil and tumult in which the existence of a common culture and national identity was being questioned by the forces of economic consolidation and social change, the Exposition was the staging ground for a dramatic dialogue on what Henry Adams called in 1894 the "tendency of history."[18]

It is with this approach to culture in mind that I have attempted to incorporate the diverse commentary on the fair into the framework of this book. Each chapter, more or less, is organized around a series of observations about the fair, be they the expressed ideas of Henry Adams, Frances Willard, William Dean Howells, Ida B. Wells, Edgar Lee Masters, or an immigrant girl named Hilda Satt. I have tried to allow the different and diverse people who find their way into this narrative to speak for themselves, to allow their voices to be heard. Each chapter is further arranged around a series of creative tensions, or dualisms, which were present in the Exposition ensemble and evident in the broader cultural climate of Victorian America.

One finds, for example, a contrast between the commercial and cultural imperatives of the Exposition itself, as well as practical conflict between the international, national, and local dimensions of the event. In the buildings and exhibits, visitors saw other tensions present in society: an artistic and mechanical ideal, themes of progress and nostalgia, domesticity and feminism in the women's programs, and the contrast between elite and mass entertainment. By denying black Americans an official role in Exposition affairs, the management further exaggerated one of the most striking contrasts in the so-called White City. And by following a policy of exclusion in the program of days, the directors perhaps unknowingly amplified the growing tension between natives and newcomers in American life, while giving immigrant groups their own voice. Although the directors sought to distinguish between so-called highbrow and lowbrow entertainment, those boundaries did not always hold in the schedule of events or in the popular culture of the day.

In my reckoning of the larger importance of the event, the Columbian Exposition was part of what I would call a "culture of renewal" that permeated the last decade of the nineteenth century. "Renewal" in this sense had an elastic quality that could accommodate a respect for the past with a sense of expectancy for future possibilities. In the summer's deteriorating social and economic conditions, a heightened sense of urgency came to inform cultural discourse, and it gave to this rhetoric of renewal an immediacy to events. One need look no further than the Exposition's wide-ranging social reform congresses for evidence of a rhetorical tradition that while mindful of serious imbalances maintained a faith amounting to a kind of religious belief in a new order. In its rituals and rhetoric, the fair reaffirmed the possibilities of renewal and reinvention in a time of profound social and economic reorganization.

Although expressed in different forms, the melody of renewal has had a recurrent quality throughout American literary history. Embedded in the rhetoric of the Puritan jeremiad and passed on to succeeding generations, the theme of renewal was remade and refashioned to meet the changing circumstances of national life in the nineteenth century.[19] Present in Revolutionary ideology as well as Emersonian individualism, the rhetoric of renewal was consciously appropriated by Josiah Strong in *The New Era*. In its most imaginative form, this rhetorical tradition possessed a quality of romantic innocence that interpreted American experience in terms of *promise* and *progress* conferred by a transcendent authority. As critics of American exceptionalism have pointed out, however, such an ideology could just as easily obscure from view the harsher realities of national life.[20]

When visitors to the Columbian Exposition associated the fair with the biblical "New Jerusalem," they were not merely engaging in rhetorical excesses. This rhetoric of renewal, as I would call it, resonated in the culture, and it had a meaning for people in the late nineteenth century. I can think of no better parallel for purposes of illustration than a new song heard regularly throughout the summer of 1893. Combining themes of pastoral innocence and divine authority, "America, the Beautiful" gave the possibilities of national renewal a redemptive or regenerative quality. Americans were drawn to the song's lyrical melody and sustaining imagery and to its overt patriotism in a way that resembled the appeal of the Chicago world's fair, itself a ritual of renewal. It was no accident that "America, the Beautiful" became the unofficial anthem of the Exposition season.

My interest in the study at hand is not to celebrate the Columbian Exposition but rather to explore what its celebratory rhetoric reveals about an emerging national society struggling to reconcile conflicting tendencies in its passage from a rural and agrarian to an urban and industrial order. In this effort, I have operated (somewhat cautiously) from the belief that those who spoke of the fair meant what they said, and I have resisted a tendency to "deconstruct" their words to conform to more contemporary sensibilities.

The Columbian Exposition was not simply a nostalgic retreat into the American past, as some critics have claimed. It was more than a "grand illusion" detached from social realities, as one recent study has suggested.[21] The Chicago world's fair offered instead a deliberate and meaningful engagement of the present aspect of American society near century's end. However imperfectly its embrace of national renewal was realized, the fair bore a striking relationship to its times.

Those familiar with the Chicago world's fair remember the first Ferris Wheel positioned on the Midway Plaisance or the sparkling marble-like edifices beside the lake. Even the apocryphal story of Little Egypt's presence has been passed down from generation to generation. But what has been overlooked is the Exposition's most potent piece of statuary, the allegorical *Statue of the Republic*. Designed by Daniel Chester French, the *Republic* was not only the tallest piece of sculpture ever cast in America (to that time), it stood at center stage in the Court of Honor as a reminder of the nation's noblest and highest ideals. Like the better-remembered *Statue of Liberty* dedicated in 1886, the *Republic* represented maternal strength and domestic stability.[22] Whereas *Liberty* was a gift from France, *Republic* was homegrown; and in 1893 the two feminine images encouraged national confidence and self-assurance. *Liberty* looked to the ocean and the East to greet incoming immigrants. As the most telling figure of renewal in the Exposition ensemble, *Republic* looked quite deliberately across the central basin to the prairie and the West beyond.

In its celebration of American life, the Columbian Exposition revealed more than its promoters intended. As a meaningful symbol, the Chicago world's fair reflected and gave fresh expression to the subversive voices of dissent. In the exhibits and the program of days, and in the unprecedented number of social reform congresses, one finds the dominant voices of the era—dominant in terms of class, race, and gender interests—and the presence of social critics who were more cautious in their expressions of approval of the present state of affairs. For a country still struggling with deep-seated, seemingly ancient antagonisms, as well as new challenges and conundrums, Chicago's Columbian Exposition was a place of remembrance and renewal. Throughout its season Americans participated in a far-ranging conversation, a dramatic dialogue that engaged diverse voices on the present aspect of national development. Wrapped in Renaissance finery and hailed as the handmaiden of progress, the Chicago fair was a fitting symbol to the age—a symbol that by its very nature encapsulated the prevailing sentiments and conflicting ideals in American life.

Notes

1. Marietta Holley, *Samantha at the World's Fair* (New York, 1893), pp. 235, 226.

2. On the multiple uses of Columbian imagery in the late nineteenth century, see Thomas J. Schlereth, "Columbia, Columbus, and Columbianism," *Journal of American History* 79 (December 1992): 951–68.

3. Henry Adams, *The Education of Henry Adams* (1918; Boston, 1961), see especially pp. 339–43 for Adams's comments on the fair.

4. Josiah Strong, *The New Era; Or the Coming Kingdom* (Chicago, 1893).

5. Strong, pp. 10–12.

6. On the enduring power of millennialism and an apocalyptic view of history in American thought, see Ernest L. Tuveson, *Redeemer Nation: The Idea of America's Millennial Role* (Chicago, 1968); Catherine Albanese, *Sons of the Father: The Civil Religion of the American Revolution* (Philadelphia, 1976); Ruth Bloch, *Visionary Republic: Millennial Themes in American Thought, 1756–1800* (New York, 1985); Paul Boyer, *When Time Shall Be No More: Prophecy Belief in Modern American Culture* (Cambridge, Mass., 1991).

7. John Higham, "The Future of American History," *Journal of American History* 80 (March 1994): 1292–94.

8. Robert N. Bellah, *The Broken Covenant: American Civil Religion in Time of Trial* (New York, 1975), p. 3.

9. Marty's quote is found in his Introduction to Albanese, p. xii. On the relationship of history to theology in public ceremonies, see David Glassberg, *American Historical Pageantry: The Uses of Tradition in the Early Twentieth Century* (Chapel Hill, 1990), pp. 9–14.

10. Robert N. Bellah et al., *Habits of the Heart: Individualism and Commitment in American Life* (Berkeley, 1985), p. 37; George Armstrong Kelly, "Civil Religion," in *Politics and Religious Consciousness in America* (New Brunswick, N.J., 1985), pp. 209–46.

11. Leigh Eric Schmidt, *Holy Fairs: Scottish Communions and American Revivals in the Early Modern Period* (Princeton, 1990). The issue of exceptionalism is of continuous controversy to cultural historians. Jack Greene finds the origins of exceptionalism's confidence in the era of the American Revolution. See Jack P. Greene, *The Intellectual Construction of America: Exceptionalism and Identity from 1492 to 1800* (Chapel Hill, 1993). Other key recent works on exceptionalism include Ian Tyrrell, "American Exceptionalism in an Age of International History," *American Historical Review* 96 (October 1991): 1031–55; Dorothy Ross, "Historical Consciousness in Nineteenth-Century America," *AHR* 89 (October 1984): 912–19; Byron E. Shafer, ed., *Is America Different? A New Look at American Exceptionalism* (New York, 1991); Michael Kammen, "The Problem of American Exceptionalism: A Reconsideration," *American Quarterly* 45 (March 1993): 1–43. David M. Wrobel's study *The End of American Exceptionalism: Frontier Anxiety from the Old West to the New Deal* (Lawrence, 1993) only incidentally touches on the subject in a broader consideration of frontier mythology.

12. Bellah et al., p. 39.

13. David Hackett Fischer's *Albion's Seed* (New York, 1989), Richard White's *The Middle Ground* (New York, 1991), and Daniel K. Richter's *Ordeal of the Long-House* (Chapel Hill, 1992) have shaped my thinking about the process of cultural and social exchange in American history. I should note more conventional works of literary and intellectual history: R. W. B. Lewis, *The American Adam: Innocence, Tragedy, and Tradition in the Nineteenth Century* (Chicago, 1955); Michael Kammen, *Mystic Chords of Memory: The Transformation of Tradition in American Culture* (New York, 1991); Robert Crunden, *Ministers of Reform: The Progressive Achievement in American Civilization, 1889–1920* (New York, 1982); T. J. Jackson Lears, *No Place of Grace: Antimodernism and the Transformation of American Culture, 1880–1920* (New York, 1981).

14. Sacvan Bercovitch, "Introduction: The Music of America," in *The Rites of Assent: Transformations in the Symbolic Construction of America* (New York and London, 1993), p. 12; Lewis, *The American Adam*, p. 2; Bellah et al., p. 27.

15. John Bodnar, *Remaking America: Public Memory, Commemoration, and Patriotism in the Twentieth Century* (Princeton 1992), esp. pp. 13–20; Michael Frisch, "American History and the Structures of Collective Memory," *Journal of American History* 75 (March 1989): 1130–55.

16. Lawrence W. Levine, "Progress and Nostalgia: The Self Image of the Nineteen Twenties," *The Unpredictable Past: Explorations in American Cultural History* (New York, 1993), p. 191.

17. Several important works on cultural bifurcation are of note here. See, for instance, Lawrence W. Levine, *Highbrow/Lowbrow: The Emergence of Cultural Hierarchy in America* (Cambridge, Mass., 1988); Joan Shelley Rubin, *The Making of Middle-brow Culture* (Chapel Hill, 1991); John Bodnar, *Remaking America: Public Memory, Commemoration, and Patriotism in the Twentieth Century* (Princeton, 1992).

18. Henry Adams, "The Tendency of History [1894]," in *The Degradation of the Democratic Dogma* (1919; New York, 1969), pp. 125–33.

19. Sacvan Bercovitch, "The Ritual of Consensus" and "The Typology of Mission, from Edwards to Independence," in *The Rites of Assent: Transformations in the Symbolic Construction of America* (New York, 1993), pp. 29–67, 147–67, respectively.

20. Bercovitch, "The Ritual of Consensus," pp. 29–67.

21. Neil Harris et al., *Grand Illusions: Chicago's World's Fair of 1893* (Chicago, 1993).

22. Alan Dawley, *Struggles for Justice: Social Responsibility and the Liberal State* (Cambridge, Mass., 1991), pp. 1, 17. Both Chauncey Depew and Grover Cleveland played important roles in the dedication ceremonies for both the *Statue of Liberty* and the Columbian Exposition.

Prologue

As President Grover Cleveland looked out from behind the curtain of his Lexington Hotel window shortly after dawn on May 1, 1893, the day did not appear to hold any special promise. A torrent of rain had fallen in Chicago during the preceding week, and the lingering blanket of dark clouds suggested that a damp, dreary day was in store for him. Cleveland had come to Chicago to help open its world's fair, one of the duties he was obliged to perform by the nature of his office. Chicago's fair was known formally as the World's Columbian Exposition, an international exhibition to celebrate the four hundredth anniversary of Christopher Columbus's discovery of the New World. Popular fancy had already dubbed the event the "White City" because of the appearance of its principal buildings.

Unknown to the president, several miles south at the fairgrounds a British journalist contemplated the weather as he meandered through a deserted Jackson Park. "The great city rose like a dusty Venice out of an Adriatic of mud," he remembered.

The great white city which rose before me, silent and awful, seemed to belong to an order of things above the common world. . . . The cluster of buildings hung together there in a sort of city in the clouds, yet severe and unmistakable in outline. It was a vision of the ideal, enhaloed in mystery.[1]

As President and Mrs. Cleveland breakfasted, Chicagoans jammed the platforms of the Alley L, the elevated train that serviced Jackson Park and the fairgrounds. Among the thousands of invited guests in town for the occasion were the Duke and Duchess of Veragua, the lineal descendants of

Christopher Columbus. Shortly after nine o'clock, a bugler's signal started the procession of several dozen carriages filled with visiting dignitaries on a southbound trek to the park. Thousands of spectators lined Michigan Avenue and saluted as the Clevelands passed, flanked by the celebrated Chicago Hussars and legions of military troops. For more than an hour the parade of celebrities made its way along congested streets through South Side neighborhoods, cheered along by enthusiastic crowds.

At the western entrance to the fairgrounds, the procession turned east to enter the Midway Plaisance, and down the so-called Avenue of Nations the carriages continued, greeted by residents of the international villages. Egyptians, Samoans, Laplanders, tribesmen of Dahomey, and the maidens of Eire were among those who cheered the celebrities. Above the roar of lions in Professor Hagenbeck's zoological menagerie, the faint strains of "America, the Beautiful" could be heard from some distant band. Once inside the main grounds, Cleveland and the others were ushered quickly to the Grand Plaza platform at the steps of the Administration Building. Fifteen hundred Columbian Guards separated the crowd of a half-million spectators, some of whom had stood for hours in ankle-deep mud to be part of the festivities. As the president looked out over the sea of humanity sprawled across the Court of Honor, its towering classical facades and statuary must have seemed more reminiscent of ancient Rome than of the most rapidly industrializing city in the country. The Duke and Duchess of Veragua could not help but be taken aback at a spectacle that had all the outward markings of the Renaissance, positioned on the shoreline of Lake Michigan.

When, a few minutes past eleven, President Cleveland appeared on the platform with Governor John Altgeld and the Spanish nobles, the tide of humanity lunged forward as manners and courtesies were abandoned. Sensing the crowd's impatience, maestro Theodore Thomas put his one hundred and fourteen–member Columbian Orchestra (billed as the largest in the world) through the paces of John Paine's *Columbian March*, a spirited piece commissioned for the day. The ploy had little effect on the audience, and it was not until the Reverend W. H. Wilburn, the blind chaplain of the United States Senate, offered a benediction that the multitude assumed what the *Chicago Daily Tribune* called a "respectful obeisance."[2]

Once again the crowd became restless as Miss Jean Couthoui extolled Christopher Columbus's foresight in what seemed to many an especially lengthy recitation of W. A. Croffut's poem "The Prophecy." Thomas's orchestra performed the overture to Wagner's *Rienzi*, but for many people, anxiety had given way to boredom and to speculation about the nature of the tall, shrouded figure that stood at the far end of the central basin.

Few persons heard George Davis, the Exposition's Director-General, when he summed up the central theme of this world's fair. "It is our hope," Davis intoned above the noise, "that this great Exposition may inaugurate a new era of moral and material progress and our fervent aspiration that the association of nations here may secure not only warmer and stronger friendships but lasting peace throughout the world."[3] When President Cleveland rose from his chair to follow Davis to the podium, a contagious cheer rippled through the mass of humanity that now filled the entire Court of Honor.

In his remarks, Cleveland praised Chicago, marveling at the "stupendous results of American enterprise and activity" that surrounded him. But he was quick to temper his national pride with a note of caution. "The enthusiasm with which we contemplate our work," he reminded his listeners, "intensifies the warmth of greeting we extend to those who have come from foreign lands to illustrate with us the growth and progress of human endeavor in the direction of higher civilization." As the chief executive extolled the beneficence of American progress, a band of seventy-five Sioux Indians listened intently from the balcony of the Administration Building. It was less than three years since the incident at Wounded Knee, and here these Sioux stood observing the festival to American greatness. At one point, reported the *Tribune*, an elderly chief turned to his companions and in a disapproving tone grunted, "Cleveland!," to which the others nodded their heads in silent agreement.[4]

While his eyes scanned a page of notes, the president's forefinger blindly sought out a telegraph key at his side. "We have built these splendid edifices," Cleveland proclaimed with a gesture to the crowd, "but we have also built the fabric of popular government, whose grand proportions are seen throughout the world." "Let us hold fast to the meaning that underlies these ceremonies," he implored his fellow citizens as his finger found the key and maestro Thomas raised his baton, "and let us not lose the impressiveness of this moment. As by a touch the machinery that gives life to this vast Exposition is now set in motion, so at the same instant, let our hopes and aspirations awaken new forces which in all time to come shall influence the welfare, dignity, and the freedom of mankind."[5]

With that, the president turned sideways on cue and gently pressed his finger to the gilded telegraph key, which directed an electrical current across three thousand feet of wire to a mammoth switchboard in the Palace of Mechanic Arts. Instantly, to the president's and everyone else's delight, cannons boomed and steam whistles shrieked, flags and bunting unfurled from the tops of buildings, and a gigantic American flag waved over the speakers' platform. From the distant caverns of the power plant there came at first a dull roar and then the quickening cadence of the leviathan Allis-Corliss quadruple expansion engine and the legion of lesser machines that breathed life into the Exposition. Simultaneously, the tritons and mermaids and dolphins in the Columbian Fountain appeared to come to life and frolic amid the spray of one hundred and sixty-eight jets, which sent water two hundred feet in the air. At the opposite end of the basin the shroud was loosed to reveal the statue *Republic*, the gilded image of a woman standing sixty feet tall.

Behind her stood the magisterial Peristyle, with the figure of Columbus atop the imperial *Quadriga* looking back across the basin to the figure of Columbia proudly at the helm of the allegorical *Ship of State*.[6]

The crowd's roar of approval was deafening, and its infectious cheer enraptured even the stolid Sioux. "One of them started to yell," the *Tribune* noted, "and the others quickly took it up and for a few moments the upper dome resounded with the yell that from the eventful day in October 1492, to the present has been more often the cry of battle and death than the tribute to progress and civilization." As the applause faded, the crowd scattered across the court joined the Columbian Chorus in singing "America, the Beautiful." The old chief, who the paper was certain "did not understand the sentiment," listened intently for a moment and then began to hum the melody with his tribesmen. When the song was finished the Indians gave one more yell with the crowd below. Those who had the presence of mind to look skyward found the sun in all of its brilliance shining down on the festivities. For some, this was a transcendent moment filled with patriotism and national pride, the likes of which they would never witness again. For Jane Addams of Hull House, however, this day would be remembered for another reason. In that exultant moment of community, a thief snatched her purse and disappeared into the throng.

Notes

1. "The Opening of the World's Fair," *Review of Reviews* 7 (January–June 1893): 656.

2. *Chicago Daily Tribune* (hereafter CDT), 2 May 1893; Daniel H. Burnham, "Final Report of the Director of Works of the World's Columbian Exposition," 8 vols. (Chicago, 1894), 7:5, Papers of Daniel H. Burnham, Burnham Library of the Art Institute of Chicago; *Daily Columbian*, 1 May 1893.

3. CDT, 2 May 1893.

4. CDT, 2 May 1893.

5. *Chicago Times*, 2 May 1893; *Dedicatory and Opening Ceremonies of the World's Columbian Exposition*, ed. under the direction of the Joint Committee on Ceremonies (Chicago, 1893); Benjamin Truman, *History of the World's Fair* (Chicago, 1893), p. 160.

6. CDT, 2 May 1893; Burnham, "Final Report," 2: 65–67. The *Tribune* reported that there was a false start on the water pumps, allowing for the immediate burst as Cleveland pressed the key. The Allis engine had been tested only once prior to the ceremonies, and there was some concern that it would not operate properly.

1

⁓

Building the Altrurian City

Standing along the great basin, with eyes uplifted to the imposing *Statue of the Republic*, William Dean Howells's fictional Altrurian Traveller was filled with emotion. "I was at home once more," Aristides Homos recalled of his visit to the World's Columbian Exposition, "and my heart overflowed with patriotic rapture in this strange land, so remote from ours in everything, that at times Altruria really seemed to me the dream which the Americans think it." "It is like our own cities in being a design," this otherworldly wanderer explained to his fellow Altrurian Cyril, "the effect of a principle, and not the straggling and shapeless accretion of accident."[1] For Howells as Homos, the Exposition stood in sharp contrast to the character of life in modern American cities, and its artistic ensemble reflected a unity of purpose he found absent in American life. For Howells's fictional Altrurian, as for many Americans in the summer of 1893, the Exposition's monumental beauty seemed, at least on the surface, an authentic incarnation of the nation's highest ideals.

Variously known as the White City, the Dream City, the Magic City, and finally the Vanished City after its destruction in a post-season fire, the 1893 Chicago world's fair lingered long in the imaginations of its visitors. For some of a religious bent, the Exposition took on the form of the biblical New Jerusalem, and for others it seemed to revitalize the dream of promise and progress in a more temporal mode. Architectural critic Montgomery Schuyler applauded the ensemble's transformative power: "The whole is better than any of its parts and greater than all its parts; the effect is one and indivisible." "It is what you will," Schuyler wrote, "so long as you will not take it for an American city of the nineteenth century, nor its architecture for the actual or the possible or even the ideal architecture of such a city."[2] Enamored of the Exposition's Altrurian possibilities of national renewal, Chicago reformer Charles Zueblin found the enterprise "a prophecy of what we could do if content with nothing but the best . . . it [the fair] was a miniature of an ideal city; a symbol of regeneration."[3]

The design of the 1893 World's Columbian Exposition represented an unprecedented collaboration of American artists, engineers, and architects. Never before had so many talented and creative designers cooperated in a municipal project on the scale of the Chicago world's fair. Contemporary observers associated the spirit of the Italian Renaissance with this most American of endeavors, and later historians have judged the fair to be the crowning achievement of an "American Renaissance" in arts and letters.[4] Reminiscent of the Italian model, commercial and cultural agendas informed the Chicago fair, creating a tension between mercantile and artistic interests that was also present in the larger urban landscape of Victorian America. The conflict between commercial and aesthetic interests also exaggerated other tensions in the management and construction of the enterprise.

The Exposition's designers had as their collective intention the creation of a powerful statement of the possibilities of urban life in the industrial age. In its towering edifices and well-manicured lawns and in the careful arrangement of its parts, the so-called White City was to serve as a model for future urban planning. The power of art—of beauty—might redeem and renew the rough features of America's sprawling and unplanned industrial wastelands. Any intimation of cultural heirarchies was unintended by the architects, engineers, and artists who labored to build what became the embodiment of Howells's Altrurian metropolis by the lakeshore.

Depending on how one measures the meaning of the expression, the 1893 Columbian Exposition was one of a dozen or more international exhibitions or world's fairs in the last half of the nineteenth century. Beginning with London's 1851 Crystal Palace in Hyde Park, international exhibitions flourished during an age of Western commercial and cultural expansion. In contrast to local and national fairs of the eighteenth and early nineteenth centuries, so-called world's fairs were, in the words of Burton Benedict, a "phenomenon of industrial capitalism." Producers from participating countries, now called exhibitors, demonstrated their wares in specific competitive categories in an effort to appeal to an emerging middle-class consumer culture. Manufactured products and heavy machinery were given privileged status in these great fairs, and the display of novel technological apparatus proved an indispensable drawing card. International exhibitions were not only an acknowledgment of the expanding trans-Atlantic market economy, as "tournaments of industry" they quickly became anthems to modernization at the end of the nineteenth century.[5]

In addition to being genuflections to the industrial revolution, international exhibitions were also urban enterprises. Great cities vied for the right to host world's fairs, as much to promote commercial growth as to demonstrate their degree of cultural refinement. Separate spaces within cities were set aside for the exhibitions' use, often creating the effect of a city within a city. But as the scope and scale of world's fairs grew, their nature and importance changed as well. By the time (1890) Chicago secured the right to host a Columbian celebration, great fairs had evolved into monumental extravaganzas that touted the prowess of the host country and city. Greatness and bigness were synonymous in the Victorian era, in cities and in world's fairs. Each successive fair sought to outdo its predecessor not only in size but also in an ever more comprehensive and sophisticated ensemble of buildings and grounds and exhibits.[6]

Late nineteenth-century expositions built upon and transformed the legacy of the Crystal Palace Exhibition, and as a result their nature changed substantially. Exhibitions in the 1870s and 1880s were emporiums of consumer capitalism, but they were also purported purveyors of culture. As "statements" of civic and national character for the host country, world's fairs were routinely commissioned to commemorate great historic events in the life of a nation.

As their planners became more preoccupied with greatness, fairs developed more elaborate ensembles and more sophisticated categories of exhibits. To attract larger crowds and to guarantee that patrons returned for subsequent visits, international exhibitions developed new forms of entertainment to accompany the expanding array of exhibits. London (1851) had its Crystal Palace, Philadelphia (1876) had its Tower of Light, and Paris (1878) had the Trocadero and, in 1889, the Eiffel Tower. Chicago, in its effort to upstage the Eiffel Tower, commissioned George Ferris to design the world's first Ferris Wheel.

In the four decades which followed the Crystal Palace, no fewer than ten international exhibitions were held, all but three hosted by European cities. And only two cities posted profits (Paris in 1867 and 1889, and Chicago in 1893).

Perhaps the most ambitious world's fair in the interval between the Crystal Palace and the Columbian Exposition was Paris's 1889 Universal Exposition (see Table 1.1). Commissioned to celebrate the hundredth anniversary of the French Revolution, the Universal Exposition was set on more than two hundred acres beside the Champ de Mars and the Seine River. Seven general categories, ranging in interest from industrial machinery and fine arts to horticulture, contained more than sixty thousand exhibits. Towering more than nine hundred feet above the decorative French Renaissance buildings, including the mammoth Galerie des Machines, was Alexander Gustav Eiffel's steel tower. Reflecting Eiffel's experience as a bridge engineer and the growing influence of the Art Nouveau movement, the Eiffel Tower remained after the exhibition as the most famous landmark in Paris.[7]

TABLE 1.1 Comparative Summary

Exhibition	Number of Exhibits (Est.)	Number of Admissions	Acres Covered by Buildings
London (1851)	14,000	6,039,195	21
Paris (1855)	22,000	5,162,330	24.5
London (1862)	29,000	6,211,103	23.5
Paris (1867)	52,000	10,200,000	37
Vienna (1873)	42,000	7,254,687	40
Philadelphia (1876)	33,000	9,910,996	56
Paris (1878)	52,000	13,000,000	60
Paris (1889)	60,000	32,354,111	75.5
Chicago (1893)	65,000	27,539,521	187.69

Another important innovation in the Universal Exposition was the Rue de Caire, a collection of "ethnographic exhibits" that amounted to little more than a bazaar of sideshows and theaters committed to mass amusement. Visitors were particularly intrigued by the so-called model villages from Senegal, Indo-China, Gabon, Tahiti and other exotic environs. Scantily clad villagers, imported for the season, paraded before European audiences as evidence of Western civilization's triumph over barbarism.

Although promoters stressed the scientific nature of the exhibits, the villagers were the objects of bemused voyeurism to a generation of Europeans enamored of evolutionary speculation on lower and higher forms of existence. The villages were lucrative investments for the managers, helping to assure the profitability of the exposition.[8] Parisians visited the fair time and again in the summer of 1889, and when the exposition closed the final report recorded that more than thirty-two million people had passed through the gates during the season. No other international exhibition in the nineteenth century recorded as many admissions.

Although New York City hosted a meager exhibition in 1853, the first real international exhibition in the United States was hosted by Philadelphia in 1876. Conceived by the Smithsonian Institution and commissioned by Congress in 1871 to celebrate a century of American independence, the Centennial Exhibition opened in May 1876, in the midst of a debilitating national economic depression. Thirty-six nations sponsored exhibits arranged in seven general buildings in Fairmount Park. The majority of the thirty-three thousand exhibits were housed in a Main Building and the Machinery Hall.[9]

Without question, the most important and the most memorable exhibit was the fourteen-hundred-horsepower Corliss double-acting, duplex vertical expansion engine, which stood in the Machinery Hall and powered the mechanical displays. Marietta Holley's fictional "Samantha" called it the "great Careless Enjin," and Edward Bruce said the machine "claims the possession of a will, and is by the latest philosophical advices credited with the same."[10] In addition to the Corliss engine, American manufacturers of mechanical and electrical equipment dominated the displays in Machinery Hall. Alexander Graham Bell exhibited his electric telephone and other novel inventions, Thomas Edison sent a quadroplex telegraph and an electric pen, and Elisha Gray, who had battled Bell over the telephone patent, demonstrated his harmonic telegraph-analyzing instruments. Not surprisingly, the United States presented more exhibits than any other country, and American participants won more awards, receiving over one-third of the thirteen thousand awards of merit presented by exhibition juries.

The Centennial's art galleries have been credited with inaugurating an "American Renaissance" in the fine and decorative arts. While such claims may be a bit excessive, the Centennial gave fresh encouragement to a younger generation of American sculptors and painters. American artists exhibited some six hundred paintings and works of sculpture at the Centennial. Thomas Cole, Asher B. Durand, and practitioners of the Hudson River School were represented in the competition. Frederick Church's *Niagara* was very popular, as were paintings by Thomas Eakins, Winslow Homer, and Eastman Johnson. In the category of sculpture, America's premier sculptors dominated the show. Augustus Saint-Gaudens, his disciple Daniel Chester French, and Olin Warner each received medals of distinction. Edward Kemeys, who like Saint-Gaudens and French would have a role in designing the Columbian Exposition, contributed several popular animal groups.[11] For a largely uninitiated popular audience, the Centennial Exhibition's artistic displays were a revelation of the creative talents of native artists who were just beginning to develop national and international reputations. If not a "renaissance," the Centennial certainly spawned an awakening of artistic appreciation in the United States. Though judged a cultural and mechanical triumph, the Centennial was not a financial success. Investors lost nearly four million dollars, a consequence of the bleak economic conditions in the summer of 1876.

To a nation barely a century old, however, a country still engulfed in sectional antagonisms and the political controversy of Reconstruction, to say nothing of labor turmoil and the Indian Wars in the West, the Centennial Exhibition served as a potent if temporary unifying symbol. It underscored the meaning of world's fairs as patriotic enterprises that celebrated commercial and cultural development, and it stimulated American interest in subsequent international exhibitions. The successes in Philadelphia outweighed the losses contained in the accountant's final report. Furthermore, as the Centennial Exhibition closed, rumors began to circulate that Congress might authorize another American fair to commemorate the four-hundredth anniversary of Christopher Columbus's discovery of Europe's New World.[12]

Chicago's civic and corporate leaders were aware of the commercial and cultural legacies of international exhibitions when, in the summer of 1889, they began to organize for a rumored Columbian celebration. "Our city," Chicago businessman Harlow Higinbotham remembered, "looked upon the coming quadro-centennial of the discovery of America as an opportunity for this city to vindicate its position as a great center of industry and intellectual activity, and by reason of the eagerness for this opportunity the citizens were willing to do everything within their power to make the event worthy of the nation."[13] "The spirit of the Exposition," explained architect Daniel Burnham in a moment of exaggerated enthusiasm, "was that of Chicago, vital and dominant. . . . This spirit finds men, it makes occasions, it attracts, holds together and vitalizes an organization until it rises to heights never known elsewhere."[14]

In Chicago, city and fair became synonomous. Its corporate elite seized upon the idea of a Columbian celebration as a way to showcase the city's meteoric rise to prominence since the Civil War, and especially their triumph over the devastating 1871 Great Fire, which had left much of the city in ashen ruins. William Cronon has suggested that the Columbian Exposition was the logical culmination of the city's emergence during the nineteenth century. This contemporary observation bears a striking resemblance to how Chicagoans in the 1890s understood the meaning of their international exhibition.[15]

A unique alliance of political and corporate interests orchestrated Chicago's campaign to host the fair and then to supervise its construction. Months of intense lobbying marked by fierce civic and regional loyalties, more than a touch of bragging and boasting, exhortations from the Bible, and even a bit of good-natured humor preceded the Congressional appointment of a host city. It was in the course of this feuding that Chicago received its most famous sobriquet. Appalled by Chicago's unabashed boosterism, Charles Dana of the *New York Sun* dubbed her nothing more than a "Windy City." His remark had nothing to do with the weather.

In announcing the formation of a Committee of One Hundred (later enlarged to 250) to guide the city's campaign, Mayor Dewitt Creiger suggested this would be "an organization representing all classes of citizens." But from its inception the Chicago group represented a coalition of elites who saw their own interests, as well as those of the city, tied to the fair. One estimate placed the combined wealth of the Chicago directors in excess of $70,000,000.[16] In an age of managerial capitalism, it is not surprising that these financiers developed a corporate bureaucracy to parcel out responsibilities and more efficiently manage their efforts. As an executive committee developed plans for a city-wide subscription campaign, representatives were dispatched to Washington, D.C., to coordinate the city's lobbying efforts.[17]

Philadelphia, Washington, D.C., St. Louis, and especially New York City were Chicago's chief rivals for the Columbian fair. Each presented detailed bids to a special U.S. Senate Quadro-Centennial Committee, which held hearings in January 1890, but few doubted the choice would fall to either New York or Chicago.[18] In addition to being America's two largest cities in population and manufacturing, the two also represented two distinct regions of the country—a circumstance the Chicago men exploited with considerable success. New York was the established giant in the East, the center of trade and finance. Chicago was the self-proclaimed "Athens of the West," the prairie upstart that had emerged from its devastating Great Fire in 1871 to dominate the course of trans-Appalachian commercial and social expansion.[19] While conceding New York's preeminence in commercial affairs, Chicago's deputies stressed their city's representative character. To understand America in its diversity and newness, the midwesterners argued, visitors must come to Chicago. It was a classic confrontation: Chicago versus New York, the West against the East, America's noble future as against her proud past. Or so the Chicago men thought.

On the morning of January 11, former Governor Chauncey Depew made a persuasive case for New York's selection. No world's fair had proven financially profitable unless it was located in the first city of the host nation, Depew argued. (He failed to mention that only two previous exhibitions had recorded a profit.) This fair was a necessity, Depew agreed, but for it to be a success it must go to New York. Its location on the eastern seaboard made the city convenient for foreign visitors, and New York had numerous sites that would be suitable for a world's fair. Depew was confident that New York's offer to absolve Congress of any financial liability for exposition expenses would carry the day.[20]

When their chance came on the afternoon of January 11, Chicago's representatives brushed aside the intense political maneuvering that had been going on for weeks. "I desire here," DeWitt Creiger began with a note of sarcasm, "in the name of the people of Chicago, to fully reciprocate the kindly expressions of fraternity which I have heard through eloquent channels this morning." "There is no rivalry between the Empire City of America—New York," he continued, "and the Empire City of the Great West—Chicago." This observation brought laughter and light applause from the audience. "Her people," Creiger said of Chicago, "are actuated on high and noble motives. She desires . . . the greatest good for the greatest number."

Creiger argued that while New York spoke for herself, Chicago spoke for sixteen western states that publicly supported her selection. New York was America's largest city, but Chicago, city of the West, was America's most representative city. Playing on the theme of regional identity, Creiger added, "Gentlemen, we do not forget to accord to the other gateway to the

Mississippi Valley—St. Louis—her advantages, but in so doing we ask that your judgment shall not be swerved from the marvel of the nineteenth century, Chicago."[21]

"Give the fair, therefore, to the West where it belongs," Thomas Bryan continued, "and New York and Washington will thank us for sparing them its cares and embarrassments, whilst they profit by its visitors. . . . The mighty empire of the West points to Chicago as her trysting-place for the Exposition and for fair-dealing." As a practical demonstration of the West's (and the city's) potential, Bryan told the senators that New York's plan for a two-hundred-acre fairground paled by comparison with the ten thousand acres Chicago had available for the asking.[22]

Creiger and Bryan's unabashed boosterism was complemented by Edward Jeffery's assurances of the prarie upstart's financial stability. Manager of the Illinois Central Railroad and a member of a Chicago delegation to the Paris Universal Exposition, Jeffery presented a detailed analysis of what Chicago would do if given the fair. Based on initial cost projections, Jeffery expected to spend $14,000,000 on the fair; moreover, he guaranteed Congress that all expenses would be met by private subscription. Chicago's financial resources, as well as its favorable summer climate and excellent rail transportation system, argued for its selection. Most of all, Jeffery stated, what recommended Chicago—and the West—was the "high and noble motives" of its citizens. What better way to demonstrate the virtue and industriousness of the American people, he asked, than to give this American fair to the most representative city?[23]

Once the hearings were concluded, the House of Representatives moved quickly to approve legislation designating Chicago as the host city of the next world's fair. Remembering Chicago's dig at St. Louis during the hearings, Missouri's George Vest attempted unsuccessfully to derail Chicago's selection in the Senate: "Like the lion and the lamb, they have lain down together," Vest told the Senate, speaking of an unholy alliance between New York and Chicago. Despite misgivings about Chicago's grand designs, most senators agreed with Ohioan John Sherman's observation: "The people of Chicago can do it. . . . They will do it, and they will make money by doing it." On April 21, 1890, by a margin of forty-three votes to thirteen (with twenty-eight abstentions), the full Senate ended debate on House legislation that had been passed two months earlier and designated Chicago as the site of the next international exhibition.[24] By the time President Benjamin Harrison signed the compromise bill on April 25, 1890, what was being promoted as the greatest international exhibition in history was scheduled to open in three years and one week.[25]

Lofty expectations and escalating costs, combined with the burdensome administrative structure contained in the enabling legislation, virtually assured that corporate and cultural agendas would collide in the management of the Columbian Exposition. The imperatives to control costs and turn a profit ran up against the creative vision of the consulting architects and artists, exacerbating tensions created by a dual system of authority meant to reconcile local and national interests in the project. Commerce and culture might be seen to cooperate in the White City ensemble, but behind the scenes they reflected conflicting agendas and expectations. Daniel Burnham, the Chicago architect who served as Director of Works, found the administrtive structure so clumsy that he recommended it be discarded in future American exhibitions.[26]

Two authorities were recognized in the management of the Chicago world's fair: the World's Columbian Commission, commonly known as the National Commission, and the Chicago-based World's Exposition of 1892. Based in Washington, D.C., and composed of presidential appointees from each state and territory, the Commission had broad administrative powers but no financial stake in the enterprise. Its chief duties were to coordinate foreign exhibits and judging, provide for the dedication of the buildings and grounds, and, perhaps most important, approve the formal site and plans for the fair.[27]

The Chicago corporation, on the other hand, was responsible for the finance, construction, and operation of the Exposition. Its list of stockholders, choice of site(s), and design plan were all subject to approval by the Commission before construction contracts could be let. Once its plan was accepted, the Corporation was allowed to set rates and admission fees, and to fix the "rights, privileges, or interests of the exhibitors or the public," subject to modification by the Commission. In the final bill, Chicago's financial guarantee was raised from five to ten million dollars. Although the Corporation's executive committee had no choice but to agree to this amendment, it steadfastly refused to open its subscription books to congressional inspection.[28] The potential for conflict between a public agency under political control and representing a national interest and a private corporation faced with mounting expenditures and dwindling revenues was considerable.

In addition to these two agencies and their various standing committees and bureaus, Congress established a Board of Lady Managers under the supervision of the National Commission. Directed by Chicago women, the Board of Lady Managers evolved into a formidable and quasi-autonomous power in its own right, overseeing the most comprehensive participation of women in a world's fair to date.[29] Like the Board of Lady Managers, the World's Congress Auxiliary existed somewhat apart from the squabbling of the Corporation and the Commission. The brainchild of Chicagoan Charles Bonney, the Auxiliary coordinated a wide-ranging lyceum-style program of meetings and conferences as an intellectual counterpart to the more material aspects of the fair.[30]

Contrary to DeWitt Creiger's early championing of an association representing "all classes," Chicago's proverbial "best men" controlled the local management board. Although nearly thirty thousand persons pledged more than $5,467,000 through the purchase of ten-dollar shares of stock in the "World's Exposition of 1892," the local organization was controlled by the city's political and financial elite. Sixteen private citizens each pledged more than $50,000, and the initial forty-five-man Board of Directors included the likes of C. H. McCormick, Frederick Peck, Charles Yerkes, and Potter Palmer.[31] Noticeably absent were several of the company's largest stockholders: Marshall Field, George Pullman, and the meatpackers Phillip Armour and Gustavus Swift.[32]

In a similar fashion, these corporate titans turned to their own to give formal leadership to the enterprise. At the April 30, 1890, meeting of shareholders, financier Lyman Gage, later to serve as secretary of the treasury, was elected president of the Corporation, and Judge Thomas Bryan assumed the responsibilities of first vice president. Potter Palmer, who stood against Bryan, agreed to serve as second vice president. A week later, William K. Ackerman was elected company auditor, and Anthony Seeberger was selected as treasurer. Dewitt Creiger chaired the Committee on Grounds and Buildings, the most important of ten standing committees created to supervise the company's administrative duties.[33]

In June, the National Commission met and organized itself in a similar fashion. Filled with political appointments, the Commissioners' stake in the enterprise was very different from that assumed by the Directors. Perhaps the most important of the Commission's standing committees was the Committee on Classifications, charged with developing a scheme for exhibits and their placement in the park. Although it might seem a mundane task, setting the system of classifications had far-reaching implications for the character of the Exposition. No determination of the number and size of exhibition buildings could be made until a plan for identifying and arranging the expected sixty-thousand exhibits was settled. In turn, the Corporation's Committee on Grounds and Buildings could not approximate the scale or dimensions of individual buildings until it was furnished with the classification system established by the Commission. The Corporation would not begin construction until the Commission approved its plan, and that plan could not be fixed until the Directors were informed of the exhibits' arrangement. In essence, at every turn the Corporation was held in check by the Commission, as time passed and anticipated costs of construction mounted.

In June 1890, stockholders voted to change the name of the company from the "World's Exposition of 1892" to the "World's Columbian Exposition." This decision reflected the change in the opening date—seven months later than originally intended—and gave the enterprise a formal designation more in keeping with the its commemorative purpose. Investors also accepted Frederick Peck's recommendation to double the company's capital value to ten million dollars. Such a move required the city of Chicago to increase its own bonded indebtedness to cover the amount, a matter that had to be approved by a special amendment to the state constitution. In acceding to the city's request, the state legislature also granted the Exposition "use and occupation of all lands, or right therein, of the State of Illinois, whether submerged or otherwise, within the city of Chicago, or adjacent thereto."[34]

Benjamin Butterworth, the Ohio congressman whose election as secretary to the Corporation had drawn fire from organization labor, recognized immediately the bureaucratic entanglements engendered by the dual system of authority.[35] Less than two weeks after his appointment by the Directors, he wrote to James Ellsworth in words which proved prophetic. "I am apprehensive that there will be more trouble than we anticipate in disentangling the jurisdiction of the two Boards," he wrote on July 11, 1890. "It will have to be done without wounding the pride of the National Board, while securing for the Local Board the control, which obviously should belong to it."[36] The persistent bickering between the two agencies persuaded Butterworth to resign his position prior to the April 1892 annual meeting.

No issue better illustrates the difficulties between the Chicago-based Corporation and the National Commission than the so-called site question. It also reveals the competing interests behind the Exposition from its inception. Although the Commissioners had acquiesced to the Board of Directors' decision to appoint George Davis as director-general, they did not concede the location of the fair to the Directors' discretion.[37] Indecision and competing interests, exacerbated by the conflict between commercial and aesthetic agendas, kept the Board of Directors from recommending a formal site to the Commission for seven critical months.

When the Committee on Grounds and Buildings began to consider the site question, most people believed with Frederick Peck that the fair had to be situated "somewhere upon the shores of Lake Michigan." Public hearings did little to alter the sentiments within the Board of Directors, which on June 18, 1890, narrowly approved a resolution favoring the Lake Front Park adjacent to downtown as the Exposition's official site.[38]

Impatient with the deadlock within the Board of Directors, James Ellsworth decided another approach was needed. Ellsworth was a director, a prominent banker, and president of the South Park Commission, which had jurisdiction over Jackson and Washington Parks. With Lyman Gage's consent, on July 29, 1890, Ellsworth wrote a letter to Frederick Law Olmsted that would substantially change the character of the Columbian Exposition. Olmsted, of Brookline, Massachusetts, was the nation's premier landscape architect, best known for his plan of Central Park in New York City and the planned suburb of Riverside, fifteen miles west of Chicago. Familiar with Olmsted and his partner Henry Sargent Codman's work, Ellsworth felt it imperative that the Exposition retain their services.

"My position is this," Ellsworth wrote with a sense of urgency, "the reputation of America is at stake in this matter, and the reputation of Chicago is at stake. As an American citizen, you have an equal interest in furthering the success of this great and grand undertaking, and I know from talking with you, that on an occasion like this you grasp the whole situation and will be confined within no narrow limits."[39] Himself about to leave for Europe on Exposition business, Ellsworth encouraged Olmsted to come immediately to Chicago. If appeals to patriotism were insufficient inducement, Ellsworth offered to pay Olmsted's expenses and a thousand-dollar honorarium for the visit.

Frederick Law Olmsted and Henry Sargent Codman arrived in Chicago on August 8 and proceeded to make a cursory study of seven possible sites— four inland parks and three along Lake Michigan. Despite the business community's growing enthusiasm for the lakefront, on August 12, Olmsted and Codman recommended that Jackson Park be designated the principal site of the Columbian Exposition.[40] Jackson Park was along the lake, but it was seven miles south of the commercial Loop. Olmsted knew of the park from a preliminary study he had done in the early 1870s, on which the city had never acted. Now, nearly two decades later, Olmsted saw virtually the same expanse of swamp and scrub pine, frequently inundated by lake waters.

Two other reasons might have persuaded Olmsted to recommend Jackson Park. Jackson Park was nearly identical in size to New York City's Central Park. Olmsted's success in carving out a natural reserve in Manhattan had been his greatest triumph. But where Central Park offered the challenge of reclaiming nature from the city, Jackson Park and the fair provided a very different opportunity. Olmsted must have recognized that here, in a similar expanse of land, was a natural setting waiting to have a city (of sorts) fashioned from its untamed features. In addition to the similarities in size, Jackson Park offered something new and experimental for the landscape architect at the height of his career.

Without acting on the site recommendation, on August 21, 1890, the Board of Directors appointed FLO and Company the Consulting Landscape Architects. At the same time, Chicago architect John Wellborn Root was retained as consulting architect, an assignment that was rescinded two weeks later when the firm of Burnham and Root was commissioned as consulting architects. This was not a reproach of Root, but a formal effort to include his partner Daniel Burnham, who had so far acted in an unofficial capacity. Along with engineer Abram Gottlieb, Olmsted and Codman and Burnham and Root formed a Consultants Board that advised the Board of Directors in the matter of a site and the preparation of the grounds.[41] Each favored Jackson Park as the site of the Columbian Exposition, a position that set them at odds with the National Commission and a formidable bloc of directors.

To further complicate the matter, under pressure from the National Commission, the South Park Commission on September 22 tendered Washington Park and the Midway Plaisance (a one-mile strip of land that connected Washington and Jackson Parks) for the Exposition's use. Daniel Burnham wrote the Committee on Grounds of the consultants' disapproval: "We decidedly favor a compact, condensed and orderly arrangement for the layout of the Fair and strongly urge that all ideas of scattering buildings over the vast area that has been tendered not be entertained."[42] "They," Codman wrote Olmsted the same day of the Board of Directors, "have got to make certain decisions and they might as well face it instead of putting us off so continually." In his reply, Olmsted encouraged Codman and Root not to lose heart, reaffirming Jackson Park and the "great natural feature" at its edge as the proper site.[43]

By mid-October, with Root in Chicago and Codman in Brookline poring over geological surveys of Jackson Park, the Board of Directors was no closer to making its site recommendation. The dedication ceremonies were only two years away ,and ground had not been broken. Furthermore, it appeared the Commission was going to insist that Washington Park be included in any plan. On October 10, John Root cabled Henry Codman to come to Chicago at once. "It seems to me that things are approaching a sort of crisis . . . ," Root told his colleague. "I confess to you that it does not look very bright for the use of Jackson Park."[44]

Two weeks later Codman wrote Olmsted, "I am beginning to feel about the World's Fair, that if they finally insist upon going to Washington Park and doing this and other things against our advice and judgment we shall be so hampered and interfered with that a good result, or what we would consider a good result, will be impossible, and that we shall have good cause to resign." "I think that we should bear in mind," Codman continued,

that, apart from the advertisement of this thing, the work will be of such a temporary character that it will soon be entirely forgotten, and even if we do make a success of it, in a few years no one will be able to recall it [the Exposition plan], all of which is so different from the Parks, or from Biltmore, for instance.

Henry Codman's prediction was shortsighted, but his gloomy letter revealed an added fear that Edward Jeffery, rather than Daniel Burnham, would be appointed chief of the Bureau of Construction. Jeffery, a railroad manager, had no professional experience for the post, and for Codman his advocacy of Washington Park further undermined his credibility. If Jeffery was appointed chief of construction, Codman told Olmsted, their firm would be "in a very unpleasant position . . . one which I should be unwilling to assume."[45]

In a decision that did not please either the consultants or the Commissioners, in early November the Board of Directors voted to place the principal buildings on the lakefront, a position favored by merchants and financiers.[46] This judgment seemed to confirm to the designers that aesthetic considerations were secondary to whatever commercial profits were to be won in the enterprise. As the rift widened between the local and national agencies, the consultants felt handicapped by the vested interests and personal jealousies within the two bodies. With Olmsted sick in bed in Brookline, Codman contemplated the firm's resignation from the project. For their part, Burnham and Root were engaged in surveys of multiple sites for which they had no enthusiasm.

In the increasingly tense atmosphere of mid-November 1890, John Root saved the day—and very possibly the world's fair itself. With Henry Codman's assistance, Root produced a preliminary plan that showed a general distribution of buildings, waterways, and roads in Jackson Park. Known as the "brown paper plan"—it was sketched on plain brown wrapping paper— Root's scheme was accompanied by Daniel Burnham's manifesto. As Burnham explained, the central features of the November plan were "a great architectural court with a body of water therein," combined with a system of interior waterways and canals connecting the exterior regions of a six-hundred-acre park and an undisturbed wooded island placed in a northern lagoon.[47] Even in this preliminary sketch the consultants contemplated the contrast of a formal architectural court at the south end of the grounds with a more secluded and forested area at the northern perimeter.

Combining unique and derivative features, Root's plan suggested several influences. Chief among them were elements of Olmsted and Calvert Vaux's 1871 study of Jackson Park (then called South Park) and their experience at Central Park. Another prominent influence was the sculptured gardens of the Champ de Mars, the grand court of the 1889 Paris Exposition familiar to Harry Codman. What the early plat also hinted at in its juxtaposition of waterways and elegant buildings was the influence of Venice on late-century artistic sensibilities.[48]

On November 21, 1890, the Committee on Grounds and Buildings approved Root's plan, followed four days later by the National Commission's acceptance. At the same time, the Board of Directors created a Bureau of Construction under Burnham's direction, with responsibility to "select, organize, and control all forces needed to produce and operate the Exposition, except the exhibits."[49] (The exhibits remained under the authority of Director General George Davis and the National Commission.) All of the consultants now reported directly to Burnham, who functioned as chief operating officer with authority to select superintendents and supervise work on the grounds. Following the December 1, 1890, approval of this "November Compact," Frederick Law Olmsted expressed his relief when he wrote to a friend, "The main features of the Columbian Exposition are now determined and further definite elaboration on the plan will be effected probably in a few days."[50]

The struggle over the site issue cost precious time and introduced the otherwise inexperienced managers to the test of wills that could lay behind international exhibitions. Furthermore, it revealed to Burnham, Root, Olmsted, and Codman the potential conflict between their artistic expectations for the fair as a cultural statement and the commercial motivations of those who provided the financial backing for the enterprise. Last, it indicated the practical impediments in a dual system of authority that pitted national against local interests in an *international* event. These lessons would be learned time and again in the next three years.

With the acceptance of the site plan, Daniel Burnham turned his attention to the selection of a group of architects to design the principal exhibition buildings. Stressing the national character of the proposed fair, the editors of the influential *Inland Architect* argued that only the best architects in the country should be trusted with its design.[51] Burnham agreed and nominated the firms of Richard M. Hunt; Peabody and Stearns; McKim, Mead and White; Van Brunt and Howe; and George B. Post. With the exception of Van Brunt and Howe, whose headquarters was Kansas City, the firms were located in New York or Boston, a circumstance that did not sit well with the Board of Directors. Despite a protracted debate over Burnham's choices, on December 13 the Committee on Grounds and Buildings approved his recommendation and instructed the chief of construction to issue invitations to the five firms.[52]

Like Ellsworth's appeal to Olmsted, Burnham's letters to the architects had far-reaching implications for the architectural integrity of the Exposition. These same letters are also the source of the continuing controversy among cultural critics who have followed Louis Sullivan's personal indictment of Burnham for betraying what he, Sullivan, saw as the signs of an authentic democratic culture in America. Sullivan's belated judgment of the Exposition's neo-Renaissance motif as an "appalling calamity" has shaped much of the criticism of the fair's imperial architecture.[53] Burnham's motives, however, were neither so sinister as Sullivan suggested nor so at odds with the developing character of international exhibitions in the late nineteenth century.

To secure their cooperation, the Chief of Construction promised the eastern firms complete freedom in the choice of style and guaranteed that no one would interfere with their collective decision. "The Committee are [*sic*] disposed," Burnham told each firm on December 13, "to leave the method of design to the five Architects, and you may determine among yourselves whether to make a joint design of the whole as one, or each to take up separate parts to be modified to meet such views as shall be expressed in your confidence from time to time."

John Root's preliminary sketches favoring a Romanesque motif were now moot. Neither he nor John Root would design a building, Burnham said, but Root (as consulting architect) would serve as an "interpreter" of their work, "without importing into the work anything of his own feeling."[54] Burnham presumably had his partner's concurrence on this point, as the nature of the invitation surrendered the character of the Exposition's design to other designers. Burnham reasoned the invitations were a necessary concession to the national and artistic aspect of the pageant.

Only Henry Van Brunt cabled his immediate acceptance of Daniel Burnham's offer. The easterners were skeptical of the enterprise, and perhaps suspicious of Chicago's great boasts for its fair. On December 22, Burnham went by train to New York to persuade the architects to join him in the enterprise. That evening the Chief of Construction, one-half of the Chicago firm that had designed more skyscrapers than any other, listened respectfully to the easterners' doubts. They doubted Burnham's ability to complete his grand-scale exhibition in the two and one-half years that remained. Though they did not commit to the fair, representatives of the four firms agreed to come to Chicago in January for a meeting with the Board of Directors.

On his return to the city, Burnham was confronted with determined opposition to his plan. Two days after Christmas, Frederick Peck and Potter Palmer, respectively the chairman of the Finance Committee and second vice president of the Corporation, raged against the use of "outsiders" to design Chicago's world's fair. They shared a growing sentiment within the Board of Directors and the business community that local men of talent had been slighted by Burnham's hasty actions. Peck, for one, wanted the invitations rescinded.[55]

Burnham interpreted the issue as a conflict between commerce and culture and between the mercantile and the artistic mind. "This was not a question of men but of Art," Burnham recalled in his final report, and Chicago had an obligation to the nation and the world that transcended local chauvinism. Commercial loyalties and favoritism should not be allowed to confuse the issues, Burnham as much as told the directors. In the showdown vote, his invitations stood by a margin of one vote; as a concession, Burnham acceded to a Board directive to issue offers of employment to five local firms. On January 10, 1891, local representatives joined the eastern architects in Burnham's office at the Rookery Building.[56]

For reasons of economy and practicality, on February 20, 1891, the Corporation's Budget Committee recommended the abandonment of any effort to place major exhibition buildings on the lakefront. This was the exact position taken by Olmsted and Codman six months earlier, and much to Henry Codman's relief the Commission approved the decision a week later.[57] By then the eastern firms had agreed to participate and Burnham had set about completing his Bureau of Construction.

"It was one of those cold winter days," Burnham remembered of January 10, 1891, when he took the easterners on a carriage ride through Jackson Park.

The sky was overcast with clouds and the lake covered with foam. We looked the thing over. [George] Peabody got up on a pier and said, "Do you really say that you expect to open this Fair in '93?" I told him yes. He said he did not think it could be done. I told him it was settled.[58]

That evening, Burnham told the easterners that the Columbian Exposition was the "third great American event," reminiscent of the trials of 1776 and 1861. "All left the dinner," he later recalled, "united like soldiers with a campaign, and Pettiness and Jealousy never raised their heads in the councils of the designers of the Fair thereafter."[59]

Along with Frederick Law Olmsted and Henry Van Brunt, the easterners remained the week to discuss design concepts and the formal treatment of the grounds with their Chicago counterparts. Consenting to the enterprise, they established a Board of Architects, with Richard M. Hunt, dean of American architects, as its chairman, and Louis Sullivan as its secretary. In addition to making minor alterations to Root's plan for Jackson Park, the second of four such alterations, the Board of Architects agreed to several substantive changes that fixed the character of the Exposition plan.[60]

Their most important and in retrospect controversial decision was the adoption of an eclectic classicism, the neo-Renaissance motif of the Parisian Ecole des Beaux Arts, as the style of the principal exhibition halls fronting the central Court of Honor. As a concession to several of the Chicagoans, latitude was granted for other buildings, with the understanding that the dominant motif of the Exposition would be classical and academic. To effect a sense of unity, the architects concurred on a common cornice height of sixty feet in the Court of Honor, with an approximate height for the corresponding terraces.[61] Later came the decision to paint the great halls white.

Although it has proven controversial to later historians, the architects' decision to adapt the historical style of the Parisian academy to the Chicago world's fair made sense. The offer of artistic freedom proved a sufficient incentive to bring the country's leading architects into the project, but it also surrendered the decision to them. As Van Brunt noted in 1892 in *Century Magazine*, a precedent had been established in recent international exhibitions that encouraged the festive, ornamental classicism adopted by the consultants. The architectural facade, he said, acted as a cosmetic "screen" that provided an air of "monumental dignity" in keeping with the spirit of world's fairs. Furthermore, the Renaissance motif was popular in America, and it was a style with which all of the principal architects were familiar. In addition to Richard Hunt and Charles F. McKim, four of the remaining eight consultants had studied at the Parisian Ecole. Such shared knowledge would allow the architects to get about their business more expeditiously.

Henry Van Brunt noted a further consideration: This was no time for artistic innovations that might jeopardize the success of the commercial enterprise. "The show might have contained some elements of the great 'American Style,' " Van Brunt reasoned, "but as a whole it would have been a hazardous experiment, and it certainly would have perplexed the critics."[62]

Some have interpreted the hesitancy to "experiment" in style, to use Van Brunt's word, as reflecting the inherent conservatism behind the Exposition. It is somewhat ironic, though not surprising, that the architects drew on the historicism of Renaissance architecture to celebrate four centuries of American progress. This certainly was Louis Sullivan's lament. But in making their decision the architects were in keeping with the evolving traditions of world's fair ensembles and were comforming to prevailing architectural styles in America. To evoke a sense of triumphant American democracy, the designers drew on what they knew and what was expected. They also chose not to antagonize financial investors. "In the choice of the classical style," Talbot Hamlin observed, "the consulting architects only symbolized popular taste; in the actual creation of the tremendously impressive group of buildings . . . they did more; they astonished, delighted, and fixed popular taste."[63] Criticism often overlooks the significant degree of innovation inherent in the plan itself and in the features that lay beneath the neoclassical exteriors.

Just as the Board of Architects was settling into its business, tragedy struck the world's fair. On Monday, January 12, word spread throughout Chicago that John Root was deathly ill with pneumonia. Three days later, Daniel Burnham was summoned to his friend's bedside. With Henry Codman waiting outside, Burnham and one of Root's aunts hovered over the bed.[64]

Harriet Monroe, the poet and Margaret Root's sister, remembered that great men "sobbed like children" when they learned of the architect's death, and everyone feared for the Exposition. Some have claimed that had John Root lived the architecture of the Columbian Exposition would have reflected the Romanesque motif he seemed to prefer. There is no evidence, however, that Root disagreed with Burnham's decision of the previous December to give stylistic control to the eastern firms. What was obvious at the time was that the Exposition had lost one of its more creative artistic consultants. In recognition of his contribution to the enterprise, the Board of Directors praised the deceased Root for "possessing high genius, exquisite taste, and genuine love for all that is true and beautiful in art."[65]

Before Van Brunt and the eastern men left Chicago, Burnham confirmed each firm's assignment. Whether on his own initiative or acceding to the wishes of the group, Burnham altered the commissions he and Root had contemplated initially. With the exception of Soloman S. Beman, who was given the Building of Mines and Mining, the structures that composed the Court of Honor were assigned to eastern architects.

This decision angered some on the Board of Directors, who complained anew that local talent had been slighted, but they did not try to change the arrangement. The Directors recognized that the Court was the architectural centerpiece, and some felt the decision was an implicit statement that local architects were not up to the task. Though this was never Burnham's stated intention, allowing the easterners to design the most visible structures was one more means to secure their commitment to the project. It also reinforced Burnham's sensitivity to the national character of the fair, and perhaps his own unwillingness to experiment by taking unnecessary risks.

Richard Hunt was commissioned to design the strategically important Administration Building, considered the gem of the architectural ensemble. The firm of McKim, Mead and White was given the Agriculture Building, and Peabody and Stearns the Palace of Mechanic Arts (Machinery Hall). Directly opposite these structures on the north side of the Court would be George B. Post's Manufactures and Liberal Arts Building and Van Brunt and Howe's Electricity Hall.[66]

Of the major exhibition buildings outside the Court of Honor, the Horticulture Building adjacent to the north lagoon was assigned to William L. B. Jenney, partner in the Chicago firm of Jenney and Mundie and regarded by some as the father of the skyscraper. Henry Ives Cobb was given the Fish and Fisheries Building; Holabird and Roche, the Live Stock Pavilion on the south grounds; and Adler and Sullivan, the Transportation Building. Daniel Burnham had originally offered Dankmar Adler and Louis Sullivan the Music Hall, in part because of their success with the acoustics in Chicago's Auditorium Theater. But Sullivan refused the commission as beneath the stature of the firm, and as a concession they were presented the Transportation Building. Burnham asked the Chicago firm of Burling and Whitehouse to design a Fine Arts Palace, but he quickly rescinded the offer when it became apparent the firm was not up to the commission. Each firm would receive a $10,000 fee on the acceptance of its final plans. Burnham refused several requests that he select a building for himself, content to act as general supervisor.

Louis Sullivan's Transportation Building and Henry Cobb's Fish and Fisheries Building were the only major exhibition halls to depart substantially from the established Beaux Arts motif, and Sullivan's Romanesque-like structure represented the only radical departure from the classical standard. Also, except for the enlarged, recessed "Golden Door" as the central entry, Transportation's exterior was brown, in contrast to the white paint decorating the other halls.[67]

One structure not included in the original plat of the fairgrounds was the Woman's Building. Although at Philadelphia and at Paris small pavilions were assigned to exhibit women's handicraft, no world's fair had provided for a separate full-scale exhibition hall devoted to women's interests. Under Bertha Palmer and the Board of Lady Managers' prodding, the Directors agreed to the additional exhibition category of "Woman's Progress," while still allowing women to exhibit in other categories. Palmer also won approval for a separate exhibition hall to house the displays, which was positioned adjacent to William Jenney's Horticulture Building on the north lagoon. Sophia Hayden, the first woman to graduate from the Massachusetts Institute of Technology's architecture program, won a national design competition—the only such competition sponsored by the Exposition—and women artists and sculptors were contracted to provide the decorative details. Though somewhat smaller than the other major halls, the Woman's

Building received great praise during the Exposition season for its tasteful Italian Renaissance motif.[68]

In Burnham's mind, the Exposition's plan was set after the January 1891 meeting of the Board of Architects, and he was determined to resist any major revision. In a letter dated February 8, he told Frederick Law Olmsted that if a new plan were forced on him he would submit his resignation.[69] But within two weeks the Chief of Construction's fears were allayed by the consolidation of the principal buildings to Jackson Park. For two months Henry Codman and engineer Abram Gottlieb had been directing survey crews at Jackson Park, and the plan was to proceed as quickly as possibly.

The Exposition plan had seven distinct parts: (1) the formal basin and canal with surrounding architecture—the Court of Honor; (2) a Wooded Island and surrounding lagoon; (3) government locations (headquarters for the U.S. and foreign governments); (4) state government locations with the Fine Arts Palace as a center; (5) the Midway Plaisance; (6) a Live Stock Pavilion, out-of-door agricultural exhibits, Convent of La Rabida, and the Leather, Dairy, Forestry, and Anthropology Buildings; and (7) the region of railyards, store-houses, workshops, and concessionaires. Burnham estimated that the total space encompassed in these seven general divisions—that is, Jackson Park and the Midway Plaisance—exceeded 687 acres, roughly the size of Central Park.[70]

Olmsted and Codman's landscape scheme was developed to exploit what the senior partner called Chicago's "one feature of natural—purely natural—beauty." This was Lake Michigan. "As a primary feature of the plan," Olmsted explained to Henry Van Brunt, "the dunes or high parts of the ground were to be prepared as sites for the Exposition buildings, and for suitable plateaus and terraces above them."[71] In marked contrast to the formal, academic setting of the Court of Honor, Olmsted and Codman imagined the northern lagoon surrounding the Wooded Island would "be made to look like a natural bayou, secluded, shallow and placid, but not suggestive of stagnancy or any form of foulness or unhealthiness." The island itself was to remain in a natural repose, as Burnham said, "in refreshing relief to the grandeur of the buildings, and through its sylvan qualities, to the crowded and busy aspect that must be looked for almost everywhere else within the grounds."[72] It was an ambitious plan, made all the more remarkable by the scarce two years the construction crews had to complete the task.

When the architects assembled in Chicago in late February 1891, the easterners brought tentative sketches of their buildings. They also brought Augustus Saint-Gaudens, whom Burnham hoped to persuade to accept a position with the fair. Although he refused a formal appointment, Saint-Gaudens agreed to advise the chief of construction informally on artistic questions. On Saint-Gaudens's recommendation, former pupils Frederick MacMonnies and Daniel Chester French were invited to join the Exposition's artistic council. Without dissent, MacMonnies was commissioned to execute the allegorical Columbian Fountain, and French, the *Quadriga* and towering *Republic*, each of which enjoyed prominent positions in the Court of Honor.[73]

At a breakfast meeting at Kingsley's Restaurant on February 20, each designer presented sketches for comment, and Olmsted and Codman further detailed the landscape plan. When Richard Hunt displayed different perspectives for a large gilded dome to surmount the Administration Building, which he described as a great "civic temple," he received favorable comments. George Post's sketches for a 450-foot dome atop the Manufactures and Liberal Arts Building produced a different reaction. "The moment they saw the dome," Burnham recalled, "you could hear them murmuring." At that, Post promised to alter the perspective. Charles McKim's plan for an enlarged portico to extend along the north facade of the Agriculture Building was also criticized, and he agreed to revisions. George Peabody, Machinery Hall's architect, suggested that a canal could be positioned between his and McKim's building to enhance the appearance of each. McKim liked the idea, as did the other architects, and without objection the plan was altered to accommodate Peabody's suggestion.[74]

Near the conclusion of this lengthy meeting Augustus Saint-Gaudens suggested that perhaps some "appropriate architectural feature" should be employed to close off the lake end of the Court of Honor. He proposed a structure defined by thirteen Greek columns representing the original states, which Burnham hailed as a "bully thing." In time and with some modification, this "feature" became the triumphant Peristyle.[75]

A critical shift of emphasis in the evolution of world's fairs was apparent during this all-important meeting. In highlighting the collective ensemble of the Court of Honor, rather than a particular building, the Columbian Exposition represented an important departure from previous exhibitions. The buildings, and their respective importance, reflected the importance of the exhibits within. Beneath the common Renaissance mask, which provided the appearance of unity, the diversity of modern economic and technological transformation abounded.

Unlike previous international exhibitions, Machinery Hall would not be the dominant structure on the fairgrounds. Rather, Peabody's Palace of Mechanic Arts would share prominence with at least five other major buildings forming the imperial Court of Honor. Also unprecedented was the placement of the Administration Building as the focal point of the ensemble. Yet in sheer size, George Post's Manufactures and Liberal Arts Building would be the most imposing structure in Jackson Park, dwarfing its competitors as the largest building in the world.

The next afternoon, the consultants and architects met with the members of the Committee on Grounds to explain their adjustments to the plan. It was an impressive assembly, America's most accomplished designers and the commercial giants of the nation's fastest-growing industrial city: the lords of commerce as patrons of the arts, entertaining the most gifted artists in the country, and together cooperating in the creation of the most significant public arts project in the history of the nation. Saint-Gaudens, who Henry Adams said "bore the stamp of the Renaissance," broke a prolonged silence after the presentation of designs. Turning to Daniel Burnham, Saint-Gaudens observed in all sincerity, "Look here, old fellow, do you realize that this is the greatest meeting of artists since the fifteenth century?"[76]

Harry Codman, by now managing his firm's involvement in the Exposition, wrote to Olmsted in Brookline and expressed his satisfaction that their original plan remained intact. "McKim's Agriculture was the best and fine," Codman said.

Peabody's was good and Van Brunt's very good, tho' incomplete. Jenney had several [plans] of the Horticulture which had a great deal of merit. Altogether the experiment of getting so many men together was productive of excellent results and I think when they have come a little closer together in some few particulars that the final effect will be very grand. They don't seem to be able on the whole to improve much on our first plan.[77]

Two weeks later Burnham wrote the architects that the Board of Directors had approved their plans and ordered construction to begin. Within twenty months the buildings and grounds were to be dedicated. Jackson Park's six hundred acres of scrub pine and sand dunes, frequently awash in the changing water level of the lake, were in two short years to be the scene of a fabled Venetian City brought to the shores of Lake Michigan, complete with canals, palaces, and the artifacts of the world's civilizations. To date, though, not a single construction contract had been let.

In addition to chief engineer Abram Gottlieb, Daniel Burnham relied most on Ernest Graham, his chief assistant in the Bureau of Construction. Graham managed the weekly staff meetings and the regular department reports, freeing Burnham for more important matters. Dion Geraldine acted as general superintendent of grounds, and Rudolph Ulrich, a German horticulturalist whom Olmsted lured from California, was in command of the routine affairs of the landscape department. William Pretyman, an English painter who lived in Chicago, accepted the position of "Director of Color" and coordinated the painting of the exhibition halls. At its peak the Exposition's Bureau of Construction employed more than thirteen thousand laborers and artisans.[78]

Although labor unions could complain about the use of nonunion workers, no similar criticism was made of the refusal to assign African Americans positions within the departments of the Columbian Exposition. Management followed a policy of conscious job discrimination in its employment practices, during the construction phase and the Exposition season. Several times the issue of black participation was raised within the offices of the Exposition management, and each time it was quickly turned aside. This refusal to include blacks in significant positions added new meaning to the fair's best-known nickname—the White City. In addition to their virtual exclusion from construction crews, during the season blacks could not obtain jobs as waiters and waitresses, as musicians in the cabarets, or as clerks in the many shops and arcades. Although a few applicants were accepted for positions as attendants to wheelchairs and rental carts and strollers, not a single African-American male was hired among the several thousand candidates for the Columbian Guard, the Exposition's elite security force.

By mid-April 1891, what Henry Codman called "the lack of any good designer in the Bureau of Construction since the death of Mr. Root" was hampering Burnham's effectiveness.[79] With this in mind, Richard Hunt suggested that Burnham hire Charles B. Atwood of New York to replace Root as chief designer. Atwood formed with Codman an informal "artistic council," which later included Frank D. Millet, to advise Burnham on aesthetic questions. His sensitivity to the intimacies of classical design complemented Codman's ability to pass on both the location of buildings and the treatment of their surroundings.

In his two years with the Exposition, Charles Atwood had a hand in the design of more than sixty structures at Jackson Park. In addition to the Leather, Dairy, Forestry, and Anthropology buildings, Atwood designed the Fine Arts Building and the Music Hall–Peristyle–Casino complex at the east end of the Court of Honor. Although Daniel Burnham and Charles McKim disagreed on the merits of Atwood's Fine Arts Palace, after the Exposition it became the Field's Columbian Museum, and still later the Museum of Science and Industry.[80]

"Uncle Dan," as Burnham was jokingly called by Frank Lloyd Wright and other young architects, took a personal interest in all phases of work. He was not averse to pressing a point or chastising someone who neglected his duties.[81] In late February 1891, Burnham cabled Olmsted at Brookline to request he come immediately to Chicago. The next day he sent a similar note to Codman. "I earnestly request you to make arrangements to come at once and stay a month," Burnham instructed. "Changes are being rapidly made, and they all more or less affect your work."[82]

"The delay you are causing us by not forwarding scale drawings is embarrassing in the extreme," the Chief of Construction wrote Richard Hunt several months later. "We cannot wait any longer for sake of extra refinement and must let the work at once at all hazards." Similar sentiments were expressed to Peabody and Stearns. "We are completely put out with the delay on your building," Burnham informed the Boston firm. Hunt and Peabody forwarded plans to Burnham in short order.[83]

Burnham thought the Transportation Building's preliminary design might be injurious to the overall artistic scheme, and with the balance of buildings and grounds in mind he suggested that Louis Sullivan change his perspective to allow for "one grand entrance to the east," which would be in line with the principal axis running through the park. Sullivan made no complaint; the result was the placement of Transportation's famous "Golden Door," which brought its designer universal praise during and after the Exposition. In all of his writings on the Exposition, Sullivan never acknowledged Burnham's contribution to one of his greatest successes.[84]

Once Burnham had approved the architects' perspectives, he turned them over to on-site engineers who refined each building's structural details. Foreign and state governments who desired their own headquarters building were responsible for retaining a reputable architect and contractors, subject to the approval of the Bureau of Construction. These independent contracts proved quite lucrative for architects fortunate enough to secure the commissions. In all, over four hundred buildings and structures were raised at Jackson Park.[85]

The inordinate amount of construction at Jackson Park was a boon to Chicago's economy, and it sheltered the city from the early effects of the financial panic that began in May 1893. Before the Exposition opened, more than five hundred thousand square feet of brick paving had been laid, twenty miles of chain fence surrounded the lawns, and nearly seventy miles of water and sewer pipes ran beneath ground. Twelve miles of gas pipe and four hundred and fifteen miles of electrical wiring connected the far reaches of the complex. Burnham estimated that more than seventeen million feet of lumber was used in the construction of the Manufactures and Liberal Arts Building alone.[86]

"Harry's knowledge of formal setting was greater than all the others put together," Burnham once said of Henry Sargent Codman. Although Olmsted and Company was engaged in several other major projects while working on the Columbian Exposition (including Vanderbilt's Biltmore Estate and the grounds of Stanford University), Codman found that the complicated nature of the landscape plan demanded he spend more time than he had expected in Chicago. Codman was concerned that Rudolph Ulrich, his chief assistant at Chicago, was too preoccupied with incidental details to adequately supervise a crew of over 230 laborers and a budget that eventually exceeded $600,000.[87] With the senior Olmsted attending other projects and periodically ill, the bulk of the Chicago work was left to Codman.

With the Exposition's Director of Color away in the East, Burnham accepted a recommendation from a source he later could not recall and ordered all the building exteriors be painted white (actually off-white). This decision enhanced the impression of unity that Burnham sought, and it gave rise to the sobriquet "White City." William Pretyman returned to find the decision implemented and resigned in protest over not being consulted. On the recommendation of Charles McKim and Augustus Saint-Gaudens, Burnham persuaded the Board of Directors to hire artist Frank D. Millet to replace Pretyman. Some of the businessmen on the Board objected to Millet's request for a salary of $15,000 a year, but the majority accepted Burnham's choice. Besides coordinating the decoration of the buildings, Millet organized the legion of artists and muralists who would ornament their interiors. When Charles Atwood became ill during the last year of construction, Burnham and the other architects found Millet's artistic counsel all the more valuable.[88]

Although the Renaissance design might appear excessively nostalgic, there was considerable technological innovation in the actual construction of most structures. All of the bridges within the grounds were reinforced with steel members, except through the entryway of the Peristyle. Since the major exhibition halls would be sold for their scrap value after the Exposition closed, the engineers tried to minimize the use of iron and steel in other buildings. The Woman's Building had no structural steel members, and in Transportation a combination of wood and iron trusses supported the large roof. In Mines, in Electricity, and in the domes of Administration, Horticulture, and Fisheries, iron trusses were used to reinforce against excessive wind pressure. The skylights in Agriculture and Manufactures had similar features.[89]

George Post's Manufactures and Liberal Arts Building was the clearest example of the unprecedented collaboration of artists and engineers in the Columbian Exposition. With three times the floor space of St. Peter's Basilica, Manufactures was the largest building in the world. The Committee on Grounds vetoed Post's plan for a 450-foot dome to surmount Manufactures, citing its exorbitant cost and a fear that such a dome would detract from the supremacy of Hunt's Administration Building.[90] At Daniel Burnham's request, Charles Atwood and Edward Shankland designed an alternative roof that received Post's approval: a gigantic central skylight supported by specially fabricated bessemer steel trusses that rose 206 feet from the floor, with a span of 368 feet from pin to pin. Each of Shankland's trusses had an ultimate strength of not less than sixty-six thousand pounds.[91] To add to the beauty of its raw steel and glass, Frank Millet gathered a dozen muralists, including Kenyon Cox, Walter McEwen, Gari Melchers, Edwin Blashfield, and J. Alden Weir, to decorate this treasurehouse of the world's material culture.

Chicago's famed "lake effect" weather was a nuisance to the construction crews who battled leaking skylights and domes. On April 27, 1892, galeforce winds ripped through Jackson Park and demolished parts of the west and south walls of the Manufactures and Liberal Arts Building. Less than two months later, another storm destroyed portions of the rebuilt walls and knocked several of the massive roof trusses out of line.[92]

As the fair's chief officer, Daniel Burnham was often approached by private citizens who proposed exhibits they felt must be included in the fair. The three dozen private concessions forming the Midway Plaisance were originally under Professor F. W. Putnam's Department of Anthropology, but as the scheme unfolded the Exposition management elected to put the entire arcade under the direction of a youthful Sol Bloom. More commercial than scientific in nature, the Midway displays evolved into money-making enterprises restricted to a separate zone beyond the main grounds. Inspiration for the Midway concessions came from the "ethnographic exhibitions" that had proven popular in Europe at the end of the century.[93] Among the more novel suggestions that Burnham rejected as beneath the dignity of the event were a fifteen-hundred-foot tower along the lines of the Eiffel Tower in Paris, a 193-acre iron-and-glass structure to house all exhibits, and a water palace with a two-hundred-fifty-foot-high dome carrying models of Columbus's vessels. Burnham undoubtedly shrugged at the suggestion of a colossal statue of Atlas supporting the earth on his shoulders.

The most ambitious project not included in the Exposition was Steele Mackaye's Spectatorium, a giant theater complex designed by the Chicago architects Jenney and Mundie. Situated on Fifty-sixth Street across from the northern boundary of the fair, the edifice was to house restaurants and an auditorium where the spectacle of Columbus would be performed. Mackaye abandoned the project before it was completed, and the structure remained standing during the Exposition season as the hollow shell of a once noble dream.[94] Burnham also refused to allow Colonel William F. "Buffalo Bill" Cody's enormously popular "Wild West and Congress of Rough Riders of the World" to perform at the fairgrounds, citing its "incompatibility" with the aim of the enterprise. Undaunted, Cody camped two blocks west of the grounds and enjoyed his most profitable season in the shadow of the White City.

Despite a collaborative spirit, egos inevitably clashed. Charles Follen McKim's objection to a rival firm's commission is a good case in point. "It made us all *perfectly sick at the stomach*," McKim wrote Atwood on October 28, 1891, regarding the proposed Art Institute, "to learn today that the permanent building is to be given to Shepley, Rutan and Coolidge, who besides being just out of the nursery, do not know enough about classical art to teach a primary school. Mead . . . wants you to know that he regards it as a public misfortune."

McKim found other cause for frustration in the work of sculptor Philip Martiny, hired to produce the statuary and reliefs for his Agriculture Building. Early in the Exposition season, McKim wrote to Daniel Chester French regarding Martiny's contribution: "I have nothing for instance against Martiny except that I wish I had never met him," McKim wrote as a final judgment on their working relationship.[95]

Daniel Burnham and Frederick Law Olmsted had their own artistic differences. Regarding the "boat question," Burnham failed to understand Olmsted's directive that no water vehicle interfere with "advancing the main artistic motive of the general design." After three months of exchanges on the subject, Burnham conceded Olmsted's point and ordered that only un-obtrusive and relatively noise-free electric launches and gondolas would be allowed to sail the interior canals and lagoon. To enhance the effect, the Exposition imported Venetian gondoliers for the season.[96]

A more serious disagreement involved development of the Wooded Island in the north lagoon. The original plat called for the island to remain in a state of nature, in Olmsted's words, as "a place of relief from all the splendor and glory and noise and human multitudinousness of the great surrounding Babylon."[97] Olmsted insisted on leaving the Wooded Island as a natural sanctuary untouched by the commercialism and pageantry of the main grounds. Burnham, however, favored a request from Theodore Roosevelt to allow the Boone and Crockett Club to erect an authentic hunters' camp on the island. Ever the advocate of manly rugged individualism, Roosevelt hoped to stock a lodge with "a good series of first-class heads and skins of each of the game animals of the United States."[98] Appalled by the idea, Olmsted remained firm that the island should not be disturbed.

Charmed by the suggestion of an authentic Japanese tea garden and replica of the Ho-o-den Temple (Phoenix Hall) on the island, Olmsted agreed to allow Roosevelt's club to build a modest hunters' camp at the south end of the island, with the temple and garden at the opposite end. During the Exposition season, both sites were enormously popular with the crowds. The rustic simplicity of the hunters' cabin stood out amid the splendor of the surrounding exhibition halls, and the Ho-o-den made a lasting impression on such different visitors as Frank Lloyd Wright and Henry Adams.[99]

Administrative and financial problems became more pressing by the summer of 1892. Construction delays and financial crises impeded the smooth operations of the organization, and once again the Corporation and the Commission were at odds. Benjamin Butterworth had resigned as secretary, telling James Ellsworth in a letter, "You can hardly imagine how sweet it is to be at home, and to be freed from the toil and turmoil that constantly beset me owing to the unpleasant conditions that were round about me."[100] In July, Harlow Higinbotham succeeded Thomas Baker as president of the Corporation. But it was the deteriorating relationship between the Board of Directors and the Commission that brought the management to a midsummer standstill.[101]

"The consequent uncertainties, delays and annoyances from these conflicts," Daniel Burnham wrote in his final report, "focused on the Chief of Construction and finally became so grave that he called some of the Directors together and laid the matter before them."[102] With the dedication ceremonies two months away and construction woefully behind schedule, Burnham impressed upon his superiors the need to streamline the management hierarchy. In August, the Directors and Commissioners created a joint Council of Administration with "absolute and final jurisdiction and control over all matters of general administration of the Exposition, including the installation of exhibits and all agencies employed in that behalf."[103]

Burnham was given the new title "Director of Works," and his Bureau of Construction was renamed the Department of Works. With the exception of a minor administrative adjustment during the Exposition season, the Council of Administration was the principal voice in the management of the Columbian Exposition, and Daniel Burnham was its most influential officer.[104]

Even as the Council of Administration was formed, a constricted cash flow was severely hindering work at Jackson Park. A March 1894 auditor's report revealed that pre-Exposition disbursements exceeded twenty-six million dollars, nearly twice the figure Edward Jeffery had quoted the Senate committee in January 1890.[105] During the construction phase (1890–1893), two separate municipal bond issues in support of the fair brought in ten million dollars to the Exposition's operating accounts. Although the Corporation could eventually count on revenues from a number of sources—the sale of stock, gate receipts, and concessions—on the eve of the dedication ceremonies credit lines were exhausted and the Corporation was running out of money.

Though opposed to direct financial aid, Congress was sympathetic to the Exposition's situation. Following a personal appeal from Director-General George Davis—"Gentlemen, contemplate the glorious harvest of your Exposition"—Congress authorized the Bureau of the Mint to issue five million souvenir Columbian half-dollars.[106] In a clever move, the Board of Directors decided to sell the coins for twice their face value, doubling the funds Congress intended. But despite the promise of $5,000,000 in support, the Exposition never received the full income from the sale of the coins. Months before the fair opened, Congress withdrew nearly $600,000 in a political wrangle over the expenses of judges and awards. Fortunately, a second bond issue brought in $850,000 just as revenues from the coins were lost.[107] The final auditor's report, dated June 1895, indicated Exposition receipts exceeded expenditures by more than $400,000, with actual disbursements of $28,787,532.80.[108]

Despite the setbacks, lavish ceremonies accompanied the official dedication of buildings and grounds on October 21, 1892. As the day approached, work at Jackson Park accelerated, and maintenance crews hurried to clear debris from the unfinished Court of Honor in anticipation of the quarter-million people who would attend. Amid criticism from New York and other cities of the unfinished condition of the grounds, Chicago doled out $275,000 for a three-day festival to inaugurate the Columbian Year and, in the words of the *Chicago Daily Tribune*, "a millennium of universal liberty and the brotherhood of man."[109]

A civic ball was held the evening of October 19, and the next day John Philip Sousa's Marine Band led a procession of eighty thousand participants (and 116 other bands) in a parade through the Loop. "There were ten grand divisions," one bystander recalled, "with banners and regalia, and the crash of military music was incessant."[110] Organizers estimated that more than a million people cheered the marchers. Vice President Levi P. Morton reviewed the troops from a platform at the federal building on Adams Street. As Sousa's band passed by, eighteen hundred schoolgirls formed an animated flag, whose stars were anything but fixed in the children's nervous excitement.

The actual dedicatory ceremonies were held on Friday, October 21, designated by Congress as Flag Day. Encouraging what Ellen Litwicki has called "civic education" and patriotism among the nation's schoolchildren, Flag Day celebrations in Chicago coincided with the Exposition's own gala event.[111] Federal soldiers and members of the state militia escorted three hundred and seventy-five carriages through South Side neighborhoods to Jackson Park. It took several hours to get the officials from downtown to a platform inside the Manufactures and Liberal Arts Building, but when the appropriate moment arrived the orchestra performed John Paine's "Columbus March," a festive piece commissioned for the occasion.

In his welcoming remarks, Chicago Mayor Hempstead Washburne glorified the Exposition as clear evidence of America's "wonderful material prosperity [and] high intelligence." It was a great day for Chicago, the mayor said, and equally great for the nation and the world. Harriet Monroe echoed the mayor's sentiments in her official (and lengthy) "Columbian Ode," a brief portion of which was read to the crowd. Mixing patriotism and freedom with feminine virtue, Monroe extolled Columbia's torch in celebrating America's historic commitment to the future: "Along her sacred shore/ One heart, one song, one dream—/ Men shall be free forevermore/ And love shall be law supreme."[112]

Foreshadowing the opening-day ceremonies six months hence, the dedicatory ceremonies freely mixed sacred and secular images in conveying the meaning of the occasion. After Daniel Burnham presented the principal architects and artists with commemorative medals, the Columbian Chorus saluted them by singing Hayden's "The Heavens Are Telling." Vice President Morton commissioned the fair with reference to the then-popular image of Christopher Columbus as a divinely sanctioned Christian adventurer, nothing less than the first American. "The transcendent feature of Columbus was his faith," Morton observed in announcing the Columbian Year. "That sustained him in days of trial and darkness. . . . Like him, let us have faith in our future." Morton concluded by dedicating the Exposition to "the world's progress in art, in science, in agriculture and in manufactures. I dedicate them to humanity. God save the United States!"

"This day belongs not to America, but to the world," New York Governor Chauncey Depew proclaimed in his "Columbian Oration." "The results of the event it commemorates are the heritage of the peoples of every race and clime. We celebrate the emancipation of man." Although he had opposed Chicago's selection as site of the fair, Depew now announced the Exposition as a handmaid to a new era of history, a theme heard often over the coming year. As the thunderous applause subsided, the ceremonies neared their conclusion with James Cardinal Gibbons's benediction. "Queen of Commerce . . . ," the Catholic prelate besieged, "be, at the same time, the handmaid of religion and of Christian civilization to the nations of the earth." Appropriately enough, the last items on the program were Beethoven's "In Praise of God" and a national salute.[113]

This marriage of nationalism and religion—American civil religion— informed the Columbian Exposition and the civic culture it celebrated. Material progress was the outward sign of divine favor, the argument went, and the dedicatory ceremonies evoked imagery that had a powerful resonance in the Protestant religious culture of the late nineteenth century. Teaching patriotism and promise, the dedication ceremonies announced the festival of progress still six months away. The appearance of the grounds in October 1892, however, indicated the tremendous amount of work that remained to be done. While Daniel Burnham could afford to relax in the self-congratulatory mood of the moment, he need only have glanced outside the door of Manufactures to be shaken back to reality. Winter was approaching, and with it came a growing list of uncertainties.

As Burnham had feared, the winter of 1892–3 was the most severe. During the month of January, the landscape department recorded that frost had seeped a full three feet below ground, and the workmen were forced to set off dynamite charges to break up the frozen earth that prevented further grading. On January 17, the mercury dropped to −20° F, causing Rudolph Ulrich concern for the several hundred thousand plants and shrubs in hibernation around the park.[114] On the thirty-first, Charles McKim wrote Richard Hunt that "snow did considerable damage in Post's building to glass and light woodwork at one or two points; likewise in Peabody's building." Canals and waterways froze over, and the glaze of crystalline powder that covered the buildings suggested to some nature's final triumph. "From every cornice and angle of the buildings," wrote one observer of the wintry montage, "icecycles [sic] were pendant, and when the rays of the frequent sunshine would fall upon domes and turrets they glittered as though studded with diamonds and amethysts."[115]

Quite unexpectedly, on January 13, 1893, Harry Codman died—nearly two years to the day after John Root's death. Since May 1892, the young landscape architect had been debilitated by occasional bouts of stomach trouble and intestinal blockage. While he was recuperating from what was believed to have been an attack of appendicitis, Codman died without warning. Olmsted accompanied Codman's brother Phil to Chicago and took over supervision of the landscape work while attending to his friend's personal effects. As a token of their appreciation for Root's and Codman's contributions to the Columbian Exposition, the consultants adopted Frank Millet's suggestion to place memorial tablets honoring the two in the supporting piers of the Fine Arts Building.[116]

Even as the construction crews hurried toward the May 1 opening, Burnham and his advisers set about the business of selling the fair. Escalating costs and early signs of an uncertain economy persuaded Burnham that nothing should be left to chance. Somewhat belatedly, the Director of Works commenced one of the largest public relations enterprises in late nineteenth-century America.

Although he escorted, by his own count, six thousand visiting dignitaries around the park during the construction phase, Burnham left other tasks to a seasoned veteran. Moses P. Handy, an experienced newspaper editor and one-time owner of the *Philadelphia News*, was appointed chief of the Exposition's Department of Promotion and Publicity. Handy developed a mailing list of some 50,000 names, and by the spring of 1893 his aides were dispatching weekly press releases to more than two thousand newspapers and magazines around the world. By April, C. D. Arnold's photographs had appeared in scores of booklets, guidebooks, and magazine publications.[117]

Burnham worked closely with Handy and with C. D. Arnold and Harlow Higinbotham, Jr., the Exposition's official photographers. Arnold and Higinbotham, son of the Exposition's president, took thousands of glass-plate photographs of every feature, angle, and vista at Jackson Park, from the earliest ground breaking straight through the entire Exposition season. Frances Benjamin Johnston, a young photographer commissioned by the federal government to record the work at Jackson Park, sometimes accompanied Arnold and Higinbotham on their rounds.[118]

Several prominent national magazines commissioned Exposition consultants to write feature articles on the enterprise. Most of these pieces addressed the artistic aspects of the fair and the expected benefits to world civilization. Henry Van Brunt's perceptive architectural essays for *Century Magazine* were accompanied by Kenyon Cox's watercolors of the different buildings. As opening day approached, more articles and photographs appeared in print, and so-called time-savers—commercial travel books and ready-reference guides—flooded the market. In one of those guides, *Harper's Chicago and World's Fair*, Julian Ralph estimated that the publicity department was mailing forty thousand envelopes a week, and official "views" of the buildings and grounds had reached as far as small villages on the edge of the Sahara Desert.[119]

To sustain the level of public interest needed to keep the Exposition solvent, Handy and his editorial staff published their own newspaper, *The Daily Columbian*, during the Exposition season. W. B. Conkey Co. of Chicago was given the lucrative contract of official publisher of Exposition materials—the various catalogs, programs, and guidebooks issued under the authority of the fair. Vendors were also licensed to market memorabilia and every kind of souvenir imaginable: spoons, playing cards, postcards, glasses and mugs, jewelry, and the like. The Exposition received a percentage of the return on the sale of all licensed materials.

A separate customs house was established on the southwest portion of the grounds near a railroad abatement. The station handled all sixty-five thousand exhibits, whose aggregate weight exceeded seventy-five thousand tons. Exhibitors were not charged for space, but they did have to pay a transportation cost to and from the fairgrounds. Each load that entered Jackson Park was levied a toll of six cents per one hundred pounds of cargo, with a minimum charge of fifty cents a shipment.[120] These funds helped to defray the Exposition's handling costs.

With opening day less than a month away, an unforeseen crisis threatened to shut down all work at Jackson Park. With little warning, the Carpenters and Builders Association called for a general strike to protest the absence of a minimum wage and the refusal of the Corporation to exclude nonunion workers or adopt an eight-hour workday. Labor-management conflict was nothing new to Chicago, a city that had witnessed its share of turmoil in the late nineteenth century. Organized labor was particularly strong in the "city that works," as the slogan went, but a work stoppage at Jackson Park could prove fatal at the eleventh hour.

On Monday, April 10, representatives of the trade unions met for twelve hours with members of the Council of Administration. Although contracts would be honored, Burnham informed the unions that the Board of Directors would not accede to their demands. While appealing to their sense of duty, Burnham also made it clear that he would fix the blame for any damage done to the fair squarely on their shoulders. Unwilling to risk a potential public backlash, the unions ordered their men back to work the next day and the crisis passed. In time a new "Article of Agreement" gave the unions what they wanted. In return, the unions agreed not to initiate or participate in any work stoppage until arbitration was exhausted.[121]

On the evening of March 25, 1893, more than one hundred prominent citizens and patrons of the arts attended a testimonial dinner in Madison Square Garden. Its stated purpose was to honor Daniel Burnham and, as the invitation read, "the great benefits to architecture, sculpture, and painting that have resulted from your [Burnham's] connection with the World's Columbian Exposition." Richard Hunt served as the master of ceremonies, and among the counsels of the fair in attendance were Charles F. McKim, Augustus Saint-Gaudens, Frank Millet, Daniel French, and John C. Olmsted, representing his father. Other notables included Richard Watson Gilder of *Century Magazine*, E. L. Godkin of the *Nation*, Charles Dudley Warner, and the artists Louis Comfort Tiffany, J. Alden Weir, Eastman Johnson, and William E. Dodge.[122]

Frederick Law Olmsted was conspicuous by his absence at an event which lavished praise on him as well. In his after-dinner remarks, Harvard's Charles Eliot Norton applauded Burnham's, and Frederick Law Olmsted's singular contributions to the enrichment of public life in the United States. Burnham confided to Norton that among all those present, he was most impressed with William Dean Howells, the "Altrurian Traveller" whom the Director of Works would have the honor of hosting on his visit to the fair.[123]

Two weeks later, Burnham reciprocated with a dinner in Chicago, and again on the last day in April, the Director of Works hosted a Sunday brunch for the principal architects and artists. Burnham gave his guests commemorative ribbons and special seasonal passes, which allowed the bearer free admission to the Columbian Exposition.[124] Buffalo Bill Cody was the only celebrity present who did not have a direct role in the Exposition's construction. Though excluded from the Exposition venue, Cody seemed to harbor no ill will. Sporting a large white sombrero, the self-styled "Last Pioneer of the Nineteenth Century" gave a lavish toast in praise of Daniel Burnham and his colleagues.

Throughout Chicago that last Sunday in April, ministers extolled the virtues and benefits of the coming age and the role of the Exposition as its handmaiden. Mixing sacred and secular images in a manner that would become commonplace in the months ahead, pastors assured their congregants that the fair was akin to beatific visions of old—an act of faith as well as an inspiration to a greater faith. Reverend Charles Morgan of the Church of the Redeemer told his congregation at Sunday services that the World's Columbian Exposition solemn pledge was "to inaugurate a new era of history."[125] Dr. Frederick Noble of the Union Park Congregational Church was sure that the fair "may be expected to make a fresh impression on the brotherhood of man and the solidarity of the race," showing "so conclusively [that] the marvelous progress of the past, will be prophetic of future progress." Tomorrow the world would come to Chicago, and Chicago would present America to the world.[126]

Celebrated as a compendium of past progress and harbinger of a new era, the Columbian Exposition was a civic pageant of unprecedented size and symbolism. Through his Altrurian Traveller, William Dean Howells voiced his judgment of the fair as a stunning glorification of democratic virtue and the possibilities of a national culture. But Howells was not alone in appropriating the Columbian Exposition as a sign of renewal amid the tumultuous transitions of the era. As a meaningful symbol, however, this corporate venture invested with such great cultural significance sometimes revealed more than its creators intended.

Notes

1. William Dean Howells, *Letters of an Altrurian Traveller*, ed. by Clara M. Kirk and Rudolph Kirk (Gainesville, 1961), pp. 22–23.

2. Montgomery Schuyler, "Last Words about the World's Fair," in *American Architecture and other Essays*, 2 vols., ed. by William H. Jordy and Ralph Coe (Cambridge, Mass., 1961), pp. 559, 573.

3. Zueblin is quoted in Lloyd Lewis and Henry Justin Smith, *Chicago: The History of Its Reputation* (New York, 1929), p. 203.

4. Lewis Mumford, *Sticks and Stones: A Study of American Architecture and Civilization* (New York, 1955 reprint), pp. 55–69; Richard Guy Wilson, "The Great Civilization," in *The American Renaissance: 1876–1915* (New York, 1979), pp. 11–74.

5. Burton Benedict, "The Anthropology of World's Fairs," in Burton Benedict, *The Anthropology of World's Fairs: San Francisco's Panama Pacific International Exposition of 1915* (London and Berkeley, 1983), p. 2; Merle Curti, "America at the World's Fairs, 1851–1893," *American Historical Review* 55 (July 1950): 833.

6. Neil Harris, "Great American Fairs and American Cities: The Role of Chicago's Columbian Exposition," in *Cultural Excursions: Market Appetites and Cultural Tastes in Modern America* (Chicago, 1990), pp. 11–31.

7. See *Reports of the United States Commissioners to the Universal Exposition of 1889 at Paris*, 5 vols. (Washington, D.C., 1890). These volumes contain a wealth of information on the planning and management of the Universal Exposition.

8. William Schneider, "Race and Empire: The Rise of Popular Ethnography in the Late Nineteenth Century," *Journal of Popular Culture* 11 (Summer 1977): 98–109.

9. United States Centennial Commission, *Official Catalogue of the United States International Exhibition, 1876*, 4 vols. in one (Philadelphia, 1876); James D. McCabe, *The Illustrated History of the Centennial Exhibition, Philadelphia, 1876* (1876; Philadelphia, 1975).

10. "Samantha" quoted in Lillian Miller, "Engines, Marbles, and Canvasses: The Centennial Exposition of 1876," in Lillian Miller, Walter T. K. Nugent, and H. Wayne Morgan, *1876: The Centennial Year* (Indianapolis, 1973), p. 4; Bruce quoted in Howard Mumford Jones, *The Age of Energy: Varieties of American Experience, 1865–1917* (New York, 1971), p. 143.

11. *Official Catalogue*, 3: 15–32.

12. A Dr. T. W. Zaremba, a citizen of Mexico who had adopted Chicago as his home, is generally credited with first proposing the idea of a Columbian world's fair. *Dedicatory and Opening Ceremonies of the World's Columbian Exposition*, ed. under the direction of the Joint Committee on Ceremonies (Chicago, 1893), p. 53; Moses P. Handy, ed., *Official Directory of the World's Columbian Exposition* (Chicago, 1893), p. 41.

13. [Harlow Higinbotham], *Report of the President to the Board of Directors of the World's Columbian Exposition* (Chicago, 1898), p. 12.

14. Daniel H. Burnham, "World's Columbian Exposition: Typewritten Materials," p. 10, found in "Materials by and about Daniel Burnham," Daniel Burnham Papers, Daniel Burnham Library of the Art Institute of Chicago.

15. William Cronon, *Nature's Metropolis: Chicago and the Great West* (New York, 1991), pp. 341–50.

16. Handy, Official Directory, pp. 42–3; [Harlow Higinbotham], *Report of the President* (Chicago, 1898), p. 8.

17. "Minutes of the Board of Directors of the World's Columbian Exposition of 1893," 2 vols. (Chicago, 1890–1895), 1:4–5, Chicago Historical Society, Chicago, Illinois; Burnham, "Final Report of the Director of Works," 1:1; Handy, *Official Directory*, pp. 43–47.

18. *Arguments Before the Quadro-Centennial Committee of the United States Senate,* 4 pts. (Washington, 1890), 1:4–11; pt. 4.

19. William Cronon makes the point of Chicago's intimate and reciprocal relationship with the region in *Nature's Metropolis: Chicago and the Great West* (New York, 1991), which is precisely the connection Chicago's representatives made before Congress in 1890.

20. "New York and the World's Fair," p. 8, Pamphlet File, World's Columbian Exposition Collection, Special Collections, Chicago Public Library; *Arguments,* 3:6–9.

21. *Arguments,* 2:1–14.

22. *Arguments,* 2:14.

23. *Arguments,* 2:15–19.

24. U.S. Congress, House of Representatives, 51st Cong., 1st and special session, 24 February 1890, *Congressional Record,* 21:1659–65; U.S. Congress, Senate, 51st Congress, 1st and Special Session, 21 April 1890, *Congressional Record* 21:3596–3615.

25. Because of delays, the opening date was set back to May 1, 1893, with the dedication ceremonies scheduled for October 12, 1892. Ibid., pp. 3607–15, 3871; see the Act in William Cameron, ed., *The World's Fair, Being a Pictorial History of the Columbian Exposition* (Chicago, 1893), pp. 133–39; *By-Laws of the World's Columbian Exposition, Acts of Congress, Officers, Standing Committees,* pp. 3–11, Pamphlet File, Chicago Public Library; *Dedicatory and Opening Ceremonies,* p. 55.

26. Daniel H. Burnham, "Final Report of the Director of Works of the World's Columbian Exposition," 8 vols. (Chicago, 1894), 1:71, Papers of Daniel H. Burnham, Daniel Burnham Library of the Art Institute of Chicago, Chicago, Illinois.

27. Cameron, pp. 133–39.

28. U.S. Congress, House, 51st Congress, 1st and special session, *Congressional Record,* 2:2618–21.

29. For a full consideration of the participation of women in the Columbian Exposition, see chapter five. The most comprehensive study of women in the Chicago fair remains Jeanne Madeline Weimann's *The Fair Women* (Chicago, 1981).

30. Charles Bonney, "A World's Congress at the World's Fair," *The Statesman* 6 (October 1889), in *World's Congress Auxiliary Organization,* 5 vols. (Chicago 1890–1893), Special Collections Division, Chicago Public Library. The *WCAO* consists of five bound volumes of articles, announcements, and programs for the various congresses and meetings held in conjunction with the fair. A more complete discussion of the Auxiliary's reform congresses is contained in chapter 6.

31. "Minutes of the Board of Directors," 1:4–5; Handy, *Official Directory,* p. 53.

32. "Minutes of the Board of Directors," 1:7–8.

33. Other committees and their chairmen were: Finance (Frederick Peck), Legislation (Edwin Walker), National and State Exhibits (Erskine Phelps), Foreign Exhibits (W. T. Baker), Press and Printing (Rollin Keyes), Transportation (M. M. Kirkman), Fine Arts (Charles Hutchinson), Ways and Means (Otto Young), and Machinery and Electrical Appliances (R. C. Crowly). James W. Ellsworth, *James W. Ellsworth: His Life and Ancestry* (New York, 1930), pp. 37–38, Papers of James W. Ellsworth, Special Collections, Chicago Public Library; "Minutes of the Board of Directors," 1:39–40; Burnham, "Final Report of the Director of Works," 1:15–16.

34. "Minutes of the Board of Directors," 1:58–60; "Minutes of the Executive Committee of the World's Columbian Exposition," 21 May 1890, n.p., Chicago Historical Society; "Laws of the State of Illinois," pp. 4–6, 18–9, Pamphlet File, Special Collections, Chicago Public Library.

35. Benjamin Butterworth to James Ellsworth, 1 July 1890; Butterworth to Ellsworth, 11 July 1890, Ellsworth Papers.

36. Butterworth to Ellsworth, 11 July 1890, Ellsworth Papers.

37. "Minutes of the Commission," pp. 119–20. In the Commission vote, taken after the Board of Directors had acted, the Chicagoan Davis defeated James Allison of Ohio by a margin of fifty votes to forty-two.

38. The Corporation's Executive Committee approved a resolution to that effect sponsored by Peck. See "Minutes of the Executive Committee," 18 June 1890. For six months Charles Hutchison, a director and president of the Art Institute, negotiated with little success with property owners near the park, who remained unpersuaded about locating the fair nearby. See "Minutes of the Executive Committee," 20 January 1891.

39. James W. Ellsworth to Frederick Law Olmsted, 29 July 1890, Olmsted Papers. A succinct overview of the firm's involvement is provided in Witold Rybczynski, *A Clearing in the Distance: Frederick Law Olmsted and America in the Nineteenth Century* (New York, 1999), pp. 385–99.

40. Lyman Gage to Frederick Law Olmsted, 11 August 1890, Olmsted Papers.

41. Burnham, "Final Report of the Director of Works," 1:2.

42. Burnham to the Committee on Grounds and Buildings, 23 September 1890, Burnham Papers.

43. Henry Sargent Codman to Frederick Law Olmsted, 23 September 1890; Olmsted to Codman, 25 September 1890, Olmsted Papers.

44. John W. Root to Henry S. Codman, 10 October 1890, Olmsted Papers.

45. Codman to Olmsted, 25 October 1890, Olmsted Papers.

46. "Minutes of the Board," 1:169–70.

47. Burnham to the Board of Directors, 21 November 1890, Burnham Papers.

48. On American artists and architects and their "enthusiasm" for Venice, see Margaretta M. Lovell, *Venice: The American View, 1860–1920* (San Francisco, 1984).

49. Burnham, "Final Report of the Director of Works," 1:2.

50. Burnham, "Final Report of the Director of Works," 1:2, 33–44; Olmsted to Charles Pullen, 4 December 1890, Olmsted Papers.

51. Inland Architect and News Record 14 (November 1889): 47; *Inland Architect and News Record* 15 (July 1890): 81.

52. Burnham, "Final Report of the Director of Works," 1:5.

53. Louis Sullivan, *The Autobiography of an Idea* (1924; New York, 1956), pp. 291, 321; Dimitri Tselos, "The Chicago Fair and the Myth of the 'Lost Cause,'" *Journal of the Society of Architectural Historians* 26 (1967): 259–68; David Crook, "Louis Sullivan, the World's Columbian Exposition, and American Life" (Ph.D. dissertation, Harvard University, 1963), esp. pp. 123–406; David S. Andrew, *Louis Sullivan and the Polemics of Modern Architecture: The Present Against the Past* (Urbana, 1985), pp. 136–39.

54. Burnham to Richard Hunt, et al., 13 December 1890, Burnham Papers.

55. Burnham, "Final Report of the Director of Works," 1:6–9.

93. William Schneider, "Race and Empire: The Rise of Popular Ethnography in the Late Nineteenth Century," *Journal of Popular Culture* 11 (Summer 1977): 98–109.

94. Burnham and Millet, *World's Columbian Exposition: The Book of the Builders*, pp. 38–39.

95. McKim to Charles Atwood, 28 October 1891; McKim to Daniel Chester French, 13 June 1893, Charles Follen McKim Papers, Library of Congress, Washington, D.C.

96. Olmsted to Burnham, 28 December 1891; Codman to Olmsted, 15 January 1892; Olmsted to Burnham, 6 February 1892, Olmsted Papers.

97. Olmsted to Codman, 4 November 1891, Olmsted Papers.

98. Theodore Roosevelt to William Buchanan, n.d., Olmsted Papers.

99. Okakura Kukudzo, *Illustrated Description of the Ho-o-den (Phoenix Hall) at the World's Columbian Exposition* (Tokyo, 1893).

100. Butterworth to Ellsworth, 12 April 1892, Ellsworth Papers.

101. [Higinbotham], *Report of the President* (1898), pp. 133–47.

102. Burnham, "Final Report of the Director of Works," 1:10.

103. *Constitution and By-Laws of the Council of Administration* (Chicago, 1892), p. 10.

104. Burnham, "Final Report of the Director of Works," 1:30; [Higinbotham], *Report of the President* (1898), pp. 146–49.

105. [Harlow Higinbotham], *Annual Report of the President of the World's Columbian Exposition, Year Ending April, 1893* (Chicago, 1893), pp. 4–6; "Report of the Auditor to the Board of Directors" (Chicago, 1894), in the Olmsted Papers.

106. *Remarks of Director-General Davis Before the World's Fair Committee of the House of Representatives, May 17, 1892* (Chicago, 1892), pp. 3–15.

107. [Higinbotham], *Report of the President* (1898), pp. 68–69, 72–74; Cameron, pp. 133–39; James W. Ellsworth, James W. Ellsworth: His Life and Ancestry, pp. 47–50.

108. [Higinbotham], *Report of the President to the Board of Directors of the World's Columbian Exposition* (Chicago, 1898), p. 340. This final report listed the total disbursements of the Exposition at $28,787,532.80, leaving a profit of $446,832.36.

109. *Chicago Daily Tribune*, 22 October 1892. Chicago moved the dedication ceremonies back from October 12 (Columbus Day) to accommodate ceremonies already scheduled in New York City to greet the arriving Spanish caravels.

110. Cameron, *The World's Fair*, p. 18; *Programme of Days and Order of Ceremonies* (Chicago, 1892), Pamphlet File, Special Collections Division, Chicago Public Library.

111. Ellen Marie Litwicki, "Visions of America: Public Holidays and American Cultures, 1776–1900" (Ph.D. dissertation, University of Virginia, 1992), pp. 442–45.

112. *Programme of Days*, pp. 10–12; Harriet Monroe, *A Poet's Life* (New York, 1938), p. 122. Monroe persuaded the Committee on Ceremonies to commission her to write the "Ode," and she worked in the utmost secrecy. When the *New York World* published a copy of the poem just days before the ceremony, without the poet's consent, Monroe was livid and threatened a lawsuit over the matter.

113. *Dedicatory and Opening Ceremonies of the World's Columbian Exposition*, ed. under the direction of the Joint Committee on Ceremonies (Chicago, 1893), p. 134;

Cameron, p. 207; Chauncey DePew, *The Columbian Oration* (New York, 1892), pp. 1–20.

114. [Harlow Higinbotham], *Report of the President to the Board of Directors of the World's Columbian Exposition* (Chicago, 1898), p. 131.

115. McKim to Hunt, 31 January 1893, McKim Papers; Cameron, p. 230.

116. Laura Wood Roper, *FLO: A Biography of Frederick Law Olmsted* (Baltimore, 1973), p. 430; Olmsted to John C. Olmsted, 17 February 1893, Olmsted Papers; Burnham, "Final Report of the Director of Works," 1:19.

117. Moses P. Handy, ed., *Official Directory of the World's Columbian Exposition* (Chicago, 1893), p. 188.

118. Two valuable essays on the Exposition's photographic legacy are Peter B. Hales, "At Its Peak: Grand Style Photography and the World's Columbian Exposition, 1892–1895," in *Silver Cities: The Photography of American Urbanization, 1839–1915* (Philadelphia, 1984), and more recently James Gilbert, "Fixing the Image: Photography at the World's Columbian Exposition," in Neil Harris, et al., *Grand Illusions: Chicago's World's Fair of 1893* (Chicago, 1993), pp. 99–132. Equally important and more comprehensive in scope is Julie K. Brown, *Contesting Images: Photography and the World's Columbian Exposition* (Tucson, 1994). During construction, Frances Benjamin Johnson produced hundreds of her own photographs of scenes at Jackson Park, shots of construction crews, buildings, and grounds, many of which survive in the Frances Benjamin Johnston Collection and the general photographic archives at the Library of Congress.

119. Julian Ralph, *Harper's Chicago and World's Fair* (New York, 1892), p. 132.

120. [Higinbotham], *Report of the President*, p. 192; *Rules and Regulations Governing Exhibits* (Chicago, n.d.), in James W. Ellsworth Papers, Special Collections Division, Chicago Public Library.

121. "Articles of Agreement" (Chicago, 1893), in "Materials by and about Daniel Burnham."

122. *New York Times*, 26 March 1893; McKim to Millet, 10 February 1893, McKim Papers.

123. *New York Times*, 26 March 1893.

124. Miscellaneous notes in "Materials by and about Daniel Burnham."

125. Rev. Charles Morgan, "Signs of the Times," in *World's Fair Sermons* (Chicago, 1893), p. 68.

126. Dr. Frederick Noble, "Meaning and Opportunities of the Fair," in *World's Fair Sermons*, pp. 54–55.

2

American Encounters

"It is a scene over which the gods might linger," Daniel Shepp, author of a popular guidebook, wrote of his first view of the Columbian Exposition, "and dream that heaven had descended to earth, and that once again man walked sinless in Eden."[1] Visitors like Shepp saw in the Columbian Exposition precisely what they were prepared to see, and although the fair had its critics, its popular acclaim was undisputed. Its novelty, innovation, exoticism, and unabashed materialism were celebrated in songs, poems, and novels. Cartoonists caricatured its visitors, and essayists extolled its virtues in commentaries that circulated around the world. If Daniel Shepp and his colleagues who celebrated the enterprise found a redemptive value in the fair, they could be allowed their excesses. Such hyperbole was entirely in keeping with international exhibitions in the late nineteenth century.

Popular commentaries frequently associated religious imagery with the regenerative power of the Chicago world's fair, a reminder of the sustaining influence of religion in private and public life. For Meg and Robin, the youthful characters in Frances Hodgson Burnett's novel *Two Little Pilgrims' Progress*, a jaunt around this latter-day incarnation of John Bunyan's Celestial City was sufficient reassurance that miracles did still occasionally occur. The fictional rural sage Uncle Jeremiah and his family did not escape the force of this "most favored spot on earth." For this whimsical backwoods patriarch the Exposition allowed reprieve from woeful lamentations on the world's sinful ways. "I am closing my days mighty satisfactory to me," Jeremiah remarked to his niece Fanny while in the park. "I believe I have felt more of the Lord in my soul in the last few days than I ever did in so many years."[2]

Even the philosopher William James was not immune to playful remarks on the devotional attitude many assumed upon entering the fairgrounds. "I shan't go to Chicago," he confessed to his brother Henry. "But *everyone* says one ought to sell *all* one has and mortgage one's soul to get there; it is esteemed such a revelation of beauty. People cast away all sin and baseness, burst into tears and grow religious, etc. under its influence." "Sell the cook stove if necessary and come," Hamlin Garland told his aging father, "you *must* see this fair."[3]

Celebratory exaltations were commonplace for world's fairs, but Chicago newspapers outdid themselves in expressing approval of the May 1 opening ceremonies, a pattern kept up throughout the six-month season. "The day was not for Chicago," the *Chicago Daily Tribune* counseled in patriotic rapture, "or for the Mississippi Valley, or for the continent of Columbus, but for the world. Later will come the fruits of human activity, which are stored in the vaulted buildings. What new ideas they may give birth to," the commentary continued, "what novel ambitions they may kindle, are bounded only by the horizon of time."[4] "Truly a theater worthy of the gods—something to be imagined by a dreamy poet or read of in the pages of an oriental legend," declared the rival *Chicago Daily Inter-Ocean.* "The dullest eye at once perceived that here the genius of man had done its best," rejoined the *Chicago Herald* with equal verve. The *Chicago Times* was no less timid when it announced that the day "marks the beginning of an Olympian era." "It was a day," the paper claimed, "of fearful and wonderful excitement for the boys from Podunk, Coon Creek, and the rural districts of Uncle Sam's dominions." But it was the *Tribune* that offered a note of sober realism in a headline that simply acknowledged, "THE EXPOSITION NO LONGER A DREAM; IT IS A REALITY."[5]

For both American and foreign visitors, the Columbian Exposition provided a rich variety of "encounters" spread across the 680-acre park and along the Midway Plaisance. Over its six-month season, which ran from the first day in May until the end of October, more than twenty-seven million people visited the World's Columbian Exposition. (Many of the people who purchased tickets, of course, visited the fair on more than one occasion, inflating aggregate attendance figures.) They came to inspect the more than sixty-five thousand exhibits arranged in four hundred buildings and pavilions. And they came to experience firsthand the world's exotic peoples and cultures.[6]

In the number and novelty of exhibits and in the scores of acres covered by buildings, the Columbian Exposition set a standard of size and monumental elegance by which all future exhibitions would be judged. Past and present, themes of nostalgia and progress, even civilization and savagery stood in relationship throughout the fairgrounds, as behind the outward trappings of its Renaissance motif visitors observed the latest mechanical and technological innovations of the day. They also spied a glimpse at the habits and costumes of other peoples gathered from around the world.

Where else, one might ask, could an Iowa farmer sample Japanese or Nubian cuisine while rubbing shoulders with a tribesman from Dahomey, a Spanish princess, and South Sea Islanders?

Hamlin Garland remembered that in the summer of 1893, all of Chicago was "humming" on account of the fair. The broad, tree-lined boulevards and narrow residential streets of the South Side were continuously flooded with Exposition traffic. In the late evening, it was not uncommon for residents of the neighborhoods adjacent to Jackson Park to be awakened by young couples singing "After the Ball" or some other popular tune on their way home. Circuses, sideshows, and revival tents cluttered the streets and lots west of the Midway, and their agents sought to exploit the tremendous appeal of the fair. One source estimated that Buffalo Bill's Wild West Show gave 318 performances, averaging twelve thousand customers a night.[7] There was money to be made in the Exposition—and outside it, for those hucksters denied a place within the fence.

In addition to the lively street scenes, temporary hotels and rooming houses flourished throughout the city. Some families abandoned their homes for the season, renting rooms to out-of-towners who had come to the fair. Cabarets, restaurants, concert halls, and playhouses sprang up to offer entertainment of one kind or another. Lillian Russell starred as "Teresa" in the Columbia Theater's presentation of *The Mountebanks,* and over the course of the Exposition season more than one million people saw the performance of *America* at the four-thousand-seat Auditorium Theater. In October, English actors Henry Irving and Ellen Terry were featured in Shakespeare's *Merchant of Venice* in a limited engagement at the Columbia. At Ziegfeld's Trocadero on Michigan Avenue, German-born strongman Eugen Sandow—"The Great Sandow," as he was billed—shared the stage with what the *Tribune* described as "an unusually refined vaudeville program."[8] Aspiring musicians like Scott Joplin and W. C. Handy, who were denied a place on the formal musical program at Jackson Park, sought work in some of the new nightclubs that flourished during the season. Gin joints, gambling houses, and other dens of mischief enjoyed brisk business, as did the so-called boardinghouses and brothels that catered to the more intimate recreational needs of their clientele. The Columbian Exposition was a boon to the local economy, and the festive, communal spirit it inspired took on many forms.

The Columbian Exposition was more than buildings and grounds, exhibits, and amusements. A wide-ranging program of musical concerts and theatrical performances brought many of the leading orchestras and music ensembles from Europe and the United States to Jackson Park.[9] An outdoor sylvan theater staged occasional plays. During the season, special days were designated to celebrate cities, states, and ethnic nationalities. The Exposition's World's Congress Auxiliary coordinated several hundred conferences and workshops devoted to every aspect of what was then termed "intellectual culture," as well as the leading social and political issues of the period. More than fifty-eight hundred speakers from one hundred countries participated in sessions at the fairgrounds or, more often, at the Memorial Arts Building on Michigan Avenue in the Loop (which afterward became the Art Institute of Chicago).[10]

"The Fair," Charles Eliot Norton told novelist Henry Blake Fuller, "in spite of its amazing incongruities, and its immense 'border' of vulgarities, was on the whole a great promise, even a great pledge. It, at least, forbids despair."[11] The highbrowed "pledge" that Norton referred to was that art and commerce, nature and civilization, could be joined into an idyllic urban landscape where beauty transforms the industrial wasteland into what William Dean Howells called "a real civic life." This was the spirit of Howells's Altrurian parable, and it was carried forward into the urban beautification programs of the twentieth century.

In this sense the Exposition was not a retreat from the discordance and disruption of the industrial age. Rather, with the imperial Court of Honor as its center, the fair offered the possibilities of renewal amid the social and economic disarray of the Gilded Age. Wrapped in the self-congratulatory rhetoric of exceptionalism and masked in the ornamental classicism of the Renaissance, the *form* of the Exposition had a particular *function* to perform.

The Chicago world's fair was a constructed reality of ordered space that incorporated commercial and imaginative elements in an ensemble meant to uplift and to enthrall. Like Frederick Law Olmsted's plan for Central Park, the Exposition ensemble was intended for enjoyment—to be pleasing to the eye—and for education. Natural and artificial elements were juxtaposed in a harmonious relationship wherein commercial, recreational, and cultural activities flourished.

In what has become a popular association, Chicago's White City stood in marked contrast to the Black City, a reference to the towering smokestacks and darkened skies of industrial Chicago. But the White City also stood in juxtaposition to the Grey City, the neighboring towers of learning at the University of Chicago. The Exposition's impression of unity disguised, at least momentarily, the sheer diversity of features and activities contained within the fairgrounds.

The Exposition was also a place of commemoration and remembrance, in which mixed what might be called the "official" and "vernacular" voices essential to all public memorials.[12] In addition to the classical motif and the common white exteriors, various forms of public iconography conveyed the impression of artistic unity. And in the cultural agenda of world's fairs, impressions carried great meaning.

The artistic unity had a broader purpose; the outward appearance was meant to engender an inner appreciation for a common basis for culture amid the growing diversity in society. Art was put to the ends of ideology, with the hopes of enlarging the realm of patriotic devotion among groups on the margins of Howells's "civic life." But as was often the case in the larger society, the diversity of the scheme could restrict the impression of unity, giving rise to the incongruities of which Norton wrote.

Critics have tended to read elements of cultural hierarchy and cultural hegemony in the physical arrangements of space within Jackson Park and along the Midway. There was a conscious effort to order space in the arrangement of exhibits into distinct categories of human activity and in the general distribution of buildings and grounds. Although a distinction was drawn between the main grounds and the Midway Plaisance, in practice the cultural boundaries associated with the division of space were more elastic than their critics have suggested.

With its towering edifices dedicated to the higher and nobler pursuits of humankind, the main grounds became something akin to sacred space. The Court of Honor in particular reflected what Lawrence Levine has called the "sacralization of culture" that was so evident at the end of the nineteenth century.[13] Time and again the great exhibition halls were referred to in reverential tones as "palaces" and "temples" (the "Palace of Mechanic Arts," the "Palace of Art," the "Palace of Electrical Arts," or the "Woman's Temple").

If the main grounds reflected the "genteel tradition," the Midway Plaisance's exoticism was more profane or worldly in its intentions and in its tolerance of crass commercialism, humbug, and fakery. Its international "villages" and Oriental theaters conjured up images of primitiveness and barbarism, as contrasted with the serene dignity of the Court of Honor. In the juxtaposition (and separation) of the Court and the Midway, ethereal and worldly pursuits, the aesthetics of art and the imperatives of commercial culture intermingled in a not-so-comfortable alliance.

Any anthropology of the Exposition would increasingly consider the noticeable contrast of ideals represented in the Court of Honor and the Midway villages. But anthropology per se was not on Reverend William White Wilson's mind when he attempted to explain the fair to his congregation. Mixing secular and sacramental images in an unintended benediction for American civil religion, the rector of Chicago's St. Mark's Episcopal Church said of the White City, "It is a great thing to appreciate opportunities when they come. God has placed the triumphs of the ages in our midst. At our door we have the whole world with its tribute of art and science."[14] "To see this miracle of harmonious form at sunset," echoed Candace Wheeler in *Harper's New Monthly Magazine*, "with all its lovely length shining down the lagoon, is easily to believe in its heavenly origin."[15] Inspiration for the Midway, on the other hand, was of more earthly lineage.

By contrast, Burton Benedict has observed that world's fairs were important institutions in the rise of a consumer culture at the end of the nineteenth century. They served, he says, to "rearrange status hierarchies and to validate the rise of the middle class."[16] In its appeal to the consumptive habits of a burgeoning urban populace, the Columbian Exposition did reflect a hierarchy of values that emphasized modern bourgeois acquisitiveness. In its great exhibition halls, the fair paid homage to expanding market economies and a reordering of habits of production and consumption throughout the nineteenth century.

But one element of the Columbian Exposition, and perhaps of international exhibitions in general, has been largely overlooked. As much as the manicured lawns and towering edifices at Jackson Park sought to create the vision of an ideal urban consumer society, the sheer size and scale of the ensemble also dwarfed the individual visitor. In this sense the Columbian Exposition anticipated elements of the coming mass society of the twentieth century. With little appreciation for the economies of scale, the designers sought to overpower and overwhelm sightseers, and they largely succeeded.

In their vision of a colossal City Beautiful, the artists had the unintended effect of creating a city that lacked human scale and proportion. In the parlors of consumerism, in the miles of aisles of exhibits and displays, and along the congested avenues of Jackson Park and the Midway, the person was lost in a sea of anonymity. Perhaps more than its attachment to consumerism and materialism, the Columbian Exposition unexpectedly exposed the anonymity of the mass culture embedded in the temper of the imagined new era it heralded.

"Progress" was the watchword of the Exposition season, as if by some detailed accounting of growth and movement and speed one could give tangible proof of humanity's moral and social improvement. Readers heard much about the fair as an "object lesson" or "catalogue" of the material, artistic, and mechanical progress since Christopher Columbus's maiden voyage to Europe's New World. When the enabling legislation called for an "International Exhibition of the arts, industries, manufactures, and products of the soil, mine and sea," many observers understood implicitly that the Columbian Exposition would be a yardstick by which to measure the advances of civilization in the nineteenth century.

In its simplest form the Exposition's classification of exhibits distinguished between the products of Nature and the products of Civilization, while recognizing a link between abundant resources and manmade devices, in the form of machinery or finished goods. Therefore, there were thirteen general departments, which corresponded roughly to the major exhibition halls. Certain smaller groupings of exhibits, such as dairy and forestry products, were given their own buildings or pavilions (see Table 2.1).

The Chicago exhibition was the first world's fair to reserve separate full-scale exhibition halls to the interests of horticulture, transportation, fish and fisheries, mining, electricity, agriculture, and women (see Table 2.2).[17] Unlike previous exhibitions, women were encouraged to participate in every exhibit category and in the separate Department of Women's Progress in the Woman's Building. Nor had any previous exhibition attempted such an integration of private amusements and concessions as was found on the

TABLE 2.1 Buildings and Grounds

Building	Square Feet	Acres
Administration	51,456	1.18
Agriculture	589,416	13.53
Fine Arts	261,073	5.99
Electricity	265,500	6.09
Fisheries	104,500	2.39
Government	155,896	3.57
Horticulture	237,956	5.46
Machinery	796,686	18.28
Manufactures	1,345,462	30.88
Mines	246,181	5.65
Transportation	704,066	16.16
Woman's	82,698	1.89
Subtotal	4,840,894	111.12
Minor Buildings	1,630,514	37.43
State Buildings	450,886	10.35
Foreign Buildings	135,663	3.11
Concessions	801,238	18.39
Miscellaneous	317,699	7.29
Total	8,176,894	187.69
	SUMMARY	
Buildings	8,176,894	187.69
Lawns	7,240,386	166.21
Water	2,630,105	60.37
Roads	11,146,184	255.88
Piers	695,125	15.95
Total	29,888,694	686.10

Midway Plaisance. Similarly, the use of mechanical and electrical power at Jackson Park surpassed all previous efforts. No previous world's fair could boast of a program comparable to the World's Congress Auxiliary.

Like its predecessors, the Columbian Exposition was touted for its educational value. "Instruction is the primary object of the Fair," wrote Royal Cortissoz, "and it is tacitly demanded of every one who comes to it that he take his pleasure seriously." Its lessons had a particularly patriotic purpose,

TABLE 2.2 Classification of Exhibits: General Exhibit Departments

Department	Chief
A—Agriculture	W. I. Buchanan
B—Horticulture	J. M. Samuels
C—Livestock	W. I. Buchanan
D—Fish and Fisheries	J. W. Collins
E—Mines and Mining	Frederick J. V. Skiff
F—Machinery	L. W. Robinson
G—Transportation	W. A. Smith
H—Manufactures	James Allison
J—Electricity	James P. Barrett
K—Fine Arts	Halsey Ives
L—Liberal Arts	Selim H. Peabody
M—Ethnology	Frederick W. Putnam
N—Forestry	W. I. Buchanan
O—Publicity and Promotion*	Moses P. Handy
P—Foreign Affairs*	Walker Fearn

*Departments O and P, though part of the classification scheme, did not pertain to exhibits.

however, what John Brisben Walker likened to a "College of Democracy" by which to judge American achievements against its competitors. "As an educational factor and as a means of culture," George Sparks boasted in *The Dream City*, "the World's Columbian Exposition possibly did more for the progress of humanity than has ever before been accomplished."[18]

The exhibition halls were filled with historical and retrospective displays meant to record the pace and scope of human progress. In this context, the Chicago world's fair was a laboratory for a comparative study of the accomplishments of the Orient and the Occident. One speaker in the Anthropology Congress saw the fair itself as one great ethnographic exhibit, wherein the world's peoples and cultures intermingled. Another observer said that to walk the fairgrounds and stroll across the Midway Plaisance was to go around the world and "pass the ages in review."[19]

Critic Mary Griswold Van Renssalaer offered potential visitors some useful advice in the pages of *Century Magazine*. Take three days to see the fair, she told those of the "usual American mind," "as alive with mere curiosity as it is with a craving for instruction—pleased to look everywhere, discontented only to think that other people are seeing things with which it [the American mind] cannot make acquaintance." To avoid unnecessary distraction, Van Renssalaer thought everyone should go alone, or in the company of someone of like mind. After a day given over to rest, everyone should "spread your wings" and visit each of the great exhibition halls. For those who cared little for the education of the main grounds, there was always the Midway Plaisance.[20]

On the main grounds, patrons could choose from a variety of transportation systems at their disposal; although walking was most common, with strollers and carts available for hire, only gondolas and electric launches were permitted on the lagoon and canals. Travel between any two points cost twenty-five cents, while ten cents secured a seat on the elevated Intramural Railway, which serviced ten passenger stations on its three-mile route along the southern, western, and northern perimeters of the park. More sophisticated than the simple elevated train that had traversed the Centennial grounds in 1876, the Intramural Railway proved to be one of the highlights of a day spent at Jackson Park.

Equally innovative was the so-called Movable Sidewalk, which ran the length of the main pier from the Peristyle complex. Rather than walking the forty-five hundred feet to the end of the pier, visitors could sit on one of two canopied wood benches, as hidden electric motors propelled the "sidewalk" at variable speeds up to six miles an hour. In all, more than twelve million fairgoers availed themselves of some form of intramural transportation while visiting the fair.[21]

After disembarking from the Terminal Station or the elevated train that served the fairgrounds, the Court of Honor was the first port of call, so to speak. "At first glimpse of the City Beautiful," Frederick Cooke wrote of the Court of Honor, "my heart gave a bound, unbidden tears filled my eyes, and I felt as one translated into an ideal world."[22] The Court and its great basin ran on an east-west axis, with majestic buildings and statuary throughout. In addition to the *Republic* and the *Ship of State* in the Columbian Fountain, Daniel Chester French's *Columbian Quadriga* surmounted the Peristyle at lake's edge. Its inscription read: "Ye Shall Know the Truth, and the Truth Will Make You Free." In words that would be remembered at New York's Coney Island, Walter Besant simply said of the Court, "It is Dreamland!"[23]

Most visitors were captivated by the towering image of the *Republic*, whose feminine cast reinforced maternal vigilance and triumphant democracy. For all of the attention directed at *Republic*, Frank Millet thought MacMonnies's Columbian Fountain stole the show. "Anything more typical of the youth and hope we fondly believe to be the characteristic of our nation is hard to conceive," he wrote of the allegorical *Ship of State*; "and if, as is to be so greatly desired, the monument is to be made permanent, . . . it might well stand to represent an era."[24]

The east-west axis running from the lake through the Administration Building was intersected by the other principal artery, which ran on a north-south line from the South Grounds through the Fine Arts Building at the far end of Jackson Park. Each of the six major exhibition halls fronting the central basin addressed the enormous technological and material development of the nineteenth century. Whereas Richard Hunt's Administration Building rose above the scene as the architectural gem of the Court, George Post's Manufactures and Liberal Arts Building sprawled across the landscape, a giant emporium of the world's material culture. To the west of Manufactures across the North Canal stood the Electricity Building and Mines and Mining. Directly across the basin on the south side of the court were Machinery Hall, also known as the Palace of Mechanic Arts, and the Agriculture Building. The Casino–Peristyle–Music Hall completed the ensemble.

If the ethos that more is better had any meaning, if progress could be measured by the multiplication of things, then the place to begin was Manufactures and Liberal Arts. A pantheon of mass production, which left little room for the talents of individual artisans and craftsfolk, Manufactures was a striking testament to the transformative force of the market revolution. Its wares revealed the tremendous commercial expansion of the market economy since the Crystal Palace Exhibition, with new items that would become commonplace in the years to come. So large was the structure (it measured 787 feet by 1,887 feet), and so comprehensive its exhibits, that one commentator observed playfully, "Little boys have been seen to enter at one end, and old men to come out at the other."[25]

In addition to the United States, thirty foreign countries and colonies exhibited in the building, including the European states, Japan and China, Sumatra, Bolivia and Nicaragua, and the African Cape Colony. Collectively, the exhibits represented the most auspicious accumulation of the world's manufactured products and material artifacts ever assembled. Almost the entire court and gallery were given over to a display of manufactured products, with only the southeastern corner reserved for what were called the liberal arts. Known as "Columbia Avenue," the central aisle ran the length of the main floor, and to each side stood the assorted pavilions sponsored by manufacturers from exhibiting nations.

With thirty-five separate classes of exhibits in the Department of Manufactures, virtually any kind of manufactured product was on display in the building, from small arms weapons and war ordnance and model battleships to fine lace and silks from the Orient. Swiss glassware and clocks, Japanese lacquerware and bamboo ornaments, British woolen products, and French perfumes and linens were shown in their respective pavilions. The German pavilion included numerous pieces of finely crafted wooden furniture, as well as Gobelin tapestries, porcelain, and jewelry belonging to the ruling family. In the Austrian section stood two large vases representing "Liberty" and "Progress," themes associated with the fair. Historical incidents commemorating each theme were painted on the vessels, including the Signing of the "Magna Carta," the Signing of the "Declaration of Independence," the Discovery of Electricity, and the Abolition of Slavery.[26]

"[A] magnificent showing of domestic industries," to quote the *Official Guide*, characterized the exhaustive display of manufactured products found in the United States section. Pottery, musical instruments, furniture, safes, paper products, inks and dyes, displays of industrial chemicals and solvents, sewing machines, and every manner of tool and mechanical device attested to the manufacturing revolution of the nineteenth century. Two very different kinds of exhibits found the greatest favor with visitors. The display of lamps, ornamental metalwork, and fine jewelry in the Tiffany pavilion was universally praised; one Tiffany case contained more than a million dollars worth of precious stones and pieces of jewelry. Juxtaposed against the Tiffany finery was a general display of firearms in the Colt, Remington, and Smith and Wesson galleries. One jewel-studded, shell-ejecting revolver in the Colt pavilion was valued at more than six hundred dollars.[27]

Novelties and curiosities abounded in the American section. At the north end of the main aisle stood the Yerkes telescope, the largest of its kind in the world and a gift from transportation magnate Charles Yerkes to the University of Chicago. There was also a thirty-foot-long, fifteen-hundred-pound model of the Roebling brothers' Brooklyn Bridge carved in soap, complete with vehicles, pedestrian crossing, and a boat plying the waters beneath. An enjoyable machine was the "Graphophone"; for five cents the customer could put two hard rubber tubes into his or her ears and listen to a recording of the popular tune "The Cat Came Back." For many, this was a first experience with reproduced sound. Soaps, perfumes, and other emblems of the public hygiene craze were on display, and housewives delighted in kitchenware, electric dishwashers, carpet sweepers, and other labor-saving devices for the home.[28]

Though less ambitious than Manufactures, the Department of Liberal Arts had its own reasons for careful scrutiny. Unlike the finished goods in Manufactures, one commentator saw Liberal Arts as a "mecca of the mind . . . as the greatest and most serviceable educational feature of the Exposition."[29] Of the sixteen classes of exhibits in Liberal Arts—which included government and law, medicine, literature, maps and printed materials, hygiene, the physical sciences, and engineering—the most important division was devoted to literary and educational displays. Libraries exhibited systems of organization and rare documents, and publishers offered inspection of authors' manuscripts. The "Lincoln manuscripts"—original presidential proclamations dating to the Civil War—attracted a great deal of attention. So too did an extensive collection of historical bibles presented by the American Bible Society. Mark Twain, Joel Chandler Harris, Bret Harte, Edmund Stedman, and Thomas Nelson Page had books on display. Original poems by James Russell Lowell and a portion of the first draft of Frances Hodgson Burnett's *Little Lord Fauntleroy* could be viewed from behind glass cases.

American and foreign systems of public education drew considerable attention. With no reference to the growing inequalities between the races during the era of Jim Crow, Louisiana took great pride in its separate display of "schools for its colored children." Yale, Johns Hopkins, Harvard, and other universities and colleges contributed small displays of their undergraduate and postgraduate curricula. Women's colleges displayed contemporary approaches to higher education, combining elements of classical education with programs of physical hygiene and athletics.

Two educational exhibits provoked a measure of controversy. More than thirty thousand square feet of space was given over to an exposition of Catholic education in the United States. As members of an "immigrant church," Catholic leaders were engaged in a dramatic battle against the forces of Protestant nativism in the 1890s. Their message was that Catholicism and Americanism could be hospitable partners in mutual progress, a view set forth in the parochial school displays. A separate Catholic system of instruction was not a threat to republican values and democratic principles. Just the opposite, the organizers suggested, it encouraged conscientious citizenship and sound spiritual formation.[30]

Like the Catholic parochial exhibit, Pennsylvania's Carlisle Indian School display addressed concerns about assimilation and inclusion in America. Divorcing himself from the U.S. government's presentation of Native American accomplishments, which seemed to fall back on stereotypical views of Indians as unproductive savages incapable of responsible citizenship, Richard Henry Pratt refused to allow the Carlisle Indian School to be placed in the official government exhibition spaces. Instead, Pratt sponsored a separate display in Liberal Arts that presented his students in a more constructive light. An advocate of "benevolent assimilation" as in the best interest of American Indians, Pratt's message—at Carlisle and in its exhibit—was that if given the oppportunity American Indians were equally capable of contributing to American progress.

Crowned by Augustus Saint-Gaudens's statue *Diana* (removed from Madison Square Garden and shipped to Chicago for the occasion), the Agriculture Building stood directly opposite Manufactures and Liberal Arts on the south side of the basin. Devoted to "the discoveries and energy of the agricultural interest and its allied industries," as well as "progress in agricultural thought," the exhibits were more a testament to the rise of commercial agriculture than a celebration of the family farm.[31] Within its walls, visitors heard little of the Populist revolt and the rumbling of agrarian discontent that enlivened political discourse in the 1890s. Entrants did find, however, "a city of pavilions, pagodas and kiosks" scattered across ten acres of exhibition space. In addition to the customary displays of foodstuffs and cereal grains from around the world, there were exhibits of the brewing industry, agricultural colleges, and tobacco, sugar, canned goods, and textile products. The comparative theme was continued, with tobacco and teas from India, Irish whiskey, fertilizers from England, and pastries and confectionery products from Germany and France suggesting the scope of agricultural interests around the world.

Like Agriculture, Mines and Mining was devoted to the economic development of products of the soil. The Exposition's official guide declared that no other department had such a "great diversity of exhibits."[32] A warehouse of fossil fuels and precious and semiprecious stones—diamonds, opals, emeralds, and other gems—greeted the visitor to the U.S. and foreign pavilions. Copper, tin, zinc, and other mineral resources were also on display by mining and development companies from the United States and abroad. South African gold mines, Italian marble, and silver from the American West were featured in separate government pavilions. In addition to an extensive display of mining technology and the techniques for locating and extracting mineral resources, the American section contained a retrospective exhibit on the development of bituminous and anthracite coal.

As might have been expected, the coal-producing states of Pennsylvania, West Virginia, and Kentucky provided statistical information on the development of the industry, a measuring rod of progress in the field. Though the Pennsylvania pavilion boasted its "needle of coal," a small mountain of coal, the state exhibit also catalogued the contribution of iron and steel in the transformation of the Commonwealth's economy. Accenting the theme of progress, there was no mention of the tremendous conflict between labor and management that engulfed both bituminous and anthracite coalfields across the nation.

As an indication of the trend in the industrial age toward corporate consolidation and exploitation of natural resources, more than a dozen large corporations sponsored private exhibits in Mining. John Rockefeller's Standard Oil Company occupied the entire north end of the gallery, and the Frick Coal and Coke Company displayed a miniature model of its Connellsville, Pennsylvania, production facility. Few visitors were unfamiliar with Rockefeller's tactics for gaining control of the oil industry, and Pennsylvanians remembered Henry Clay Frick as general manager of Andrew Carnegie's Homestead (Pennsylvania) steel mill during the previous summer's "Battle of Homestead." No mention was made of these less-noble achievements.

After stops at Machinery Hall and the Electricity Building, whose exhibits will be discussed in a different context, only a tour of the Administration Building remained to complete a visit to the Court of Honor. As its name suggests, the Administration Building was not a formal exhibition building, but the organizational center of the fairgrounds. Richard Hunt's imperial dome towered over its surroundings, and within its walls were offices of the directors and department chiefs, a branch bank, and other management concerns. Decorative plates commemorated the great inventions and discoveries of human history, from the compass to the steam engine. Names of the great explorers and inventors as agents of progress were inscribed on its walls.[33]

Having completed the circuit of buildings and perused the statuary about the Court of Honor, fairgoers might go north or south or go directly to the Midway Plaisance for reprieve. The southern section of Jackson Park, known to the Columbian Guards as "Siberia" because of its remoteness from the rest of the park, was filled with smaller buildings and outdoor pavilions clustered around the South Pond. Windmill displays, an agricultural implements exhibit, several restaurants and a French bakery, and an antique whaler bark were all placed on the South Grounds. One woman thought the German munitions exhibit out of place in the ethereal splendor of the park. She described a giant Krupp cannon on display as "a fearful, hideous thing, breathing of blood and carnage, a triumph of barbarism crouching amid the world's triumphs of civilization."[34]

Between the pond and the lake shore stood the Leather Exhibit, the Forestry and Dairy Buildings, and the larger Anthropology Building. The most unusual feature of the Forestry Building was its rough-hewed timber construction, which made it stand out from the other classical structures. In addition to a full display of what was called "forest culture," Forestry contained Gifford Pinchot's display of scientific woodlands management at the Vanderbilt's Biltmore Estate near Asheville, North Carolina.

A large area was reserved for livestock exhibits during the summer months and an open-air livestock pavilion. When animal and cattle shows were not in progress, the pavilion doubled as an out-of-door gymnasium for athletic competition among ethnic fraternal associations like the Hibernians, Turnerverein, and the Sokol Society. One of the more noticeable features of the South Grounds was the aromatic fragrance that lingered in the air around the livestock pavilions during the hot summer months.

Perhaps the most memorable structure on the South Grounds was also the exhibit most evocative of the fair's commemorative purpose. This was the tasteful Convent of La Rabida, a facsimile reproduction of the monastery at Palos from which Columbus sailed on his first voyage. Benjamin Truman called the structure the "shrine of the White City." Valuable artifacts loaned by the Spanish government and the Vatican archives possessed what one visitor thought was "the air, the remembrance of feudal times, the age of chivalry, and the achievements of Columbus." Gold coins, precious mosaics, papal manuscripts, and rare books were among the material artifacts that filled La Rabida's retrospective exhibit.[35] The popular Spanish Caravels, reproductions of the *Nina*, the *Pinta*, and the *Santa Maria*, which had sailed with much fanfare from Spain to Chicago for the season, were moored nearby.[36]

The Convent of La Rabida was actually part of a large outdoor archeological exhibit attached to the Exposition's Department of Anthropology. Frederick Putnam of Harvard University's Peabody Museum hoped to use the Columbian Exposition to cultivate a popular appreciation of anthropology and archeology. In addition to the exhibits in the Anthropology Building, Putnam and his assistants supervised several museum-like attractions that brought the study of human society to a general audience. The Yucatan Ruins, a giant staff (plaster of Paris–based material) and papier-mâché reproduction of the ancient village discovered near Uximal, and the Cliff-Dwellers, a facsimile of cave dwellings found near Battle Rock, Colorado, were featured attractions. Complete with implements and artifacts that might have been used by its early inhabitants, Cliff-Dwellers was presented as an authentic representation of "probably the earliest civilization of the American continent."[37] These exhibits were intended as serious scientific displays, as teaching instruments for the education of the audience. By comparison with the magnificence of the Court of Honor, they were supposed to demonstrate the scope of progress from primitive to modern times. With whatever intention, after the fair a group of writers, including Henry Blake Fuller and Hamlin Garland, appropriated the name "Cliff-Dwellers" for a new literary club in Chicago.

In addition to the archeological exhibits, the Department of Anthropology managed several ethnographic exhibits on the main grounds. Following closely on the conclusion of the western Indian Wars, these "living museums" labored unsuccessfully to offer an accurate rendering of aboriginal cultures while avoiding the condescension and overt racism of the Midway villages. The Esquimaux Village at the Fifty-Seventh Street entrance to Jackson Park and the Village of the Penobscot Indians on the South Grounds were extensions of a detailed ethnographic display found within the Anthropology Building itself. A two-story model Indian School demonstrated the accomplishments of Indian education programs. Putnam and his chief assistant, Franz Boas, hoped their villages would be culturally authentic and avoid the stereotypes of Indians shared by many American and European visitors.

An immigrant professor who taught for a time at Clark University in Massachusetts, Boas had an abiding scholarly interest in African-American and Native American cultures. He was considered something of a maverick within academic circles for his advocacy of a more progressive and pluralist view of human society. By the time he joined Putnam at the Exposition, Boas was well known within academe for his defense of environmental factors rather than biological determinism as an explanation for differentiation within the human species. Under Boas's influence and with Putnam's cooperation, the ethnographic exhibits within the Anthropology Building made an important if subtle statement in favor of cultural factors in history, instead of the popular pseudoscientific racism that pervaded serious discourse in the late nineteenth century. Boas also had the unspoken agenda of supporting pluralism and racial acceptance within the confines of the White City. In the years after the Chicago fair, Boas became the single most influential anthropologist in America, championing the message (largely missed) of the 1893 exhibits.[38]

The Exposition's official guidebook claimed that the Indians on the South Grounds performed "all the appurtenances of Indian life," while "living in the exact way their forefathers lived before the white man invaded their lands." "They cook, make trinkets, perform their songs and dances, and go through the ordinary routine of life in their tribes." "This illustration of Indian and pioneer life is intended as a great background to the Exposition," the commentary continued, "bringing out by comparison with greater force the advances made during the past four centuries" (as shown in the great exhibition halls). Unfortunately for Putnam and Boas, the outdoor exhibits seemed to reinforce the popular perceptions of primitiveness and savagery rather than a more scientific basis of cultural comparisons. More often, the Native Americans appeared as "anthropological artifacts" rather than as conscientious and productive human beings.[39]

The inscription above the main entrance to the Anthropology Building read: "Anthropology—Man and His Works." Inside were exhibits from the United States and more than twenty foreign countries and territories, dedicated to a diverse grouping of subjects that ran from charitable works and public hygiene to eugenics and sanitation, each appropriating a measure of scientific importance. Comparative tables and charts analyzed the physical and mental characteristics of the world's races and peoples, as well as retrospective and contemporary exhibits that assessed the social habits of various population groups. Franz Boas's anthropometric laboratory was the most important of several workstations operating within the building.

In contrast to the South Grounds which was a hodgepodge of attractions and exhibits squeezed into a relatively small area clustered near the pond, the North Grounds (directly north of the Court of Honor) was suburban, with its spacious grouping of buildings and concessions spread across a more expansive terrain. In addition to the several major exhibition halls—Transportation, Women's, Horticulture, Fish and Fisheries, and Fine Arts—there were the United States Government Building, nineteen foreign government headquarters, and thirty-seven state buildings.[40] Festival Hall (also called Choral Hall) stood between Horticulture and Transportation and hosted hundreds of special programs and musical concerts throughout the season. Private corporate pavilions, ample public comfort stations, outdoor cafes, a weather station, a naval exhibit and military hospital complex, and numerous smaller exhibits and concessions were scattered about. There was also the great natural feature of the park proper, Olmsted's Wooded Island on the lagoon.

The Wooded Island stood in marked contrast to the developed, congested areas of the fairgrounds. Conceived by Frederick Law Olmsted as a place of repose amid the edifices of civilizations, the island was a popular place to stop and catch one's breath. In addition to a large rose garden, the island contained a Japanese tea garden and temple. The clean lines and simple beauty of the Ho-o-den Temple proved especially appealing to such different travelers as Henry Adams and Frank Lloyd Wright.

By contrast, at the southern end of the island stood the Boone and Crockett Club and an Australian squatter's camp. Sparsely furnished, with animal hides and pelts serving as interior decoration, the cabin was a shrine, a nostalgic celebration of the rituals of Victorian manhood and the pleasures derived from the natural life. In keeping with the anthropological theme, some could have read the exhibit as a testament to the conquest of aboriginal peoples, with Indian-fighter Kit Carson's rifle proudly displayed above the fireplace mantle.[41]

Nature was again codified and celebrated in the Horticulture Building, an enormous greenhouse containing "hundreds of arboreal curiosities." The exhibits reflected the Victorian interest in gardens and the decoration of natural spaces. It also suggested the recovery of nature in the urban age on more genteel terms than the Boone and Crocket Club. Vines and mosses draped the walls and balustrade beneath the enormous metal and glass dome, and tall palms and bamboo shoots spread their feathery crests to drink in the sunlight. Virtually every kind of plant, vegetable, and fruit grown around the world was exhibited in the building, the largest of its kind devoted to such interests. Pomology, the science of fruit growing, was represented in displays from such distant places as Sicily and New South Wales. Domestic wines augmented California's presentation of thirty different varieties of citrus fruit. Vegetables, canned foods, and what were called "horticultural appliances" were grouped in the building's north pavilion, and on the Midway stood the department's two-acre nursery and cranberry bog. Over three hundred varieties of pears and one hundred seventy strains of gooseberries were among the exhibits offered by the forty-four states and territories that sponsored pavilions.

Every imaginable variety of shrub and flower and aquatic plant was displayed, and several large gardens and raised beds stood behind the building, with floricultural and horticultural exhibits arranged so that something was always in bloom. "The profusion of sweet peas, clematis, and fleur-de-lis were [sic] a delight," read an admiring *Official Guide*. "Geraniums also put forth their petals, not ashamed of the more pretentious agaves, cacti and yuccas."[42]

Like Horticulture, the Fish and Fisheries Building celebrated nature's bounty, with special attention to marine life. The structure was an aquatic wonder, which anticipated the popularity of commercial aquariums in cities across the country. Especially in those landlocked regions of the country, direct experience with marine life was growing more limited as people moved to cities. Paralleling other exhibits, however, the strong emphasis was on the commercial value of aquatic resources, not the simple pleasures derived from a day on the lake.

The exterior of the Fish and Fisheries Building was novel in appearance, with classical columns carved with figures of fish, mammals, and aquatic figures. As described by the *Official Directory*, Fish and Fisheries contained "materials and collections illustrative of the commercial fisheries, fish culture, angling and scientific invention bearing upon the inhabitants of the seas, lakes and rivers."[43] Fishing, for pleasure and for profit, was celebrated in the department's exhibits, with commercial fisheries featured in the central pavilion and sport fishing and angling reserved for the western pavilions. At the opposite end of the building stood the world's largest aquaria of live fish, with freshwater and saltwater tanks with capacities up to seventy-eight thousand gallons; the total capacity of the aquaria facility exceeded one hundred forty thousand gallons. A large pond with a brilliant cascading waterfall stood just inside the main entrance, with a myriad of fish and aquatic life.

Columbian Guards had the thankless task of trying to keep young children's hands and faces off the glass barricades, as picture-book images danced before their eyes. Fearsome sharks patrolled their tanks as hapless remora held on for life, and the many-hued sea anemones provided an underwater rainbow of colors. There were spoonbill from the murky Mississippi and brilliant Japanese goldfish. Speckled trout, little darters, turtles, winged sea robins, salmon, and every manner of crustacean to inhabit land or sea were represented in the exhibit.

The United States Government Building, which served the dual purposes of a headquarters and an exhibition building, was adjacent to the Fish and Fisheries compound. Each of the major government departments—War, Interior, State, Treasury, Agriculture, and so on—contributed to the display of memorabilia, as did the Post Office and the Smithsonian Institution. The U.S. government's exhibits ranged from scientific and ethnographic displays to those of the military. A separate naval exhibit with a papier-mâché replica of the battleship *Illinois* was docked at the north pier. Purely historical or retrospective exhibits complemented murals denoting the development of the nation. Attracting considerable attention was the natural science area, particularly the display of birds and mammals of North America. William Palmer, the chief taxidermist at the Smithsonian Institution, spent two years collecting and cataloguing animals that were stuffed and mounted to "counterfeit life" to all but the expert eye. Included in the presentation on the birds of America was every known type of common pigeon under domestication: the rare blue-tailed turbit, the regal bald-headed tumbler, and the more serene yellow magpie.[44]

The most controversial exhibit in the government building was prepared by the Smithsonian Institution, which offered its own ethnographic exhibits under the direction of Otis Mason, curator of the Bureau of American Ethnology. In arranging an extensive display of the history and culture of North American Indian tribes, the Smithsonian built upon anthropologist John Wesley Powell's research on Native American speech patterns. The extensiveness of the exhibits betrayed a public fascination with American Indians amid the military and cultural conflicts in the western territories. Unlike the Department of Anthropology, however, the Smithsonian did not incorporate living subjects into its ethnographic exhibit; it offered instead a retrospective display of "primitive Indian industries" and culture through the use of statues and models.[45]

Although Mason and his colleagues hoped that incorporating the concept of "culture groups" would illustrate the theme of racial progress, the exhibit had an unfortunate and unintended effect. Contrary to the hopes of the government anthropologists who cooperated in the Smithsonian exhibit, the manner in which Native American culture and handicraft were presented seemed to give scientific justification for popularly held racial stereotypes. (Like the Anthropology Building exhibits, the Smithsonian gave virtually no attention to the culture and social habits of African Americans, reinforcing the place of American blacks as invisible or at least marginal beings in American social development.)[46]

"In the [Smithsonian's] Anthropology exhibit," noted the Exposition's *Official Guide*, "an attempt is made to show the characteristics of the principal races of men and the progress of civilization as shown by the evolution of some of the more important arts and industries."[47] Life-size mannequins—their resemblance to living beings was so convincing that some wondered if they too were not stuffed like the animals in the adjacent aisles—were dressed in native tribal costumes to depict the characteristics of various tribes. Visitors were told the scenes depicted Indians in common labors: buffalo hides being cleaned, warriors working on shields and tents, and women preparing meals. A separate case contained numerous plaster casts and busts of famous Indian chiefs, portraying to one author "the last true records of a dying race of men." No mention was made of the tragedy at Wounded Knee, still fresh in people's minds, nor of the ongoing dispossession of Indian tribes. The curators presented these materials as "authentic data upon which to build accounts of the American aborigines after they shall have passed away, if civilization entirely overwhelms them."[48]

Whatever scientific purpose the Smithsonian intended in the exhibit, its very nature reflected the condescending paternalism which informed the demonstration. One scene in particular drew a good deal of comment. Advertised as "representative" of Indian folkways, this scene depicted a Hupa mother and her two children in tribal dress at work on the crafts for which the California tribe was known. An admirer of the display commented, "The baby is laced into the cradle with buckskin thongs, and smiles like a white child, showing the taciturnity of the savage is a lately-acquired characteristic."[49] Fear of just such a reaction had persuaded both Richard Pratt of the Carlisle Indian School and the government's own Office of Indian Affairs to object to the Smithsonian presentation and to mount separate exhibits of their own elsewhere on the grounds.

Relics of the American past were spread throughout the Government Building, part of an effort to promote a shared understanding of the past. Colonial artifacts were found throughout the building, including the purported first Bible brought to the New World, Miles Standish's pipe, and

General Burgoyne's spurs. In the Army section, maps and battle flags from important military campaigns adorned the walls, surrounding a bronze cannon captured at the Battle of Yorktowne in 1781 and the "Long Tom," a gun used by privateers to capture British vessels off the Azores in 1814.

Civil War memorabilia abounded. Weapons, medical supplies, a rickety Union ambulance, and litters used to carry bodies from the battlefield conjured up memories of the not-so-distant struggles for a national society. Within the rotunda a plaster model commemorated a scene from the 1882 Greeley expedition to the Arctic. It showed General Greeley welcoming group members Lockwood and Brainard on their return from north latitude 82°/24 minutes. Near the Greeley model stood the hollowed-out trunk of a giant California redwood tree; an incandescent lamp illuminated the inner cavern to reveal a montage of photographs taken of its primeval forests.[50]

Headquarter buildings of the American states and foreign nations stood beyond the United States Government Building. Here too, visitors found a deliberate effort to invoke history to inform the present. Thirty-seven states sponsored buildings that functioned as their official headquarters, as well as celebrating their respective citizens and resources. In what became a commonplace occurrence, visitors to the fair often proceeded first to their state building and signed the registry, informing friends and acquaintances of their whereabouts in Chicago.

The State of Illinois built the largest and most elaborate structure, an impressive neoclassical building that afterward was used as a model for a new capitol building in Springfield. Most states commissioned Exposition architects to design buildings modeled on famous historic structures, such as Florida's Fort Marion in St. Augustine, New York's reproduction of the great Van Rensselaer mansion, and Pennsylvania's Independence Hall. The exterior of the Massachusetts Building was a replica of the John Hancock House, and Virginia recreated Washington's Mount Vernon plantation house as its headquarters. A Joint Territories Building rounded out the American headquarters buildings and allowed the several existing territories a formal place in the Exposition ensemble.[51]

The appearance of the foreign government buildings reflected the diversity of peoples and countries represented in the fair. There were no competitive exhibits in the headquarters buildings, and the exhibits that were presented reflected the culture and traditions of their homelands. Because of the recent extension of the 1882 Chinese Exclusion Act, which prohibited Chinese immigration to the United States, China did not sponsor a building, nor did its government have any official representation at the fair. Not so with such countries as England, Germany, France, and Spain, whose national exhibits commemorated their historical development while celebrating the rewards of colonialism. Not surprisingly, Spain played to the Columbian theme in a presentation of artifacts, patents, and letters pertinent to the mariner and the country's subsequent New World settlements.[52]

Though most of the structures created little interest, the very presence of one government did create a stir: Haiti, whose government spent over $20,000 on the construction of its headquarters building and another $100,000 on exhibits. Commemorating the first autonomous black republic in the Western Hemisphere, the Haitian building served as a reminder of the violent struggle to wrest the island of Santo Domingo from French colonial control, a struggle accompanied by the only successful slave rebellion in the hemisphere. Quite coincidentally, the headquarters building opened just in time to commemorate the hundredth anniversary of the 1794 insurrection that had so startled American slaveholders. There were displays of agricultural staples and other finished goods produced on the island. Sacred relics of the rebellion filled the exhibition space, including the sword of Toussaint-Louverture, the "Black Napoleon" and liberator of the Haitian people.

As compelling as Toussaint's battle regalia was the person of Haiti's commissioner to the Exposition and official host of the government building, the American Frederick Douglass. Perhaps the most famous living African American, Douglass accepted the Haitian government's invitation to act as its commissioner, giving him a prominence denied other blacks in the White City.[53]

Except for the Woman's and the Transportation Buildings, which will be discussed in a different setting, one last stop remained on the North Grounds before one proceeded to the Midway to relax. For lovers of beauty and the connoisseurs of taste, the exhibits in the Palace of Fine Arts represented the largest and most comprehensive display of artistic accomplishment ever assembled. More than ten thousand works of art from twenty countries were arranged in seventy-four galleries. The displays in the Fine Arts Building, the only permanent structure on the fairgrounds, summarized in retrospective and contemporary salons nearly every major movement in art from antiquity to the current trends and fads.

Halsey C. Ives, director of St. Louis's Museum of Fine Arts, was appointed chief of the Department of Fine Arts after a protracted search by Exposition officials, and together with Charles Kurtz and Sara Hallowell he solicited the participation of nearly four thousand artists in the states and abroad.[54] Hundreds of private collectors were also asked to lend works for the season. Where continental painters and sculptors had dominated previous international exhibitions in Europe, the Chicago fair marked a moment of triumph for American artists.

The American galleries reflected Ives's decision to showcase American art since the Centennial Exhibition, as well as earlier American painters and muralists. At Paris's 1889 Universal Exposition, the French and American sections in fine arts were the largest, with more than fifty-seven hundred French works on display—ten times the number of works from the United States. By comparison, the Columbian Exposition reversed the

order with some three thousand separate pieces in the American galleries—
more than double the number of works from France.[55] Dozens of paintings
and pieces of sculpture afterward were purchased for or donated to the Art
Institute of Chicago.

Cincinnati painter Henry Farny echoed the central theme of the Exposition when he observed of the cumulative effect of the art galleries: "This
Chicago fair will start a new era in American art."[56] William A. Coffin, art
critic of *The Nation*, wrote that the chief benefit of the Exposition's art exhibition was to be found in its demonstration of the present generation of
American artists' talent. Coffin commented on what he saw as the marked
improvement in technique and form displayed by American artists since the
Centennial Exhibition.[57]

Comparative themes abounded, in Fine Arts as elsewhere on the grounds.
If sheer numbers counted for anything, then in its effort to record the
"progress" of American art in the last quarter century the Exposition galleries showed a telling preference for established works rather than recent
and innovative trends in the art world. Close inspection of the American
sections also revealed the exclusive nature of the art establishment in the
United States. Few works by women artists and sculptors were included in
the exhibition, and no women served on the regional or national advisory
committees or on juries that awarded prizes.[58] This, despite the Exposition's
decree that women should be involved in all stages of exhibition and competition on the grounds. Similarly, there was a virtual absence of academic
or vernacular art produced by African-American and American Indian
artists, whose interests were not solicited. In this sense, the American art
exhibit reflected the exclusion found elsewhere at Jackson Park and
throughout the larger culture.

Romantics and the precursors of Modernism were represented in retrospective and contemporary galleries meant to chart progress in the arts.
Classical statuary, medieval tapestries, church art, and works of the Renaissance masters and nineteenth-century Romantic painters filled the fifteen
general groups of exhibits in the Department of Fine Arts. There were no
Van Gogh or Gauguin watercolors, but there were numerous works by the
French Impressionists. Also prominent was American vernacular and folk
art, along with the landscapes of the Hudson River School and the Lumin-
ists. A strong showing was made by a generation of American exiles who had
sought training and respectability in the art schools and salons of London,
Paris, Dusseldorf, and Munich.[59]

Like the Centennial Exhibition, the Columbian Exposition's galleries
have been credited with inaugurating a new era of artistic appreciation in
the United States. One art historian went so far as to claim that the exhibition at Chicago was the "first apparent attempt to define a historic development in American art."[60] Through the integration of galleries devoted to
contemporary artists with galleries containing historical or retrospective col-

lections, the American section represented the largest and most diverse exhibit of native artists ever mounted. In the retrospective galleries, one hundred and ten paintings from seventy American artists reflected patterns of taste in the nineteenth century. Pastoral scenes by Thomas Cole and Asher B. Durand—allegorical rural landscapes in the tradition of the Hudson River School—were among the most popular works in the historical collection. Charles Wilson and Rembrandt Peale, Benjamin West and John Trumbull, John Singleton Copley, and Gilbert Stuart sketches invoked an idealized past rich in imagery, which continued to resonate with meaning at century's end. William Morris Hunt, Robert Weir, Henry Inman, C. C. Ingham, and the western artist George Catlin were among the other notable figures represented in Fine Arts.[61]

Lorado Taft, the Chicago sculptor and critic who exhibited at the fair, thought the number and variety of oil paintings by contemporary Americans certified that an artistic renaissance was underway in the United States.[62] More than eleven hundred oils hung in the American gallery, representing virtually every contemporary artist of significance in the United States. The American gallery was dominated by paintings that fell into several broad subject categories: rural life and landscapes, maternal and family scenes, portraiture, and works that captured images of gentility and the leisure class. With fifteen representative oil paintings, Winslow Homer offered the most works for exhibit, but what one observer described as his "native, self-taught genius" stood in contrast to the more academic portraits from the most commercially successful artist, John Singer Sargent.[63]

Many of the leading figures in American painting exhibited their works in the United States section. The list of their names in the exhibition catalog read as a veritable who's who in American art. From Philadelphia, Thomas Eakins offered several oil paintings, including his widely praised *Portrait of Dr. Gross*. Eakins's *Gross Clinic*, as it was also known, did not stir the controversy at Chicago that it had at the Centennial; one measure of its general acceptance was its inclusion in 1893 in the art gallery. Numerous commentators remarked on the large crowds that stood before Eakins's work, but it is uncertain whether they pondered the realism of the clinic sketch or the large portrait of a nude woman that hung alongside the masterpiece.

J. Alden Weir, John La Farge, George Inness, William Chase, Eastman Johnson, Frederick Remington, Childe Hassam, and Homer Martin were a few of the talented artists who exhibited in the Fine Arts Building. (Many of the most prominent painters and sculptors also served on the state and national advisory councils that screened the final selections.) Like Elihu Vedder, Walter McEwen, Edwin Blashfield, Kenyon Cox, and Mary Fairchild MacMonnies, Frank Millet and others commissioned to create murals for the great exhibition buildings at Jackson Park showed more personal works in the American painting sections.[64] Vedder, who in 1893 completed his murals for the Fine Arts Building while working on new murals for the

Collis P. Huntington estate mansion, exhibited eleven of his paintings at the fair. These works were as different as his early *Lair of the Sea* (1864) and the allegorical *A Soul in Bondage* (1891).[65]

James McNeil Whistler was one of the more celebrated exiles who cooperated with the Columbian exhibition. While his selected works reflected the gallery's preference for traditional and romantic tendencies, Whistler was also one of the few Americans with modernist leanings to exhibit in the fair.[66] Four of his paintings hung in the American gallery, including *The Chelsea Girl* and *Harmony in Blue and Silver*. Perhaps because of his reputation for eccentricity, Whistler's paintings were not particularly well received by some critics. "Overwhelmingly egotistical, possessing an insatiable love of notoriety," one critic said in Whistler's defense, "he is, nevertheless, one of the greatest painters in the world."[67] Whistler would have agreed, as did the judges who awarded his fifty-some etchings and drawings more medals than went to the work of any other artist. Albert Pinkham Ryder was one American painter who did not exhibit at the fair. Ryder's dark, bereaved, black-and-white and oil paintings had much in common with Whistler's brooding nocturnal scenes.

The display of American sculpture was equally impressive. Although Augustus Saint-Gaudens did not loan works for the competitive galleries, he did serve on the National Board of Judges, and his studio produced two pieces of sculpture found in the Court of Honor. Philip Martiny, Frederick MacMonnies, and Daniel Chester French were among several of Saint-Gaudens's former studio assistants who did participate in the competitive exhibition. MacMonnies and French seemed to have been the master's favorites—and the most talented of the group. For that reason Saint-Gaudens had recommended them to design the principal statuary in the Court of Honor.[68] In addition to exhibiting in Fine Arts, Martiny had designed the reliefs for the Agriculture Building, and not by coincidence Saint-Gaudens's statue *Diana* surmounted the building's central dome. There seemed to be little disagreement that the most significant piece of sculpture by an American was French's *Death Staying the Hand of the Young Sculptor*, which Lorado Taft, a competitor in the show, said "speaks to every imagination."[69]

Along with Taft, numerous younger sculptors exhibited in the Fine Arts Building. They included Edward Kemeys, A. P. Proctor, Carl Rohl-Smith, Philip Martiny, and Karl Bitter, each of whom like Martiny had designed reliefs and pieces of statuary found throughout the fairgrounds. For many of the younger sculptors who were not as well established as Augustus Saint-Gaudens, such as J. Q. A. Ward or Olin Warner, participation in the galleries at Jackson Park proved critical to later success in obtaining lucrative commissions for public buildings and private collections.[70]

Perhaps no American artist benefited more from the exhibition at Jackson Park than Louis Comfort Tiffany. Tiffany, who served on the national jury for watercolors, was already well established as an artist and designer within

East Coast circles. His triumph at Chicago in 1893 brought him international attention and a host of new clients. In addition to the several stained glass windows and leaded-glass lamps exhibited at the fair, Tiffany designed a bejeweled Romanesque-Byzantine chapel especially for the Columbian Exposition gallery. By one estimate, more than one and one-half million visitors came to marvel at the chapel with its brilliant windows and decorative mosaics. The altar, tabernacle, and lectern were ornamented with precious and semiprecious stones that glistened in the coordinated lighting effects. Window settings were bold experiments in glass, which would come to characterize Tiffany's later work. Critics have agreed with Tiffany's own assessment that the Columbian Exposition Chapel was among "some of my finest work." What pleased Tiffany most was that it was a personal project and not the result of a client's commission.[71]

In one of the great ironies of the Fine Arts exhibits, France chose not to exhibit paintings of what was called the Modern Art movement, and visitors had to go to the American Loan Collection to see the works of the Impressionists and the emerging Art Nouveau. Here, gathered from private collections throughout the United States—principally from New York, Chicago, Philadelphia, and Boston—were 122 paintings and four pieces of sculpture from sixty-two European artists, denoting a revolt against formalism in art. Reflecting the manner in which private wealth had been put to cultural use, the Loan Collection demonstrated how aggressive American collectors had become since the days of the Centennial Exhibition.[72]

The American Loan Collection featured three major movements in Western art: Impressionism, the Barbizon School, and Romanticism. Among the Romanticist painters represented in the collection were Delacroix, Fromentin, John Constable, Constant Tyron, and Decamps. Of the practitioners of the Barbizon School, there were numerous representative works on display. Jean Baptiste Camille Corot had a dozen paintings exhibited, and there were eight landscapes and peasant scenes by Jean-Francois Millet. Rousseau, Dabigny, Dupre, and Diaz each had paintings in the collection. Jules Breton's *The Song of the Lark*, which afterward was donated to the Art Institute of Chicago, was judged to be the most appealing foreign painting exhibited in the Fine Arts Building. Perhaps the only European work to rival the enthusiastic response to *The Song of the Lark* was Carl Marr's enormous canvas, *The Flagellants*.

If Breton's pastoral *Song of the Lark* was judged the most popular European painting, the French Impressionists offered the most important challenge to the authority of the Romantics. After visiting the Loan Collection, Hamlin Garland wrote a widely circulated essay on Impressionism that heralded the movement and its leading practitioners to a wider American audience.[73] Garland praised the revolutionary technique mastered by the French Impressionists, and what he saw as a bold confrontation with tradition. Citing in particular Eduoard Manet and Claude Monet, Garland talked about their sense of a new relationship between nature and the artist and, by inference, their new view of reality. Garland acknowledged that the Loan Collection introduced many Americans to the form and manners of modernism in artistic expression and therefore to a questioning of conventional certainties.

In addition to numerous works by Manet and Monet, the Loan Collection also contained at least one painting each by Camille Pissarro, Degas, Renoir, and the Englishman Alfred Sisley, but apparently none by Paul Cezanne. The collection featured several pieces of sculpture by August Rodin.[74]

Whatever the importance of the modernist works hung in Fine Arts's galleries, none of them rivaled the appeal of a vernacular painting of rural innocence. Of the thousands of paintings, etchings, drawings, and pieces of sculpture, none was more appealing than Thomas Hovenden's *Breaking Home Ties*. In a scene packed with cultural resonance, Hovenden drew the moment when a man-child bids farewell to his family on the farm and sets off into an uncertain future.

No refined theory was needed to appreciate the draw of Hovenden's work. *Breaking Home Ties*, one of three Hovenden paintings on display, captured in a very personal and poignant way the powerful emotions many Americans still held about family as the ordering point of community, particularly community rooted in the land.[75] Visitors lingered in front of the painting, contemplating its image and emotions. Juxtaposed to a work like Eakins's *The Gross Clinic*, Hovenden's *Breaking Home Ties* reflected the enduring appeal of traditional values amid the glamour and glitter of the changing landscape of sensibilities in American life.

If claims of an American renaissance were too grandiose, the Fine Arts exhibit nonetheless made an important statement concerning American artistic development since the Centennial Exhibition. More than that, it offered the American public the most comprehensive international display of paintings and sculpture ever staged in this country. Positioned beyond the Court of Honor, the "Palace of Fine Arts" represented the enshrinement of culture so characteristic of the Exposition's White City, and it offered an important corrective to a heavy emphasis on mechanical and technological displays elsewhere on the grounds. A reminder of the nobler pretensions of the Columbian Exposition, Fine Arts was a fitting last stop in the main grounds before a visit to the decadence and diversions of the Midway Plaisance.

If the main grounds and its lofty exhibition halls embodied a City Beautiful, the concessions of the Midway Plaisance reflected an obverse reality. In its rich diversity of sights and sounds and in the sheer diversity of its human inhabitants, the Midway offered cultural encounters of a different order than those found on the main park. With forty-some theaters, cabarets, and amusements straddling either side of the mile-long Avenue of Nations, the Midway was a sideshow melting pot of distractions and deceits. Originally conceived as a division of the general Department of Anthropology, the Midway was actually a collection of private venues choreographed by the entrepreneurial Sol Bloom. Each attraction levied its own admission fee, with one-fourth of the take returned to the corporation's coffers. If visitors were startled by the difference in ambiance between Jackson Park and the Midway, one can only imagine the thoughts of the academic dons of the University of Chicago, whose greystone Gothic spires could be seen immediately beyond the fence that enclosed the Plaisance's northern boundary. Recently endowed with Rockefeller monies, the university offered a completely different and seemingly more sober education than the Midway cosmopolitan curriculum.

"We are aware of a great change in our spiritual atmosphere," Denton Snider wrote of his passage from the fairgrounds to the Midway, "we have passed into a new environment of the human soul, foreign to us but very fascinating." To cross beneath the Stony Island viaduct and emerge onto the Avenue of Nations was for another traveler to step into "a strange land, peopled with outlandish folk, echoing with barbaric noises, and given over to strange customs, costumes, tongues, diets, dwellings and gods." Fashioned as something of a latter-day Babylon—"this paradise of Babel," Benjamin Truman called it—the Midway was a genuflection to popular tastes, with a strong fragrance of crass commercialism in the air.[76] "But one can observe for five dollars in the Plaisance what it would cost twenty thousand dollars to see if he traveled purposely to see it," observed the enthusiastic Truman, "and no one complains."[77] This latter point was an overstatement.

What lured many visitors was an intoxicating and often voyeuristic delight in the Midway's exotic ambiance, its suggestive mimicry and departure from respectable decorum. In an age that counseled self-control and restraint, particularly in sexual matters, the Midway theaters had an air of licentiousness that seemed not only to permit but to encourage a deviation, if only temporary, from Victorian standards of propriety. Young girls with exotic names and little clothing danced in public theaters, before audiences composed of men and women who frequently came back for a second or third inspection.

One of Finley Peter Dunne's characters, an Irish saloon-keeper named "Colonel McNeery," offered an amusing recollection of a visit to the Midway. After McNeery takes in the sights and sounds of the Plaisance, he ends up at a bar, surrounded by "a lot of black fellows with red towels around their heads an' knives stickin' out of their yellow cloaks . . . and half-a-dozen gur-rls with earrings as big as barrelhoops in their ears." "I dunno what happened at all," McNeery told his friends, "at all, with dancin' gur-rls an' snake cha-armers an' Boolgarian club swingers an' foreign men goin' around with their legs in mattresses."[78]

The Midway Plaisance reflected an emerging culture of mass entertainment that would flourish in the early twentieth century, and it provided important precedents for the developers of Coney Island and other amusement parks. A loose collection of concessions and attractions that conformed to no particular internal hierarchy or spatial arrangement, the Midway, like Coney Island, was a separate zone of entertainment set off from the other activities and enterprises that informed the urban landscape.[79] Devoted to the commercial appeal of the exotic and sometimes overtly sexual in its message, the Midway capitalized on the popularity of so-called ethnographic exhibits of "polyglot peoples" that had succeeded at European fairs in the late nineteenth century. More than a concessionaire's boardwalk, the Midway also was less than the scientific venue some promoters claimed. Its controversial departure from Victorian precepts, its willingness to follow the line of least resistance in public entertainment, was a source of truant, but great, fun.

Numerous shops and arcades along the Avenue of Nations sold their goods to the public solely for profit, with no promise of entertainment to follow. Other concessions disguised their mercantile motive behind the masque of amusement. Mechanical rides, games, a circus, restaurants and cafes, and regularly featured attractions filled the Midway venue. There were rival Irish villages, each with its own fake castle. One could kiss the replica stone in Blarney Castle on the southern side of the avenue or meander through the Castle at Donegal located, appropriately enough, on the northern side of the Plaisance. Purely commercial shops included the Libbey Glass Works, the Parisian Store, the Adams Express pavilion, and the Diamond Match Company display.

In one of the more commercial venues, the International Dress Company lured customers by hosting a daily beauty contest of "Midway types," sturdy women whose figures and fashions reflected the Victorian appreciation for robust beauty. The Vienna Cafe was among the most popular eateries and watering holes on the avenue, frequented by the likes of lawman Bat Masterson, the Austrian Archduke Franz Ferdinand, heavyweight boxing champion "Gentleman Jim" Corbett, and the aspiring poet Edgar Lee Masters, who lost his first love to Corbett at the Midway cafe.

Commercial amusements abounded. Two mechanical rides foreshadowed the technological wizardry of Coney Island: the Barre Sliding Railway, in which cars glided over a broad flat rail lubricated by water, and the Ice Railway. Described as "gaily-painted sleighs" which swept "merry crowds across an elliptical, undulating plane 850 feet long" covered with artificial snow, the railway was a refreshing alternative during the hot summer months.[80] Visitors could indulge a fascination with natural disasters in stops at the Panorama of the Kilaueau Volcano and the Diorama of the "Destruction of Pompeii." The Westinghouse Company sponsored an electric Scenic Theater, where with the use of electricity technicians affected the appearance of an Alpine village passing through stages of daylight and darkness.

There was an ostrich farm for children, the swimming pool–Natatorium complex, hot-air-balloon rides, and the famous Hagenbeck Animal Show, a self-styled "zoological menagerie" whose animals rode bicycles and whose tropical birds played a variety of card games. Several rustic log cabins were located on the Midway, one said to belong to Sitting Bull. The Ottomans Arab Wild East Show—complete with Bedouin horseman—imitated the appeal of Buffalo Bill's doings. On the Midway visitors found nurseries and cranberry bogs and a "Tree of Wonder," as well as miniature models of St. Peter's Basilica and the Eiffel Tower. But what dominated the landscape of the Plaisance was an enormous metal wheel, which became the Exposition's most remembered attraction and its most important technological innovation.

Dissatisfied with several proposals for a tower-like edifice that might rival or surpass the appeal of the Universal Exposition's Eiffel Tower, Daniel Burnham accepted Pittsburgh engineer George Ferris's proposal for a two-hundred-and-fifty-foot-tall revolving wheel as the centerpiece of the Midway ensemble. Modeled on the principle of the bicycle but appearing more like a spider's web, this first "Ferris Wheel" was a metallic masterpiece that it was said reaches "over science and sweeps into the domain of art."[81] The wheel itself (actually two wheels connected by metal rods and wood struts) was eight hundred and twenty-five feet in circumference and weighed, with a full complement of passengers, twelve hundred tons. Thirty-six pendulum cars were fixed to the wheel, each twenty-seven feet long and able to hold forty passengers. This made for a maximum passenger load of fourteen hundred people for every ride, which lasted two complete revolutions. There were seats and counters in each car, and for a time Ferris contemplated installing Bell telephones so that sky-bound travelers could talk to their friends below.

Though the Ferris Wheel was not put into operation until June 21, by mid-September the concession had paid for itself. At the Exposition's close, more than a million and a half passengers had taken a ride on the great wheel, surpassing the management's wildest dreams.[82] When the wheel was filled to capacity, receipts from the attraction were more than $1,440 an hour, and Sol Bloom recalled observing families who bought tickets by the dozens and spent whole afternoons on the wheel.[83]

"All feel its deep suggestiveness," Denton Snider wrote of his ride on the wheel, "and catch its flashes afar into the past and future; it fills the soul with glimpses of meaning not quite beyond what we can at first tell; an unspeakable, overwhelming element lurks in it which picks up our struggling spirit and makes a bold dash for the Infinite." "The rise is smooth and magnificent," remembered an enthusiastic passenger. "The crowds of the Midway grow thinner by a more nearly vertical perspective, and after a time the eye runs away and looks bravely abroad."[84] Passengers and commentators alike recognized the element of fear that was a part of the Ferris Wheel's appeal—the precarious feeling of being suspended high above the ground, which was exhilarating and timorous at the same moment.

From the top of the wheel, as it began its slow, even descent, travelers were given a spectacular vista of the Midway and the towering palaces of the Exposition grounds beyond. What also came more clearly into view was the

Midway's other great topic of conversation, the foreign theaters that gave the Plaisance an alien ambiance. As one walked down the Midway, it was said, one traveled around the world, and the cafes, shops, and makeshift habitats added to the allure of the scene.

"Old Vienna," the Austrian Village's beer garden, was the most popular of the restaurants on the Plaisance. Nearby stood the Hungarian Concert Cafe, where a Gypsy band performed haunting melodies as visitors sampled the fare. The German Village had its own concert garden and "ethnographic museum." "Cottages from the Black Forest and Westphalia cluster round a typical town hall of Hesse," wrote one visitor, and in the garden imported orchestras performed rhapsodic Bavarian tunes as the audience tasted imported wines and beers.[85] Though without official representation in the fair, a group of Chinese investors sponsored a private Chinese village and theater complex. There were also cafes and eateries attached to the Algerian Village, the Moorish Palace, and the Street in Cairo concession.

Veiled in mystery, or so its sponsors claimed, the Street in Cairo was the most discussed of the several "Oriental" villages on the Midway. Like the Persian and Turkish villages, the Moorish Palace and the Algerian Village theaters, the Street in Cairo promised an education unlike any found elsewhere on the grounds. Visitors were intrigued by the babble of unfamiliar tongues and the contrast of cultures promised by solicitors. Even more, they were drawn by the anatomical gyrations of young dancing girls, whose nimble movements questioned customary standards of propriety. Each of the Oriental bazaars had exhibits and shops, but it was the theaters that brought patrons back again and again—and again.

The entrance to the Street in Cairo was disguised beneath a towering facade, said to be a replica of the ancient temple at Luxor. Inside, visitors found the recreation of a street scene, complete with donkeys and "donkeyboys," camels for hire, and Nubian and Sudanese vendors in open-air shops. The complex contained an Egyptian temple and tomb with rare artifacts and supposedly authentic mummies brought for the occasion. Natives were attired in their home dress, which perpetuated the mystique.

"There is such a hubbub of strange noises," wrote one visitor, "such a medley of races, tongues and costumes, such a lavish profusion of coloring, and so much bustle, humor and variety of incident that the visitor is apt to lose sight of the architectural features, and therefor [sic] the educational purpose of the show."[86] Masked behind the vernacular architecture were sixty-two separate shops, a temple, a mosque, and the infamous Egyptian theater complex.

In a scene repeated in the other Eastern theaters of the Midway, but never with quite the flair, young Nubian girls performed exotic dances that attracted larger and larger crowds as word of their provocative expressions spread. As disinterested musicians lounged on couches and pillows at the rear of the stage, the troupe of one dozen teenage girls performed the "danse du ventre," a style of dance later popularized as the "Hootchy-Kootchy." A regular customer who seemed unable to resist the young women's appeal described the dance as "a suggestively lascivious contorting of the abdominal muscles, which is extremely ungraceful and almost shockingly disgusting."[87] Another observer noticed that:

[As] the "orchestra" accelerates its measure, the girl sways her lithesome body in a curiously rhythmical fashion. Suddenly she seems to tremble with violent emotion, the "orchestra" plays with furious fervor while the hips and waist [sic] of the dancer appear to undulate and quiver in what might be called an ecstacy of delirious delight.[88]

Contrary to popular lore, there was no dancer named "Little Egypt" in the Egyptian theater; she would surface several years later. But there was "Fatima," perhaps the Midway's best-known resident. The mere mention of her name, said one commentator, gave young men shivers and incensed their female companions. It is possible that Fatima became Little Egypt, but more likely the latter was the creation of clever managers who remembered the appeal of the former during the Columbian season.

Mrs. D. C. Taylor, who penned a popular account of her visit to the fair, was one of those patrons disturbed by Fatima's interpretation of the dance. "And oh! that dance!" Taylor wrote in disbelief. "She takes a few light steps to one side, pauses, strikes the castanets, then the same to the other side; advances a few steps, pauses and causes her abdomen to rise and fall several times in exact time to the music." "No one seems to linger long," Taylor concluded of the audience. "A little seems to go a great way with these grave, good-natured, sober-minded Americans." Though she seemed unable to explain why some "sober-minded Americans" came back for a second and third look at what she called the theater's "sensuous, oriental atmosphere," Mrs. Taylor confessed that she and her party left the Street in Cairo thanking the Almighty for progress and singing "My Country, 'Tis of Thee."[89]

The scene in the Street in Cairo theater was repeated in the other so-called Oriental theaters, and by mid-season the provocative displays of feminine sexuality created sufficient scandal that the Exposition management attempted to shut the theaters down (see chapter 6). Much of the negative comment directed at Fatima and her companions was similar to the growing censure of another style of entertainment that challenged traditional conventions of feminine behavior—burlesque. As in burlesque, which William Dean Howells called a "horrible prettiness," gender and culture issues collided in the Midway theaters. Although the Midway troupes lacked the elements of parody and masquerade that characterized late nineteenth-century burlesque shows, they raised similar conflicting emotions in their audiences. The open sexuality of the dance was at once alluring and unsettling to patrons, and the suggestiveness of gestures emanating from the stage encouraged an element of fantasy in the male spectators that ran counter to Victorian expectations of modesty and self-restraint.[90]

As appealing and as controversial as the Middle Eastern theaters became, another type of international village on the Midway was equally provocative. In decided contrast to the more dignified European villages—the architecture and attire of Teutonic and Celtic peoples—there stood on either side of the Midway five makeshift habitats populated by authentic if sometimes uninspired inhabitants gathered from around the world. Orchestrated by crafty entrepreneurs and modeled on displays of indigenous peoples popular at the 1889 Paris Exposition, the Midway villages were money-making schemes with only a veneer of scientific intent. Different from the ethnographic exhibits on the main grounds, these habitats were touted by promoters for their own educational value, their ability to expose ticket holders to the manners and rituals of the "semicivilized races" and "polyglot peoples" only lately brought under the influence of civilization (read "white colonial rule").[91] If the great palaces of the Court of Honor symbolized the highest sentiments of culture, these aboriginal villages engendered more primal prejudices with an anthropology all their own.

As sightseers walked the length and breadth of the Plaisance, they crossed an unspoken but apparent boundary regarding the international villages. Villages at the east end were marked by their thriftiness and decorum, while those habitats at the opposite end were starker and more "natural" in their settings. The discerning eye could note not only a geographic distinction of the villages' respective countries of origin, but also a racial or color demarcation loaded with cultural importance when judging degrees of civilization and savagery.

Encompassing the theater performers, this racial boundary went further to segregate indigenous people—the proverbial "other"—whose customs and manners added to the exotic nature of the scene. On either side of the Avenue of Nations stood the American Indian Village (including Sioux, Pawnee, Blackfoot, and Cheyenne Indians), the Javanese Village, the Laplander Village, the Dahomey Village, and a village of South Sea Islanders (Samoans). Not entirely divorced from the humbug and huckstering of the oriental theaters, these villages typified what the Midway was all about and why it was separated from the Exposition proper.

In an age enamored of social Darwinism and a preoccupation with lower and higher forms of existence, few people missed the less-than-subtle suggestion of how far civilization had advanced in the century. The primitive villages and the resident villagers not only occupied a different place in the Exposition scheme, but in the minds of most visitors, they occupied a lower rung on the evolutionary ladder. Science aside, the villages' entertainment value made their residents mere curios forced to endure flagrant abuse and indignities from patrons and promoters alike.

For all of their notoriety, none of the villages came close to matching the nearly two million tickets sold for the Street in Cairo. Victimized by promoters who failed to come through with the material and financial assistance they had agreed to, the villagers from the outset became objects of curiosity and derision. One guidebook author called the Samoans in the South Sea Island Village "without any exception the best natured and most amiable" of the villagers. Another suggested the subjects of "King Mataafa" were "an unmixed and pure race" who were "physically remarkably fine specimens" of primitive man. This author, though, assured his readers that the Samoans, like their neighbors in the Javanese Village, were no longer "under the spell of cannibalism."[92]

Though native to the continent, the inhabitants of the American Indian village fared no better. Treated as cultural oddities, as a vanquished people now that the western Indian wars had drawn to a conclusion, the American Indians housed on the Midway were unable to escape the popular stereotypes of the "ignoble savage."[93] Unable to keep pace with "progress," the Midway's Indians became stock characters for the amusement of the paying customer. Such had been Richard Henry Pratt's fear from the outset.

Of all the international residents, the West African inhabitants of the Dahomey Village suffered the greatest invective. Ill-prepared for the cold weather of Chicago's winter and spring seasons, the seventy-five Dahomeans, subjects of King Behazin, arrived at Jackson Park to a cool reception. In a lengthy descriptive article published in early May, the *Tribune* led the chorus of criticism that greeted the troupe's arrival at the park. The paper referred to the more than sixty men and women, "black as the shades of night, every one of them," as "Amazons, hideous with battle scars and with lines of cruelty and determination on their faces." Adajemos was the leader of the Midway village and, in the paper's words, "like the rest he was unable to speak or utter a word of any language save the guttural of his own land." "Seeing the savages eat," echoed the *Chicago Record*, "is like watching pigs at a trough."[94] Such racist comments lent additional meaning to the fair's nickname, the "White City."

As the fair season progressed, the Dahomeans fared no better. Publicity circulars routinely referred to the Dahomeans as "African savages" and erroneously reported they were cannibals who practiced human sacrifice as a part of their religious rituals. The implication was clear: Come to the Midway and witness for yourself the peculiar passions of these less-than-civilized, and for some less-than-human, Africans. Of the ceremonies in question, William Cameron remarked, "But it is in the Dahomey village, at the west end of the Plaisance, that the grossest forms of worship concentrate." "The dances and festivals of Dahomey," echoed Denton Snider, "are heathenish." Having carefully studied the folkways of those "many specimens of the semi-civilized and barbaric races" that inhabited the Midway villages (with special attention to the Dahomeans), Snider expressed his certainty that slavery among civilized people was preferable to this form of aboriginal barbarism.[95]

Another writer caught the precise contrast of the Midway and the main grounds in a caption beneath a picture of the Dahomeans: "It was a strange but purely scientific motive that prompted the bringing from Africa of a company of savage Dahomeans, to exhibit them before the sharp and curious gaze of World's Fair visitors. But, they afforded a remarkable contrast, the extreme of barbarity in contact with the highest types of civilization."[96] Expressions of brotherhood and understanding, so eloquent in the opening-day ceremonies, seemed quickly lost as one proceeded down the Avenue of Nations on the Midway Plaisance. In ways not always intended, the Exposition managed to juxtapose the magnificent promises of progress with the primal prejudices of the era.

The Oriental bazaars and the aboriginal villages created their own measures of controversy, and throughout the Exposition season there were calls from different quarters to rid the fair of these unsightly extravaganzas. Despite the consternation of some, most visitors to the Avenue of Nations took the villages and theaters in stride, delighting in the antics and "incongruities." For many a weary traveler they were a welcoming reprieve from the pantheons of progress positioned on the eastern side of the viaduct. Lest they doubt the triumphs of the century, observers had only to take a ride on the Midway's technological wonder, the Ferris Wheel. The wheel rose high above and beyond the clutter and confusion of the Midway villages to take in the broad expanse of the idealized city that spread along the lakeshore. There the imperial *Republic* stood confidently at center stage in the allegorical assemblage, looking westward to return the sightseer's gaze.

As the Midway's most cherished memory, the Ferris Wheel was a logical link between the villages of the Plaisance and the palaces of Jackson Park. In its engineering wizardry, the "Great Wheel" had much in common with the "temples of technology" on the main grounds. Henry Adams could indulge himself in the mischief of the Midway, but he also appreciated better than most the Columbian Exposition's genuflection to the Machine Age that propelled his generation toward the accelerated universe of the twentieth century.

Notes

1. William and Daniel Shepp, *Shepp's World's Fair Illustrated* (Chicago, 1893), p. 34.

2. Frances Hodgson Burnett, *Two Little Pilgrims' Progress: A Story of the City Beautiful* (New York, 1895); [Charles S. Stevens], *The Adventures of Uncle Jeremiah and Family at the Great Fair* (Chicago, 1893), pp. 45–46.

3. William James to Henry James, 22 September 1893, in William James, *The Letters of William James*, 2 vols., ed. by Henry James (London, 1917), 1:348; Hamlin Garland, *A Son of the Middle Border* (New York, 1917), p. 458.

4. *Chicago Daily Tribune*, 2 May 1893.

5. *Chicago Daily Inter-Ocean*, 2 May 1893; *Chicago Herald*, 2 May 1893; *Chicago Times*, 2 May 1893; *Chicago Daily Tribune*, 2 May 1893.

6. Daniel Burnham and Frank D. Millet, *The World's Columbian Exposition: The Book of the Builders* (Springfield, Ohio, 1894), p. 19. Burnham and Millet cite the fig-

ures of 620.85 acres for Jackson Park and 66.5 acres for the area of the Midway, for a total of 687.63 for the entire fairgrounds.

7. Cameron, p. 851.

8. Cameron, p. 851; *Chicago Sunday Tribune*, 6 August 1893; *Chicago Daily Tribune*, 3 October 1893.

9. George H. Wilson, "Final Report of the Bureau of Music" (Chicago, 1894), in World's Columbian Exposition Collection, Special Collections Division, Chicago Public Library, Chicago, Illinois; William K. Ackerman [Auditor] to James W. Ellsworth, 7 October 1893, James W. Ellsworth Papers, Chicago Public Library; Ezra Schabas, *Theodore Thomas: America's Conductor and Builder of Orchestras, 1835–1905* (Urbana, 1989), pp. 195–212. For a more in-depth consideration of the music program at the Columbian Exposition, see chapter 7.

10. Rossiter Johnson, ed., *A History of the World's Columbian Exposition*, 4 vols. (New York, 1898), 4:6.

11. Charles Eliot Norton, *Letters of Charles Eliot Norton*, 2 vols. (Boston and New York, 1913), 2:217–18. For Norton's views on the fair, also see Kermit Vanderbilt, *Charles Eliot Norton: Apostle of Culture in a Democracy* (Cambridge, Mass., 1959), pp. 201–9.

12. Cecilia Elizabeth O'Leary, *To Die For: The Paradox of American Patriotism* (Princeton, 1999), pp. 167–68; John Bodnar, "The Memory Debate: An Introduction," in *Remaking America: Public Memory, Commemoration, and Patriotism in the Twentieth Century* (Princeton, 1992), pp. 13–20. There is a renewed interest in the issue of "memory" and American historical consciousness. See, for example, the representative articles in a "Memory and American History," Special Edition, *Journal of American History* 75 (March 1989); Michael Kammen, *Mystic Chords of Memory: The Transformation of Tradition in American Culture* (New York, 1991); David Glassberg, *American Historical Pageantry: The Uses of Tradition in the Early Twentieth Century* (Chapel Hill, 1990).

13. Lawrence W. Levine, *Highbrow/Lowbrow: The Emergence of Cultural Hierarchy in America* (Cambridge, Mass., 1988), pp. 86–168.

14. Quoted in *Chicago Daily Tribune*, 1 May 1893.

15. Candace Wheeler, "A Dream City," *Harper's New Monthly Magazine* 86 (May 1893): 836.

16. Burton Benedict, "The Anthropology of World's Fairs," in *The Anthropology of World's Fairs* (London, 1983), p. 9.

17. Although the 1876 Centennial Exhibition and the 1889 Universal Exposition had separate pavilions to display the art and handicraft of women, neither was a full-scale exhibition hall on the order of the Woman's Building at Jackson Park.

18. Royal Cortissoz, "Color in the Court of Honor," *Century Magazine* 46 (July 1893): 323; John Brisben Walker, "The World's College of Democracy," *Cosmopolitan* 15 (September 1893): 520; George B. Sparks, *The Dream City: A Story of the World's Fair* (Chicago, 1923).

19. Ella Bowes, "Ancient Religions, Games, and Folklore," n.d., n.p., Manuscript Division, Chicago Historical Society; Robert H. Thurston, "An Era of Mechanical Triumph," *Engineering Magazine* 6 (January 1894): 457.

20. Mary Griswold Van Renssalaer, "At the Fair," *Century Magazine* 46 (May 1893): 3–13.

21. Daniel H. Burnham, "Final Report of the Director of Works of the World's Columbian Exposition," 8 vols. (Chicago, 1894), 3:52–53, Daniel Burnham Library of the Art Institute of Chicago; John Ellis, *Chicago and the World's Columbian Exposition* (Chicago, 1895), p. 154; *The Vanished City: The World's Columbian Exposition in Pen and Paper* (Chicago, c.1894), n.p.

22. Quoted in *Daily Columbian*, 2 August 1893.

23. Daniel Chester French was also the sculptor of the *Republic*, and artist E. C. Potter, who contributed numerous pieces of statuary, collaborated with French on the *Quadriga*. The numerous phrases inscribed on the Peristyle were selected by President Charles Eliot of Harvard University. Walter Besant, "First Impressions," *Cosmopolitan* 15 (September 1893): 533. The name "Dreamland" would later be attached to one of the largest and most popular public amusement parks at Coney Island.

24. Frank D. Millet et al., *Some Artists at the Fair* (New York, 1893), pp. 75–76.

25. Cameron, p. 392.

26. *Official Guide to the World's Columbian Exposition* (Chicago, 1893), pp. 94–97; Shepp, pp. 64–67, 82–83; Ellis, p. 245; Benjamin Truman, *History of the World's Fair* (Chicago, 1893), pp. 211–42.

27. Ellis, pp. 248–52; Shepp, p. 68.

28. Ellis, pp. 248–52; Tudor Jenks, *The Century's World's Fair Book for Boys and Girls* (New York, 1893), p. 122.

29. Benjamin C. Truman, *History of the World's Fair* (Chicago), p. 242.

30. *The Catholic Educational Exhibit at the World's Columbian Exposition* (Chicago, 1896); Dennis B. Downey, "Tradition and Acceptance: American Catholics and the Columbian Exposition," *Mid-America* 63 (April–July 1981): 79–92.

31. *Official Guide to the World's Columbian Exposition*, p. 50.

32. *Official Guide*, p. 103.

33. *Official Guide*, pp. 43–47.

34. Mrs. D. C. Taylor, *Halcyon Days in the Dream City* (Kankakee, Ill., 1894), p. 9.

35. Truman, pp. 409–15.

36. J. W. Buel, *The Magic City* (Philadelphia, 1894), n.p.; *Chicago Times*, 8 July 1893. The caravels left Barcelona in July, 1892, participated in a pre-exposition naval review off the East Coast, and arrived at Jackson Park on July 7, 1893. Five days later the Viking Ship docked at the North Pier for the season.

37. *Official Guide*, p. 57.

38. Marshall Hyatt, *Franz Boas, Social Activist: The Dynamics of Ethnicity* (Westport, 1990), pp. 27–33. For an informative overview of Boas's approach to race and culture, see Carl N. Degler, *In Search of Human Nature: The Decline and Revival of Darwinism in American Social Thought* (New York, 1991), pp. 61–83. Hyatt details Boas's disappointment over not being selected to direct the new Columbian Natural History Museum, which opened in the Fine Arts Building after the fair closed. The debate over a director, like the exhibits themselves, exposed a larger rift within the profession over matters of heredity and culture.

39. *Official Guide*, pp. 54–55; Frederick Hoxie, *A Final Promise: The Campaign to Assimilate the Indians, 1880–1920* (Lincoln, Neb., 1984), pp. 87–90.

40. The exhibits in the Transportation and Women's Buildings are discussed in detail in later chapters.

41. Frederick Hoxie, *A Final Promise*, pp. 84–85.

42. *Official Guide*, p. 81; Ellis, pp. 129–44.

43. *Official Directory*, p. 1011.

44. Ellis, pp. 311–14.

45. Truman, p. 404.

46. *Official Guide to the World's Columbian Exposition*, pp. 117–18; Frederick Hoxie, "Beyond Savagery: The Campaign to Assimilate the American Indians, 1880–1920" (Ph.D. dissertation, Brandeis University, 1977), pp. 174–86; Rydell, pp. 55–59.

47. *Official Guide*, pp. 117–18.

48. Truman, p. 404; Smithsonian officials quoted in Ellis, p. 311.

49. Ellis, p. 312.

50. *Official Guide*, pp. 115–21; *Magic City*, n.p.

51. *Official Guide*, pp. 147–62.

52. Truman, pp. 509–28.

53. For a brief account of Douglass's appointment as commissioner for the Hatian government, see William S. McFeely, *Frederick Douglass* (New York, 1991), pp. 359, 356.

54. On the political wrangling over a chief for the Department of Fine Art,s see Carolyn Kinder Carr, "Prejudice and Pride: Presenting American Art at the 1893 World's Columbian Exposition," in *Revisiting the White City: American Art at the 1893 World's Fair* (Washington, D.C., 1993), pp. 65–69.

55. *Revised Catalogue of the Department of Fine Arts* (Chicago, 1893), pp. 5, 46; *Fine Arts at the World's Columbian Exposition* (Chicago, 1894), p. 5. The most comprehensive treatment of the art exhibits at the fair is found in Leslie S. Goldstein, "Art in Chicago and the World's Columbian Exposition of 1893" (M.A. thesis, University of Iowa, 1970), and *Revisiting the White City*.

56. Quoted in Carr, p. 91.

57. William A. Coffin, "The Columbian Exposition—I. Fine Arts: French and American Sculpture," *The Nation* 57 (3 August 1893): 79–81.

58. Apparently Halsey Ives belatedly asked Mary Cassatt and Mary Hallock Foote to serve on juries, knowing that neither artist would accept his invitation. Cassatt was living in Paris and objected to juried exhibition, and Foote was living in Idaho and constrained from traveling by modest financial resources. Three women were later appointed to one of the international juries. See *Revisiting the White City*, pp. 81–82; 394–95.

59. On the emergence of Modernist sensibilities in Americ,a see Robert Crunden's *American Salons: Encounters with European Modernism, 1885–1917* (New York, 1993), esp. pp. 5–29.

60. Goldstein, p. 45.

61. *Revised Catalogue, Fine Arts*, pp. 32–38.

62. Lorado Taft, *The History of American Sculpture* (New York, 1930), p. 11.

63. *Revised Catalogue, Fine Arts*, pp. 39–78; Goldstein, p. 85; *John Singer Sargent*, ed. by Ealine Kilmurray and Richard Ormand, eds. (Washington, D.C., 1999), pp. 13–18.

64. *Revised Catalogue, Department of Fine Arts*, pp. 10–13, 39–78; "Appendix C," *Revisiting the White City*, pp. 394–95.

65. Richard Murray, "The Art of Decoration," in *Perceptions and Evocations: The Art of Elihu Vedder* (Washington, D.C., 1979), pp. 202–4; *Revised Catalogue, Department of Fine Arts*, pp. 39–78.

66. Robert Crunden makes a persuasive case for Whistler as the preeminent precursor of modernism in American art at the end of the century. On Whistler, see *American Salons*, pp. 5–28.

67. Ellis, p. 285.

68. Kathryn Greenthal, *Augustus Saint-Gaudens, Master Sculptor* (New York, 1985), pp. 136–39; *The Reminiscences of Augustus Saint-Gaudens*, ed. by Homer Saint-Gaudens, ed., 2 vols. (New York, 1913), 2: 66–73. Saint-Gaudens also helped design the commemorative medallions presented to winning artists.

69. Taft, p. 285.

70. *Revised Catalogue, Fine Arts*, pp. 25–32; James L. Reidy, "Sculpture at the Columbian Exposition," *Chicago History* 4 (Summer 1975): 99–107. Works by Edward Kemeys, John Rogers, and J. J. Boyle were singled out for excellence by the judges.

71. Hugh McKean, *The Treasures of Tiffany* (Chicago, 1980), pp. 65–67; *Revised Catalogue, Department of Fine Arts*, pp. 39–78. Among the watercolors Tiffany exhibited in Fine Arts were *Market at Nuremberg, Bavaria* and *Pottery Market at Wurtzburg*.

72. Goldstein, p. 87; *Revised Catalogue, Fine Arts*, pp. 147–54.

73. Hamlin Garland, "Impressionism," in *Crumbling Idols: Twelve Essays Dealing Chiefly with Literature, Painting, and the Drama* (1894; Cambridge, Mass., 1960), pp. 97–110.

74. *Revised Catalogue, Fine Arts*, pp. 147–54.

75. On the appeal of Hovenden's painting, see Oliver W. Larkin, *Art and Life in America* (New York, 1949), p. 237; and Howard Mumford Jones, *The Age of Energy: Varieties of American Experience, 1865–1917* (New York, 1971), p. 184. Hovenden's *Bringing Home the Bride* was completed two weeks before the Exposition opened.

76. Denton Snider, *World's Fair Studies* (Chicago, 1897), p. 259; Cameron, p. 642; Truman, p. 549.

77. Truman, p. 551.

78. Quoted in Charles Fanning, *Finley Peter Dunne and Mr. Dooley: The Chicago Years* (Lexington, Kentucky, 1978), p. 29.

79. Some historians have insisted that the Midway's arrangement of concessions reflected the cultural hegemony of Western European values, with African and Oriental exhibits placed at the far end of the Plaisance. A cursory examination of the Midway's map shows this not to be the case, with an arrangement that was looser and less proscribed.

80. Cameron, p. 663.

81. Snider, p. 9.

82. "The Ferris Wheel at the Columbian Exposition," *Halligan's Illustrated World's Fair* 5 (September 1893): 634; "The Great Wheel at Chicago," *Scientific American* 68 (July 1, 1893): 8–9; Ellis, p. 334.

83. Sol Bloom, *The Autobiography of Sol Bloom* (New York, 1948), pp. 138–39; Shepp, p. 502.

84. Snider, p. 11; John McGovern, "On the Wheel," *Halligan's Illustrated World's Fair* 5 (August 1893): 597.

85. *Official Guide*, pp. 22–25; Truman, pp. 575–76.

86. *The Vanished City*, n.p.

87. *The Magic City*, n.p.

88. Cameron, pp. 674–75.

89. *Halcyon Days*, p. 23.

90. For an excellent discussion of Burlesque's assault on Victorian values, see Robert C. Allen, *Horrible Prettiness: Burlesque and American Culture* (Chapel Hill, 1991).

91. For a general consideration of racism and ethnographic exhibits at European fairs, see William Schneider, "Race and Empire: The Rise of Popular Ethnography in the Late Nineteenth Century," *Journal of Popular Culture* 11 (Summer 1977): 98–109; for perceptive comments on the villages on Chicago's Midway, see Robert W. Rydell, *All the World's a Fair: Visions of Empire at American International Expositions, 1876–1916* (Chicago, 1984), pp. 60-68; Rydell, "A Cultural Frankenstein? The Chicago World's Columbian Exposition of 1893," in Neil Harris et al., *Grand Illusions: Chicago's World's Fair of 1893* (Chicago, 1993), esp. pp. 158–66.

92. *The Vanished City: The World's Columbian Exposition in Pen and Picture* (Chicago, c.1894), n.p; John Ellis *Chicago and the World's Columbian Exposition* (Chicago, 1895), p. 338.

93. Frederick Hoxie, "Beyond Savagery: The Campaign to Assimilate the American Indians, 1880–1920" (Ph.D. dissertation, Brandeis University, 1977), pp. 174–86.

94. *Chicago Daily Tribune*, 4 May 1893; *Chicago Record*, 29 May 1893. See also Christopher Robert Reed, *"All the World Is Here!": The Black Presence at White City* (Bloomington, 2000), pp. 164–71.

95. Cameron, p. 644; Snider, p. 330.

96. *The Magic City*, n.p.

3

≈

Technics of Acceleration

For Henry Adams, the experience of sitting beneath Richard Hunt's magisterial dome in the Court of Honor brought back a flood of reminiscences. A historian and descendant of presidents and an inveterate world traveler, Adams was prone to viewing cultural developments through the prism of personal experiences. As he surveyed the grounds, Adams found himself pondering whether the Columbian Exposition was the symbol of renewal that so many believed it to be. Had its impression of artistic unity reconciled its competing elements, much like the larger society? Did the Chicago fair indeed prefigure the "new era" of progress and enlightenment, or was there a prophetic warning in the dissonance and fragmentation he felt throughout the grounds?

Mindful that the fair reflected national development at the end of the nineteenth century, Henry Adams found reason to study what was being taught. "Chicago asked in 1893 for the first time the question of whether the American people knew where they were driving," Adams wrote in what amounts to one of the most telling observations of the Exposition. "Adams answered," he continued in the third person, "for one, that he did not know, but would try to find out."[1]

Henry Adams visited the Columbian Exposition on two occasions. It was his second and extended visit that made the greater impression. Like Charles Eliot Norton, Adams was unprepared for the sharp contrasts and glaring contradictions that greeted him at every turn. Of his experience at the fair, Adams wrote of himself, "He found matter to study to fill a hundred years, and his education spread over chaos." "Not since Noah's Ark, no such Babel of loose and ill-joined, such vague and unrelated thoughts and half-thoughts and experimental outcries as the Exposition, had ever ruffled the surface of the Lake." Henry's brother, Charles Francis, praised the "spirit of order and decorum" at Jackson Park, but Henry concluded, "Here was a breach of continuity—a rupture of historical sequence! Was it real, or only apparent?" he asked himself. "One's personal universe hung in the balance."[2]

Adams was not above poking fun at his own peculiar angle of vision. "Of course I don't understand it," he wrote Lucy Baxter of the fair, "but then I don't understand anything—not even Beacon Street." "For a poor old ghost like me," he continued to his friend John Hay, "just barely hovering on this earth for which my ethereal nature unfits me," the "fakes and frauds" of the Midway were an especial delight.[3] But Adams's whimsical self-deprecation did not prevent him from seeing the Columbian Exposition as a great cultural moment that transcended the normal sequence of historical events.

"Education ran riot at Chicago," he concluded, "at least for retarded minds which had never faced in concrete form so many matters of which they were ignorant." Dissenting from the self-congratulatory theme, Adams remarked on his own "misdirected education," which had left him "helpless before the mechanical sequence" that marked such an abrupt departure from the past.[4] Where his brother, Charles Francis, found order and unity at Jackson Park, Henry Adams found only chaos and uncertainty, clear evidence that the Chicago world's fair did indeed prefigure a new but inhospitable era to come. In the Columbian Exposition's technological exhibits, especially in the Electricity Building, Adams discovered a personal symbol for the randomness of an accelerated multiverse he would associate with the twentieth century—the dynamo.

Society at the end of the nineteenth century took the constancy of change as a measure of its worth. The greater the output, the swifter the speed of travel, easier the modes of communication, and according to Thorstein Veblen, the more conspicuous its habits of consumption, the surer the course of progress.[5] Technology manufactured the wherewithal of material prosperity, and these technics assumed a moral authority—more is better, the saying went—which reflected the shift from a religious toward a commercial basis for culture.

It is not surprising that Henry Adams should apprehend a special significance in the Chicago world's fair's mechanical displays, considered by most observers to be a catalog of the mechanical and technological advances of the nineteenth century. More than a mere celebration of the Machine Age, the exhibition of mechanical force at Chicago prefigured for Adams the rapidly accelerating pace of existence, a rate of development with which society would increasingly fail to keep up.

Looking back on the Columbian Exposition from the vantage point of the 1900 Universal Exposition, Adams wrote: "In these seven years man had translated himself into a new universe which had no scale of measurement with the old. He had entered a supersensual world, in which he could measure nothing except the chance collision of movements imperceptible to the senses."[6] An 1893 commentary unknowingly anticipated Adams's remark in looking forward to the dawn of the new century:

Yet grand in conception and in construction as the Exhibition of 1900 may be, it will bear little resemblance to the present exhibition at Chicago. There is nothing constant but change. . . . Nearly every machine, every process and every form of art and industry that is now on exhibition in Jackson Park will in a single generation have vanished like the "Hellenic dream" that will disappear when the existing buildings are removed never to be repeated.[7]

It must have humored Adams to know that popular conversation made much of what one author called the "cathedral-like" appearance of the Palace of Mechanic Arts (Machinery Hall) and the religious dimensions of the Exposition as a whole. In keeping with the spirit of renewal, the Machine had entered this Eden-like garden to deliver humanity from centuries of backwardness into the enlightenment of the golden age.[8]

The Columbian Exposition represented a veritable temple to technology, the enshrinement of the Machine as a popular icon of the revolutionary and formative force of modernization in the new era. Though for Henry Adams the Exposition was not the epiphany of progress so many believed it to be, he would have agreed that the technics of acceleration housed in the fair's great halls demanded a kind of faith all their own.

Since the 1851 Crystal Palace Exhibition, visitors to world's fairs were accustomed to encountering larger and more varied, to say nothing of more sophisticated, displays of mechanical instruments and apparatus. In an age when mechanization took command, to paraphrase Siegfried Giedeon, the exhibits in Machinery Hall at Chicago formed the largest display of mechanical power ever assembled to that date. As such they personified the Exposition's general benediction on the industrial revolution. With eighty-six different classes of machines and mechanical apparatus, Machinery Hall was the triumphant moment in what Gilman Ostrander has termed "the first Machine Age."[9] Stretched out along three massive longitudinal aisles, the mechanical exhibits lent further comparative weight to America's emergence as the world's industrial giant.

The U.S. sections demonstrated the tremendous industrial and technological development since the first international exhibition in 1851. They also provided undeniable evidence of the transformation machinery had effected in routine processes of producing finished goods. Nearly six hundred American firms exhibited in the department, almost five times the number of its closest competitor, Germany. All manner of machines were included in the general classification of exhibits: motors and apparatus for the transmission of power; machines for working with wood, stone, metals, foods, and textiles; machines for printing, typesetting, and lithography; every conceivable type of hand implement; and miscellaneous mechanical devices. Each exhibit, read the *Official Catalogue of the World's Columbian Exposition,* "has its own mission of instruction and interest."[10]

Generally, the exhibits focused on the commercial application of machines to industrial and domestic labor. The technology of mass production and apparatus to ease household labor, as well as catalog merchandise, abounded. Steam hammers, nail cutting devices, and wood-carving saws were but a few of the industrial instruments on exhibit. Power looms and electric sewing machines for home and factory stood near printing presses that produced forty-eight thousand pages of news text per hour. The latter were used to create the fair's own newspaper, the *Daily Columbian.*[11]

Stretching for nearly a thousand feet along the building's south wall was a horizon of polished steel and whirling belts that comprised the Exposition power plant and the world's largest electric lighting plant. Absorbed by the incessant hum of working motors and the gyrations of overhead line shafting, visitors assumed a reverential pose as the great engines effortlessly went about their tasks "as though possessed of intelligence," wrote one admirer. Another visitor seemed perplexed by his visit to the machinery exhibits. The machinery "is bewildering and nerve-shattering," wrote F. Hopkins Smith. "There is a demonic energy in machinery and a vast suggestiveness, too, when one considers the transformation of society that it brings. . . . I fled [Machinery Hall] with a sense of relief."[12]

Machinery Hall's power plant was a remarkable assembly of technological innovations that performed several practical functions. In addition to supplying electrical current to the more than ninety thousand incandescent lamps that illuminated the fairgrounds, the plant brightened the fifty-some arc lamps used on the exteriors of the major buildings. Beyond providing power for the working exhibits in Machinery Hall, the power plant generated current for exhibits in Manufactures, Agriculture, Mines, Electricity, and Transportation. All the electric fountains and the air pressure in the water and sewer systems worked off the power plant. Quite understandably, Machinery Hall was acclaimed the "heart and lungs of the Exposition."[13]

The sheer force and sophistication of the power plant testified to the advances since the novel Corliss engine at the Centennial Exhibition. (These same machines also spoke to the growing prominence of a small number of large corporations able to stifle competition in the industry since 1876.) Philadelphia's power plant seemed almost primitive when compared with the advanced efficiency of the machinery that powered the Chicago exhibition. In Philadelphia's Machinery Hall, tandem condensing overhead beam engines had a combined capacity of fourteen hundred horsepower. Chicago's power plant consisted of seventy-seven engines with an aggregate of 29,830 horsepower. Furthermore, this plant furnished three times the electric lighting power than used in the entire city of Chicago, and ten times the electricity used in the 1889 Paris Exposition.[14]

The E.P. Allis Company's leviathan Reynolds-Corliss horizontal quadruple expansion engine led the accelerated cadence assumed by lesser engines and generators. With a total weight of three hundred and twenty-five tons, a fly-wheel thirty feet in diameter, and a normal operating capacity of two thousand horsepower (but able on adjustment to produce three thousand horsepower), the Allis engine was the largest ever used or displayed at a nineteenth-century world's fair. It was also the more efficient version of the two, seven-hundred-ton Corliss vertical expansion engines used at the Centennial.

Whereas the Centennial engines stood upright, towering over spectators, the single Columbian engine lay on the horizontal and stretched like a beast down the long nave, dwarfing bystanders with what seemed benign indiffer-ence. At the Centennial only one American firm (that of George Corliss) competed against European manufacturers of heavy industrial engines, but in 1893 nearly sixty domestic companies competed in the market, and most of them exhibited at Chicago. At the Columbian Exposition the American machines generally were praised for now being superior to the English and German rivals.[15]

Joined to twin ten-thousand-lamp Westinghouse incandescent dynamos, the Allis engine was the mainstay of the lighting plant. Pittsburgh's Westing-house Electric and Manufacturing Company was awarded the sole contract for the installation, operation, and maintenance of this, the largest incan-descent lamp facility in existence. Three other firms shared the contract for the arc lighting system: General Electric, Standard Electric, and the Western Electric Company. A total of thirty-three manufacturers loaned machinery to the Exposition power plant, all at no charge, and each engine had its own maintenance crew that supervised operations and repairs.[16]

In obtaining the contract for incandescent lighting on the Exposition grounds, George Westinghouse was faced with the problem of building quickly and economically a facility capable of serving the equivalent of a city of 250,000 inhabitants. In addition to furnishing the necessary conductors and dynamos, Westinghouse invented a novel incandescent bulb called a "stopper lamp" for use at Chicago. When the prototype failed to retain the necessary vacuum for a sufficient time, Westinghouse had an additional quar-ter-million bulbs fabricated and shipped to Jackson Park. Another important innovation was Westinghouse's success in adapting Nikola Tesla's alternating current motors at the Columbian Exposition. Locked in a fierce battle with Thomas Edison for control of the electrification industry, Westinghouse per-suaded a dubious public to Westinghouse's side by the triumph of "a.c."[17]

More than fifty steam-generating boilers, with an aggregate equivalent of more than twenty thousand commercial horsepower, stood hidden behind Machinery Hall. A special twenty-two-mile-long pipeline connected the Stan-dard Oil's Whiting, Indiana, reservoir with storage tanks at the southeastern corner of the fairgrounds. Separate from Machinery Hall but still part of its power-plant complex, the Worthington Pump Station had machinery capable of pumping twenty million gallons of water a day throughout the fairgrounds. By comparison, the Centennial's Worthington Station had a daily pumping capacity of six hundred thousand gallons of water.[18]

Henry Adams admitted he shared the ignorance of those at Chicago who "had not a shadow of a notion what amount of force was meant by a *watt* or an *ampere* or an *erg*, or any other measurement introduced within a hundred years." With the constant hum of wheels in motion, the procession of oscillating levers and gears, and the jungle of belts and shafts rotating in harmonic sequence, this powerhouse of mechanical force was capable of inducing vertigo. To protect against injury, broad guardrails kept the curious a safe distance from the pulsating engines as they breathed life into the Exposition. For a generation enamored of the Machine as icon, would Henry Adams have seen a similarity with the sanctuary rail at Chartres? As a temple to technology, Machinery Hall exhibited an element of force visible yet to many incomprehensible, which to Adams's way of thinking demanded a faith of its own.[19]

In a sense the entire Exposition was a testament to the new forces of acceleration, which were transforming the ordinary routines of everyday life and labor. Following this line of development, the next logical step was a visit to the Department of Electricity. Never before had an international exhibition used electrical energy so comprehensively. Apart from the intricate telephone system and the use of electric elevators in the major exhibition halls, the nights at Jackson Park were the most obvious sign of the thorough integration of electricity into the complex. So powerful was the nighttime illumination that one visitor claimed that on a clear night the Court of Honor's glow could be seen more than ninety miles away, in Milwaukee.[20]

Electricity was perhaps the most radical or novel of the new technologies demonstrated at the Columbian Exposition. Early in the construction phase, Daniel Burnham advised architect Henry Van Brunt that a suitable building "should possess utmost refinement and delicacy . . . and, I hope, be sumptuous, and in a quiet way, both rich and gay."[21] The building itself, the first dedicated to electricity at a world's fair, fit the bill with a towering arched entryway, decorative turrets and pediments, and sculptor Carl Rohl-Smith's statue of Benjamin Franklin, eyes cast heavenward in a devotional pose with key in hand, inviting the inquisitive to partake of the mysteries within. More than fifteen thousand lamps (aggregate candlepower of 240,000) solely for its interior lighting.[22]

"The primary purpose of the Electricity Department," explained its chief, J. P. Barrett, "is to demonstrate in actual operation, of [*sic*] the commercial and economic application of electricity."[23] Subsidiary goals were to form a historical document of electricity's development in the nineteenth century, as well as to perform practical experiments and tests on electrical apparatus. More than practical, electrical science was revolutionary in its implications for everyday life. "Forty years ago," wrote one observer, "such a building would not have been necessary. Then the telegraph was still young, a giant at play, hardly yet harnessed to the chariot of progress. . . . The old world seems very far away now."[24]

Seventeen groups and sixty-three more specific classes of electrical exhibits demonstrated what Hubert Bancroft termed "the greatest and yet youngest and most progressive of the sciences."[25] Amid the patterns of brightly flashing lights and the rows of polished metal objects were apparatus for illustrating the phenomena of electricity and magnetism, batteries, conductors, motors, and appliances that produced and conducted electrical current—dynamos that could generate up to one million volts of electricity. Exhibits covered electrical lighting, heating, and power; the use of electricity in dental, surgical, and therapeutic procedures; machines that adapted electrical current to the needs of transportation, mining, and manufacturing, as well as home and industrial labor. Taken in sum, the exhibits in the Electricity Building dramatized the transformation made in the most ordinary of human activities by harnessing the force of nature.

Government exhibits vied with commercial pavilions, with numerous historical and statistical displays charting breakthroughs in the "science of electrodynamics." Similar to Machinery Hall, the American and foreign exhibits stressed dramatic and novel adaptations in the field and what seemed to some the limitless horizon of commercial possibilities for electricity. "What electricity cannot do," admitted one spectator in the department, "would be easier to state than what it can do. We feel a sense of uneasiness in moving about; great staring eyes are watching our every movement; they are only lamps for railroad engines, in many different colors, but, like the eyes in some portraits, they seem to follow us. . . . What a curious playful giant electricity is."[26]

Not surprisingly, Germany occupied the largest pavilion of the ten foreign nations that exhibited in the building, followed next by France and England. Supplementing the display of dynamos, commercial motors and machines for the transmission of continuous and multiphase electrical current, the German firms exhibited models of arc lamps, searchlights, coils of wire cable, telegraphic and electric telephones, and the latest models of electric streetcars and pole lamps used in metropolitan areas. France highlighted its electric cooking apparatus, coastal lighthouse reflectors, electric music boxes, and a novel electric match. Included in the French section was a thorough exhibition of the electrical instruments used in medical surgery and in the treatment of atrophied muscles and diseases. Rounding out its extensive exposition of electricity applied to the needs of manufacturing was a hydroelectric riveter used primarily in the construction of bridges.[27]

A collection of government telegraphic instruments, the oldest telegraph dating from 1837, were among the more interesting displays in the British pavilion. Visitors were also entertained by an electric voice box, a "homacoustic communicator," manufactured by the Homacoustic Speaking Tube

Company to transmit the human voice by means of electrified tubes. Seismological instruments from the Japanese Imperial University demonstrated the detection of earth tremors and quakes and other natural disasters.[28]

Though the United States could claim few if any pioneers in the early discoveries and experiments of electrical science, many exhibits attested to America's practical and commercial application of electricity. Virtually every important domestic manufacturer of electrical machinery and instruments was represented in the department, with the largest exhibit sponsored by Thomas Edison's recently formed General Electric Company. The product of a merger between Edison Electric, the Thomson-Houston Electric Company, and several smaller competitors, in 1893 General Electric was the most diverse and commercially successful manufacturer of electrical appliances and equipment in the United States.

For nearly twenty years, Thomas Edison, the so-called "Wizard of Menlo Park," had dominated the new industry with a succession of practical inventions that created a new industry of manufactured sight and sound. In addition to his own incandescent bulb, phonograph, microphone, and various duplicating machines, Edison improved on competitors' inventions, including Alexander Graham Bell's telephone. Edison's victory was complete with the installation of America's first incandescent lighting plant at New York's Pearl Street station in 1882. In his workshop in New Jersey, the prototype for the modern industrial research laboratory, Edison invented the "kinetoscope," a forerunner of the motion picture camera. General Electric's pavilion at Jackson Park was a testament to the remarkable genius and commercial success of Edison and his research teams.[29]

General Electric's 85-foot-high glowing "Tower of Light" dominated the Electricity Building's interior. Resting atop a giant colonnade and studded with five thousand light bulbs colored red, orange, and purple, the tower was crowned by an enormous replica of Edison's first incandescent light, made of forty thousand glass prisms. The entire apparatus ran to accompanying waltz music recorded by John Philip Sousa's band, a feature that the *Chicago Sunday Tribune* said "adds to the charm of the display."[30] Magnets, induction coils, converters, transformers, voltmeters, and ammeters—the accoutrements of electrical power—were arranged around the Tower of Light.[31]

The only American firms to rival the General Electric exhibit were the Westinghouse Electric and Manufacturing Company and the American Bell Telephone Company. George Westinghouse had used his early financial success with the invention of the railroad air brake to build a manufacturing empire to challenge Edison. With the use of alternating current in the Exposition's lighting plant, Westinghouse achieved a measure of triumph in the battle. What first caught the eye of those who wandered into the Westinghouse pavilion was not the long procession of motors and dynamos on display nor the myriad of electrical inventions that lay strewn on the floor in a somewhat orderly fashion. In a curious mixing of the old world and the new, with a patriotic theme that was unmistakable, a large mural blazed on the building's south wall. A facsimile caricature of Christopher Columbus with the dates "1492–1892" was emboldened with red, white, and blue lights.

Not to be outdone, Bell Telephone Company had the third great exhibit in the Department of Electricity. Since exhibiting a prototype of his telephone at the Centennial Exhibition, Alexander Graham Bell was among the best known of a generation of admired inventors. Bell estimated that in 1893 more than a half million electric telephones were in daily use in the United States.

A retrospective display of Bell's early inventions, as well as the latest accomplishments in the field, formed the company's Chicago exhibit. Those fortunate enough to attend the Exposition during Professor Bell's first visit were able to watch as the pioneer opened the first "long distance" telephone circuit between Chicago and New York. Visitors to the company's pavilion were especially intrigued with the "radiophone," a device that transmitted the human voice by use of a parabolic reflector. One end of a bulbed glass tube was placed into the focus of the reflector and the other end into the human ear. Aided by a piece of burned cork in the tube, the listener was somehow able to interpret words borne by a ray of light. The radiophone was thought a marvel in 1893, prefiguring the later development of the radio and the era of optical fiber transmission.[32]

Chicago-based Western Electric Company, the only authorized manufacturer of electric telephones in the United States, exhibited telephone apparatus, electric switchboards, and other support machinery. Western Electric operated the popular Scenic Village on the Midway. The concession depicted a Swiss village passing through stages of daylight, twilight, and night and through a variety of climatic changes, the whole impression effected by the use of artificial lighting. James Barrett, chief of the Department of Electricity, estimated that an average of three thousand persons visited the theater each day, making it the most popular exhibit in the department.[33]

A variety of machines and instruments suggesting the domestic and commercial potential of electricity was scattered throughout the remaining American exhibits. Alternative arc lighting systems then in operation in several American cities, electric forges, drills, welders and plating machines, and an electric typewriter revealed the wide variety of profitable applications. An assortment of new electrical appliances, including fans, an electric carpet sweeper, clothes irons, and a model electric dishwasher and dryer promised relief from the tyranny of domestic labor. Each of these items guaranteed a measure of progress for the homemaker, allowing her to do more in less time, freeing her from monotonous household routines.

Exiting Electricity Hall, one grateful enthusiast remarked, "It is a hall of marvels, a museum of enchantments, where the eye of curiosity was almost blinded by bewilderment and dazzled by surprises." Henry Adams observed of these same exhibits, "One lingered long among the dynamos, for they were new, and they gave to history a new phase." As a device that converted mechanical power into electrical energy, the dynamo symbolized for Adams the radical disjuncture in human experience inaugurated at Chicago.

Henry Adams sensed that, like himself, fellow visitors did not understand the complexities of electrodynamics, but they marveled at its accomplishments. There was an aura of mystery to these exhibits, but what relationship they had to the experience of Americans just a generation before, Adams could not say. In a less apocalyptic but equally compelling way, Daniel Shepp acknowledged the revolutionary character of the Columbian Exposition's Department of Electricity. "How bewildered our grandfathers would be," Shepp wrote,

if they could rise from their graves and see how business is being kept cool by electric fans, and servants called by electric bells; how diseases are cured by electricity, and how it is made to do man's will in a thousand ways! Our poor ancestors would wish to retire hastily from a world that has gone so far beyond them.[34]

In addressing the Congress on Electricity, which convened in late August, Professor Elisha Gray, one of America's foremost scientists and an inventor, echoed these sentiments in his opening remarks to the Exposition's Congress on Electricity. "The rapid strides that have been made in electrical science and electrical invention in the last twenty-five years," Gray noted, "have marked a new era in our civilization, and this age may well be called the electrical age."[35] Thomas Edison, Nikola Tesla, Elihu Thomson, and the German physicist Hermann Von Helmholtz, author of the First Law of Thermodynamics, were among the leading scientists and inventors who attended the gathering, a theoretical counterpart to the electricity exhibits.

In the main address of the conference, Von Helmholtz (1821–1894) gave a perspective from which to judge the great advances of recent years. "The beginning of my career," he observed, "was when the phenomena of electricity were most delicate experiments which were performed by some physicists in their laboratory. We can move at present great machines of the greatest power and at the time when I began to study electricity we could not move a little magnetic needle suspended on a silken thread, the finest we could find." More than a thousand people attended a session at the Agriculture Building auditorium in which Croatian-born Nikola Tesla discussed and gave practical demonstration of his system of high-tension currents. Tesla, at thirty-six the "Wizard of Physics," was praised for his command of electrical theory and the English language, and his remarks drew a sustained standing ovation from the likes of Thomas Edison and Hermann Von Helmholtz.[36]

Years later, Henry Adams echoed Elisha Gray's remark on an "electrical age" when he sought to explain how the dynamo might be used to symbolize a new phase of human history. Tellingly, Adams appropriated the notion of a new "Electrical Phase" to the final chapter in his pseudoscientific "Rule of Phase Applied to History" (1909).[37] It was a new era of sensual experience, one in which the very notion of time and space was altered by the revolutionary discoveries of science. For Adams, electricity was as good or better than any other descriptive adjective in charting what he imagined "the tendency of history."

Ever the restless wanderer since his wife's tragic death in 1885, Henry Adams was prone to long excursions to Europe and the Pacific Islands. As an experienced traveler, Henry Adams was also drawn to the novel technics housed in the Exposition's Transportation Building as a last port of call in charting accelerated force at Chicago. An exile of sorts, Adams grew to appreciate the steady stream of improvements in oceanic and continental transportation in his lifetime, and throughout his wanderings he was reminded of the relationship of space, time, and force, of the conquest of space and the accelerated pace of travel. Like Machinery and Electricity, the exhibits in Transportation spoke to the astounding technological revolution of the nineteenth century and of how notions of time and space had been transformed by the technics of acceleration.

Curator James Dredge said that on entering through Louis Sullivan's much-praised "Golden Door" one found "every vehicle used in transportation . . . from baby carriages to monster locomotives." Dredge, the British Royal Commissioner to the Columbian Exposition, assured those who doubted the importance of the Department of Transportation that the building's exhibits were "the key to the phenomenal progress of the century," and he recommended close observation of the many lessons it taught.[38] Once again, comparative study was recommended as the measuring rod of progress, with retrospective and contemporary exhibits that summarized past achievements as an avenue to future invention.

There were seven general divisions in the Department of Transportation: railways, plants and equipment; miscellaneous and special railways; vehicles of the common road; aerial and pneumatic transportation; vessels, boats, and marine transportation; naval warfare and coastal defense; and streetcars and systems.[39] Of the nearly one thousand exhibitors in the building, seventy percent were from the United States. Among other popular conventions, forty-three manufacturers of bicycles exhibited in the department. This in the year when the tune "Daisy Belle" rivaled "After the Ball" in popularity.

For those with more conventional tastes there were long rows of buggies, phaetons, and coaches able to carry one or more persons on a variety of business or social errands. Enhancing the appeal of the better-known manufacturers was the high degree of craftsmanship exhibited in each of the smartly painted and brightly polished vehicles. Adjacent to the horse-drawn ambulances and hospital coaches were the hearses, their dark and somber elegance intimating the inevitability of their mission.

Among the exhibits devoted to naval warfare, visitors seemed most curious about models of German torpedo boats able to cruise undetected underwater in the shadow of enemy vessels. Few who viewed the "U-boats" could imagine their role twenty-odd years hence in shattering the hoped-for new era of international cooperation that adults associated with the Exposition.

Among the more impressive displays were models of China's lightning-fast warship, the *Ting-Yeng*, and the English battleship *Ramilles*. Included in the exhibit of heavy ordnance were cannons and long-range mortars manufactured at the Essen, Germany, Krupp Iron Works, and a fifty-ton breech-loading gun manufactured by America's Bethlehem Iron Works. Included in the Elswick, England, shipyard display were a model of the ironclad *Victoria*, whose lone turret bore twin eleven-ton guns, and models of the two recently completed steamers commissioned by Argentina, the *25 de Mayo* and the *9 de Julio*. Reflecting the modest state of the American navy, the government's naval exhibit was largely limited to the staff and concrete facsimile of the battleship *Illinois*, docked at the north pier.[40]

There were numerous comparisons and contrasts to be drawn in the Transportation Building's retrospective displays. A replica of an ancient Roman chariot stood in stark contrast to the last naval ordnance. So too did the scene of street carriers from Constantinople, their burros laden with heavy parcels, and the man- and animal-drawn carts from Sicily. "But," wrote one author apologizing for their primitive manners, "they are a contented folk, all of them, in their Eden of an island. . . . It would be almost a pity to break in upon these people with the rush and rumble of our noisy existence." By such contrasts were civilizations judged.[41]

In charting the transportation revolution of the nineteenth century, the railroad exhibits offered the greatest comparative detail. In a century of transcontinental migration and an expanding internal market economy, the locomotive was the preeminent icon of national progress. Traversing the continent beyond the eastern curtain of mountains, the locomotive symbolized for the generation of Henry Adams's grandfather the era in which the nation presumably stepped beyond its provincial folkways. Nathaniel Hawthorne, Walt Whitman, and Henry David Thoreau had each pondered its place in American culture; and Thomas Wolfe would later sum up a generation's fascination with this "miracle of man's handicraft, and everything about it is eloquent of human purpose."[42]

The last great transcontinental rail system to traverse the nation was completed in 1893, and fittingly—or coincidentally—the Exposition's exhibits comprised what Rossiter Johnson called "in all respects the greatest exhibit of railway material, appliances, and machinery ever brought together." John-

son's observation was all the more significant because of the exhibit's placement in Chicago, a city made by the railroad and for a quarter-century the
world's busiest railroad junction.

In the main building and in its car-barn annex a complete retrospective
exhibit demonstrated the revolution in transportation that paralleled the
surge of population westward in the previous two generations. Equally
compelling to the locomotives themselves were the displays of the great
manufacturing complexes or "works" in the United States and Europe. The
colossal Baldwin Locomotive Works in Pennsylvania brought a model of its
sprawling facility, as well as a number of its more famous products. From
Germany came an exhibit from the George-May Iron Works, complete with
coaches, samples of track, and switching devices found throughout the
continent.

Many visitors enjoyed the ornate passenger cars provided by the Wagner
and Pullman Palace Car companies. In the Pullman pavilion was a scale
model of George Pullman's company town constructed in 1882 south of
Chicago. Intended as a model industrial environment to satisfy workers'
every need, Pullman, Illinois, had instead come under much criticism by
Richard Ely and other reformers, who found in the company "code" a rigid-
ity analogous to the medieval manor. Within a year the Pullman facility
would become the scene of the worst labor unrest of the century.[43]

Chicagoans, no doubt, looked with nostalgia on the Chicago and Northwestern Railroad's *Pioneer*, purchased a half-century before by William But-
ler Ogden to inaugurate rail service to the city. British visitors found among
many familiar sights the *Rocket*, a locomotive that operated on a line between Manchester and Liverpool in the 1820s, and the mighty *Lord of the
Isles*, first exhibited in 1851 at the Crystal Palace Exhibition and still capable of an average speed of sixty miles per hour.

Among the relics in the Baltimore and Ohio exhibit was the *Experiment*, a
locomotive built in 1832 to cover one mile of straight track in fifty seconds.
Other mid-century locomotives of similar speed were included in the B&O's
retrospective display: the *James*, the *Henry Campbell*, and the *Crab Tree*. The
best indication of how far locomotive technology had advanced in a single
lifetime was in the separate house of the New York Central. There the
DeWitt Clinton and the *Empire State Express* stood side by side in a dramatic
representation of engineering progress. Known as a "stagecoach on wheels"
because its rough passenger car was modeled on a horse-drawn carriage, the
Clinton was the older of the two. The monstrous *Express* towered over its an-
cestor and by all measures was "the fastest long-distance train in the world."
In comparison, the *Clinton*, built in 1831, had a maximum operating speed
of fifteen m.p.h.; the more recently constructed Express, headed by the famous Engine No. 999, was capable of operating at speeds in excess of one
hundred ten m.p.h.[44]

Henry Adams felt the pull and tug of these wondrous machines. As a student of accelerated force, he found a similar lesson in the display of trans-Atlantic steamers. "Historical exhibits were common enough," Adams said of Transportation's divisions.

One of the best was that of the Cunard steamers, but still the student hungry for results found himself obliged to waste a pencil and several sheets of paper trying to calculate exactly when, according to the given increase in power, tonnage, and speed, the growth of the ocean steamer would reach its limit. His figures, he thought, brought him to the year 1927, another generation to spare before force, space and time should meet.[45]

Had one the patience to do the statistical calculations on the increasing speed of ocean travel, Adams's observations would have been sustained. In his detailed *Record of the Transportation Exhibits*, James Dredge presented a detailed analysis of trans-Atlantic travel and the vessels on display in the Transportation Building. Dredge's chart of increasing speed and efficiency reinforced Henry Adams's own definition of progress as the "economy of force."

In 1818, the *Savannah* became the first steam-propelled barque to make the trans-Atlantic passage, using steam-powered paddles for eighty hours of its twenty-seven-day crossing to Liverpool. Seven years later, a steamer named *Enterprise* made the trip from England to Calcutta, India, in a record-breaking one hundred thirteen days. Though clipper ships continued to dominate the Atlantic trade routes for the next two decades, by the late 1840s the development of the screw propeller gave the snub-nosed steamer a decided advantage.[46]

On its maiden voyage in 1840, the Cunard Line's *Britannia* carried one hundred fifteen passengers and made the passage to New York in fourteen days and eight hours, at an average speed of 8.5 knots. With an average speed of thirteen knots in 1856, the steamer *Persia* made the crossing just under nine days. By 1893, the Cunard twin-screw steamers *Luciana* and *Campania* dominated the Atlantic routes by making the oceanic passage in just under five and one-half days, each vessel with an average speed greater than 20 knots.[47]

Like the *Empire State Express* of the railroad section, the *Campania* was a fitting symbol of an age that celebrated not only a gospel of efficiency but also what might be called a gospel of haste. When compared with the mock Columbian caravels moored on the Exposition's south grounds, the *Campania* was the best and truest example of the four centuries of progress since Columbus's voyage celebrated in the Chicago world's fair. Henry Adams took note not only of the increased speed and efficiency of the great Cunard ships, but the luxurious comfort that attended trans-Atlantic travel at the end of the century.[48]

Henry Adams found in the *Campania* a fitting counterpart to the dynamo in the Electricity Building. In fact, the exhibits in Machinery, Electricity, and Transportation stood in relationship for Adams and for those who visited the fair. Collectively they were the most visible sign of the new forces that had revolutionized modes of production and transportation, to say nothing of the fabric of everyday life, at the end of the nineteenth century.

Preoccupied with the question of unity in a world he felt splitting apart, Henry Adams was fond of saying that one sees what one brings. Where contemporaries like his brother Charles Francis saw unity and order at Chicago, he found signs of a universe of accelerated force that bore no relation to the past. While he concurred that the sparkling technics of acceleration present at the Columbian Exposition heralded a new era, Henry Adams dissented from what most assumed would be the benevolent nature of that period. What others accepted as progress, the surer advance of civilization into a higher plane of existence, Adams viewed as the convergence of the menacing forces that would overwhelm the individual and society. Artist and friend John LaFarge had recognized the symptoms and had noted their shared predicament in dedicating his book, *An Artist's Letters from Japan*, to Henry Adams. Reprinted in 1893, the dedication read: "To Henry Adams, Esq. . . . If only we had found Nirvana—but he was right who warned us that we were late in this season of the world."[49]

The convergence of old worlds and new forces was visible throughout the Exposition grounds. Nowhere was it more obvious than in the classical neo-Renaissance motif of great exhibition halls and the innovative, even revolutionary, exhibits within. Where most observers proclaimed the Exposition a handmaiden of progress, Adams found only dissonance and disjuncture. Increasingly at odds with the world prefigured by the dynamos at Chicago, Henry Adams embraced instead the world of the Middle Ages, drawn to the symbol of the Virgin as a force more humanizing than the Dynamo. Adams appreciated the imagery of the Exposition's temples of technology and the reverence expressed for their relics and artifacts. Caught between two worlds, Adams preferred instead the cathedral to the powerhouse, the Virgin to the Dynamo. "All the steam in the world," Adams wrote, "could not, like the Virgin, build Chartres."[50]

Notes

1. Henry Adams, *The Education of Henry Adams* (1918; Boston, 1961), p. 343. Adams's comments on the Exposition are found in the chapter entitled "Chicago."

2. *The Education*, pp. 339–340; Charles Francis Adams made his remarks to the Massachusetts Historical Society and is quoted in Simon Schama, *Dead Certainties, Unwarranted Speculations)* (New York, 1991), p. 42.

3. Henry Adams to Lucy Baxter, 18 October 1893; Henry Adams to John Hay, 18 October 1893, in *The Letters of Henry Adams*, 6 vols. (Cambridge, 1983–1988), 4:132–35.

4. Adams, *The Education*, p. 342.

5. Lewis Mumford, *The Myth of the Machine*, 2 vols. (New York, 1967–1970); Gilman Ostrander, *American Civilization in the First Machine Age, 1890–1940* (New York, 1970), pp. 3–20; Thorstein Veblen, *The Theory of the Leisure Class* (1900; New York, 1953).

6. *The Education*, p. 339.

7. "The Chicago Exposition and Its Successors," *American Architect and Building News* 41 (July–September 1893): 170–71.

8. See Leo Marx, *The Machine in the Garden: Technology and the Pastoral Ideal in America* (New York, 1964); Justus D. Doenecke, "Myths, Machines and Markets: The Columbian Exposition of 1893," *Journal of Popular Culture* 6 (Spring 1972): 535–49.

9. Ostrander, *American Civilization in the First Machine Age*, p. 3.

10. *Classification and Rules, Department of Machinery* (Chicago, 1893), pp. 20–26; Moses P. Handy, ed., *Official Catalogue of the World's Columbian Exposition* (Chicago, 1893), pp. 6–7.

11. Rossiter Johnson, *A History of the World's Columbian Exposition*, 4 vols. (New York, 1898), 2:224; W. E. Hamilton, *The "Time-Saver"* (Chicago, 1893), pp. 16–17; Benjamin Truman, *A History of the World's Fair* (Chicago, 1893), p. 325.

12. Shepp, p. 18; F. Hopkins Smith, "The Picturesque Side," *Scribner's Monthly* 14 (September 1893): 601–11.

13. Handy, ed. *Official Catalogue*, p. 197.

14. United States Centennial Commission, *United States International Exhibition, 1876*, 8 vols. (Washington, D.C., 1880), 1:166–67; Daniel Burnham, "Final Report of the Director of Works of the World's Columbian Exposition," 8 vols. (Chicago, 1894), 5:19, Papers of Daniel Burnham, Daniel Burnham Library of the Art Institute of Chicago; Moses P. Handy, ed., *Official Catalogue*, p. 197.

15. Johnson, *A History of the World's Columbian Exposition*, 3:195.

16. A complete summary of the power plant is found in Burnham, "Final Report of the Director of Works," 5:19; 6:5–6.

17. Henry G. Prout, *A Life of George Westinghouse* (New York, 1922), pp. 134–40; Alex Groner, *American Business and Industry* (New York, 1972), pp. 178–79.

18. Daniel Burnham, "Final Report," 5:6–14; *International Exhibition of 1876*, 1:171. The Machinery Hall complex also included a machine and carpentry shop and an extensive annex on the west end of the building.

19. Henry Adams, *The Education*, p. 342.

20. J. P. Barrett, *Electricity at the Columbian Exposition* (Chicago, 1894), p. 67; John Ellis, *Chicago and the World's Columbian Exposition* (Chicago, 1895), p. 153.

21. Daniel Burnham to Henry Van Brunt, 10 February 1891, Burnham Papers.

22. Barrett, *Electricity at the Columbian Exposition*, pp. 6–7.

23. *World's Columbian Exposition: Classification and Rules, Department of Electricity* (Chicago, c.1892), p. 5.

24. Shepp, *World's Fair Photographed*, p. 50.

25. Hubert Bancroft, *The Book of the Fair* (New York, c.1894), p. 402.

26. Shepp, *World's Fair Photographed*, p. 224.

27. Shepp, *World's Fair Photographed*, p. 230; Bancroft, *The Book of the Fair*, pp. 413–15; Otis Elevator Company, *Diagrams of World's Fair Buildings* (Chicago, 1893), pp. 16–17.

28. Bancroft, *The Book of the Fair*, pp. 416–417.

29. "Thomas Edison," in *Dictionary of American Biography* 21 (New York, 1944), pp. 277–81.

30. Barrett, *Electricity at the Columbian Exposition*, p. 16; "Electricity at the Fair," *Chicago Sunday Tribune*, 8 October 1893.

31. Barrett, *Electricity at the Columbian Exposition*, p. 129; Bancroft, *The Book of the Fair*, pp. 406–8.

32. Barrett, *Electricity at the Columbian Exposition*, pp. 12–15; *CST*, 8 October 1893.

33. Barrett, *Electricity at the Columbian Exposition*, pp. 13–15.

34. Shepp, *World's Fair Photographed*, p. 50.

35. *CDT*, 22 August 1893.

36. *CDT*, 22 August 1893.

37. Henry Adams, "The Rule of Phase Applied to History," in *The Degradation of the Democratic Dogma* (1919; New York, 1947), pp. 247–311. See also Dennis B. Downey, "Henry Adams and the Rule of Phase: An Intellectual Odyssey" (M.A. thesis, Florida State University, 1976).

38. James Dredge, *A Record of the Transportation Exhibits of the World's Columbian Exposition* (New York, 1894), p. viii.

39. Handy, ed., *Official Directory*, pp. 787–88.

40. J. W. Buel, *The Magic City* (St. Louis and Philadelphia, 1894), n.p.; Dredge, *A Record of the Transportation Exhibits*, pp. 507–670.

41. Shepp, *World's Fair Photographed*, p. 206.

42. Thomas Wolfe, *You Can't Go Home Again* (1939; New York, 1973), p. 49.

43. In 1885 Richard Ely published a series of articles on Pullman in *Harper's Monthly* magazine, and the reservations Ely expressed seemed confirmed by the strike, which followed a cut in wages in July 1894.

44. Dredge, *The Transportation Exhibit*, pp. 331–32; Johnson, ed., *A History of the World's Columbian Exposition*, 3:238; Buel, *Magic City*, n.p.

45. *The Education*, p. 341. Curiously, Adams's prediction matched the year Charles Lindbergh flew the first solo flight across the Atlantic. Had Adams lived longer he would have witnessed force, space, and time converging with the advent of supersonic aircraft.

46. Dredge, *The Transportation Exhibits*, pp. 528–29.

47. Dredge, *The Transportation Exhibits*, p. 539.

48. Dredge, *The Transportation Exhibits*, pp. 529–39.

49. John LaFarge, *An Artist's Letters from Japan* (1893; New York, 1979), p. vii.

50. Adams, *The Education*, p. 388.

Directors, designers, and architects on the Exposition grounds, c. 1892. Courtesy of the Chicago Historical Society.

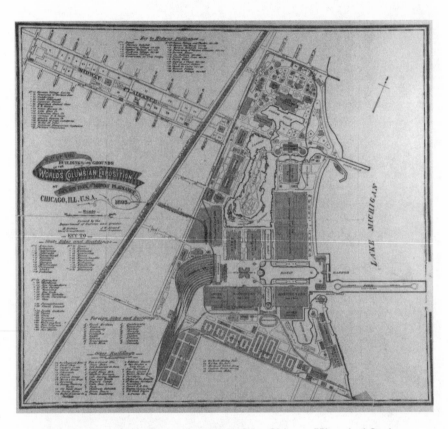

Map of the grounds, 1893. Courtesy of the Chicago Historical Society.

The Court of Honor, looking east from the Administration Building. Courtesy of the Chicago Historical Society.

Grover Cleveland on speakers' platform, opening day ceremonies, May 1, 1893. Photo by C. D. Arnold. Courtesy of the Chicago Historical Society.

The Administration Building, Richard M. Hunt, architect. Courtesy of the Chicago Historical Society.

The Electricity Building, Van Brunt and Howe, architects. Courtesy of the Chicago Historical Society.

The *Statue of the Republic* and the Peristyle Complex. Courtesy of the Chicago Historical Society.

Main entrance, the Fine Arts Building, Charles Atwood, architect. Courtesy of the Chicago Historical Society.

Interior gallery, the Fine Arts Building. Courtesy of the Chicago Historical Society.

The Woman's Building, Sophia Hayden, architect. Courtesy of the Chicago Historical Society.

Interior Hall of Honor, the Woman's Building. Courtesy of the Chicago Historical Society.

The Manufactures and Liberal Arts Building, George Post, architect. Photo by C. D. Arnold. Courtesy of the Chicago Historical Society.

The Transportation Building, Louis Sullivan (Adler and Sullivan), architect. Photo by William Henry Jackson. Courtesy of the Chicago Historical Society.

Exhibits, Machinery Hall. Photo by B. W. Kilburn. Courtesy of the Chicago Historical Society.

The Ferris Wheel, Midway Plaisance. Photo by C. D. Arnold. Courtesy of the Chicago Historical Society.

Lithograph, *Columbia Greeting the World*, 1893. Lithograph by Rodolfo Morgari. Courtesy of the Chicago Historical Society.

Lithograph cartoon, *World's Fair Puck*, 1893 (note the contrast with image on facing page). Courtesy of the Chicago Historical Society.

Street in Cairo exhibit, Midway Plaisance. Courtesy of the Chicago Historical Society.

Lapland Villagers, Midway Plaisance. Courtesy of the Chicago Historical Society.

Esquimaux Villagers braving the Chicago winter, 1893. Photo by C. D. Arnold. Courtesy of the Chicago Historical Society.

The *Statue of the Republic* and the remains of the Peristyle following fire, 1894. Courtesy of the Chicago Historical Society.

4

A Gentle Seriousness

In a manner bespeaking the solemnity of the occasion, Elizabeth Cady Stanton asked delegates to the World's Congress of Representative Women: "How can we hasten the social and civil evolution of woman?" Her answer, given to the thousand-member audience in a speech read by Susan B. Anthony, reflected Victorian sensibilities, as well as Stanton and Anthony's half-century of involvement in the equal rights movement: "Only by an education as to her true position in the physical and moral world, and as to her duty and destiny."[1]

At the age of seventy-eight, Elizabeth Cady Stanton enjoyed an international reputation as a social reformer and advocate of women's rights and as the author of a "Woman's Declaration of Independence" (1876). In her Chicago address Stanton challenged the women in her audience to overcome what she described as their "natural conservatism and conscientiousness" and take the initiative in whatever opportunities were offered. Only by asserting their true nature, Stanton suggested, could women fulfill their destiny as equal partners of men in the vicissitudes of progress.

In prepared remarks to the World's Parliament of Religions, Frances Willard, president of the Women's Christian Temperance Union, echoed the theme enunciated by Stanton. Willard reflected on what she understood as the "ideal of womanhood" and its implications for social progress. "The Women's Christian Temperance Union is doing no work more important than that of reconstructing the ideal of womanhood," she said of the nation's largest female voluntary association. Willard, who never married, spoke of marriage as "that mystic sacrament," and she went on to observe:

In an age of force, woman's greatest grace was to cling; in an age of peace, she doesn't cling much, but is every bit as tender and as sweet as if she did. She has strength, and individuality, a gentle seriousness; there is more of a sister, and less of a siren; more of a duchess, and less of the doll. Woman is becoming what God meant her to be, and Christ's gospel necessitates her being the companion and counselor, not the encumbrance and toy, of men.

"The world has never yet known," Willard concluded, "half the aptitude of character and life to which men will attain when they and women live in the same world."[2]

In their separate remarks both Elizabeth Cady Stanton and Frances Willard captured the expectations of women's organizations in the World's Columbian Exposition. At Chicago, women of diverse experiences and ideologies celebrated the past as a stepping-stone to future opportunities, and they embraced the cause of women's participation in the fair as an essential means to the end of broader inclusion of women in public life. Through the administrative structure of the Board of Lady Managers and in the far-ranging Women's Congress, women of diverse backgrounds and causes looked to this world's fair as an opportunity to expand their social and economic spheres and to heighten the attention given to what was then called the "Woman's Question."

Part exposition of women's material accomplishments and part consciousness-raising, women's organizations sought to clarify an understanding of woman's culture and its implications for individual and social development. Their common hope was that through a clarification of the relationship of women to the great issues of the day, participation at Chicago would indeed initiate a "new era" of mutual progress for women and men in American life.

The Columbian Exposition occurred at a critical juncture in the American women's movement and the emerging international women's movement.[3] In the 1890s an emerging feminism that championed equal rights in all areas of human activity challenged a Victorian domestic ideology that reinforced the notion of separate but complementary spheres for men and women. Similarly, the growing number of women—married and single—drawn to activities in voluntary associations and the club movement gave women important outlets beyond the home and neighborhood setting. In a culture that affirmed marriage and family life as the ideal foundation of a stable social order, the alarming increase in the divorce rate—to one in twelve marriages by 1900—and the growing number of urban single women who did not live under direct parental supervision raised troublesome personal and social concerns.[4]

Equally controversial for its implications for family life was the frequency of domestic abandonment, which left significant numbers of women (and their children) unprepared to manage their lives or earn a livelihood. At Chicago, women of diverse backgrounds sought to negotiate the conflicting ideologies that grew out of widely varying experiences. Put another way, traditional and modern sensibilities—feminism and maternalism—were juxtaposed in a wide-ranging reconsideration of what Elizabeth Cady Stanton meant by woman's "duty and destiny."[5]

Aware of the diversity of experiences represented in any consideration of the Woman's Question, reformers at Chicago counseled for a broader conception of "woman's culture" while remaining faithful to what Barbara Welter has called the "Cult of True Womanhood."[6] Organizers were particularly conscious of the effects of modernization—important differences in the status of women resulting from the urban-industrial transformation. The separation of the workplace from the home and the profound changes occurring in everyday life and habits provided new opportunities and new problems for women. While not departing from the traditional view of women as mothers and managers of a domestic economy, organizers sought to focus attention on a more comprehensive agenda of interests. Through the programs of the Columbian Exposition, American women sought not only self-definition but a strategy to accommodate the divergent tendencies informing the Woman's Question at the end of the nineteenth century. Women who advocated political activism debated with women who counseled greater philanthropic and charity work as the proper outlet for women's energies, and between the two a conversation of sorts on the public and private role of women in Victorian culture emerged. This was but another example of the peculiarly American significance of this international exhibition.

Political and social feminists, suffragettes and advocates of temperance, those who embraced domesticity and motherhood, and those who advocated equal rights in all spheres of human enterprise found a voice in the efforts at Chicago. Their program illuminated points of conflict and commonality within a broad spectrum of reform issues. In one of the more striking ambiguities of the Exposition season, women organizers sought greater inclusion in public life chiefly through a strategy of separation. It was through the separate, "gendered space" of the Woman's Building and the World's Congress of Representative Women that activists promoted the greater acceptance of women in all spheres of human activity. But as Frances Willard remarked, this strategy also reinforced that Chicago offered no radical departure from conventions regarding the relationship of the sexes. Public and private interests converged in the organization of women at the Columbian Exposition, and what triumphed was a middle-way strategy that sought greater choices and opportunities for women without overtly abandoning the domestic environment of the home as a basis for morality and women's autonomy.[7]

Previous exhibitions had given only limited attention (and exhibition space) to the contributions of women in civilizations past and present. At the 1876 Centennial Exhibition, a special Women's Centennial Executive Committee supervised the involvement of American women through the Woman's Pavilion. Less than a full exhibition hall, the Woman's Pavilion nonetheless allowed for the greatest involvement of women in any international exhibition to that date. Mary Frances Cordato has argued that "an enlarged notion of woman's culture shaped the activities" of women organizers at the Centennial.[8] Rather than embracing the ideology of equal rights and suffrage, the women organizers sought to enlarge women's roles while still remaining faithful to an established notion of woman's calling. But the segregation of exhibits to a separate pavilion reinforced the common perception of "separate spheres" for men and women. Economic realities—especially the lingering national economic depression—also contributed to the limited impact of the Centennial women's exhibits, as they did for the fair in general.

Perhaps the most significant accomplishment of women at the Centennial came in the form of a deviation from the formal program, and it came from reformers more committed to issues of political empowerment. At the July 4 Independence Day celebration in downtown Philadelphia, a group of suffragettes led by Susan B. Anthony and Elizabeth Cady Stanton startled the audience by assuming the stage to issue a "Women's Declaration of Independence." This departure from acceptable decorum dramatized an important ideological and strategic split in the woman's movement, a division that informed women's efforts in the Chicago world's fair. Although respectful of the symbolic importance of the separate exhibits of women's art and handicraft in the Philadelphia pavilion, advocates of political rights found the accomplishments of 1876 an important but incomplete triumph in the struggle for equality.[9]

In organizing the program for the Columbian Exposition, advocates of reform sought to build upon the legacy of the Centennial. But more than in the 1876 exhibition, conflicting personalities and competing ideologies clashed in the very agencies intended to ensure women's inclusion. These conflicts led to several highly publicized episodes of controversy within the Board of Lady Managers, and they exposed deep-seated divisions within the women's movement at the end of the nineteenth century. But at the May 1, 1893, opening of the Woman's Building, Board President Bertha Honore Palmer glossed over these differences in enunciating a theme that all could agree on: "But sentimentalists again exclaim, 'Would you have women step down from their pedestal to enter practical life?' Yes, a thousand times yes. If we can really find, after careful search, women upon a pedestal, we should willingly ask them to step down in order that they may meet and help and uplift their sisters."[10]

When the Board of Lady Managers met for the first time in Chicago in November 1891, the one hundred and seventeen appointed members had several things in common. In addition to being well educated, the members of the Board were all white women from middle- and upper-class backgrounds. But despite the racial and class harmony of the board, conflicting agendas and determined personalities would contribute to consequential divisions in their common effort to promote the interests of women in the fair. Mirroring a larger tension in the administrative structure of the Exposition, a group of Chicago women who belonged to the Chicago Woman's Club and its Auxiliary Executive Committee vied for control of the national board. Led by Bertha Honore Palmer and Ellen Henrotin, these socialites sought to use their personal and social connections with members of the Board of Directors to dominate the Board of Lady Managers.

Palmer, Henrotin, and members of the Auxiliary were confronted by suffragettes and advocates of what might be called political feminism, members of the national Queen Isabella Society. The Isabellas, as they were called, favored equal attention to Queen Isabella in any Columbian celebration, and they advocated using the Chicago world's fair to promote a broader agenda of equal rights for women. Their ranks included Susan B. Anthony, Isabella Beecher Hooker, and Phoebe Couzins. While both groups—the Auxiliary and the Isabellas—saw in the fair the "opportunity" to promote their respective agendas, the highly publicized differences undermined any conception of common identity.[11]

In the first test of influence, the Auxiliary women carried the day, with Bertha Honore Palmer's election as president of the Board of Lady Managers. The Auxiliary's influence was further secured with Ellen Henrotin's selection as first vice president. Both women were wives of prominent Chicago businessmen, and each had a reputation for charitable work with laboring women. As a concession to the Isabellas, Phoebe Couzins was chosen for the position of secretary to the Board of Lady Managers. Couzins was not of Palmer and Henrotin's social class, and she was identified with the more militant element in the women's movement. Eventually the clash of personalities and their differing ideologies brought Couzins into open rebellion against Palmer's control of the Board. By September 1891, Palmer had maneuvered to have Couzins removed from her position, in what became known as "the Couzins Affair," and amid tears and much gnashing of teeth, the Auxiliary women emerged triumphant.[12]

The conflicting social agendas that surfaced in the activities of women in Chicago reflected a broader rift within the women's movement at the end of the nineteenth century. In this sense, the woman's program at the Columbian Exposition was more "representative" than organizers had originally intended. In the Board of Lady Managers and its management of the Woman's Building and in the separate World's Congress of Representative Women, a domestic ideology clashed with an ideology of equal rights in all spheres of human activity; try as they did, partisans were unable to contain the differences between the two positions. Those who understood women's primary responsibility as being in relation to family and child-care issues, those who worried about the domestic implications of social and economic change, came at the multifaceted Woman's Question from a different perspective and with a different sense of urgency than those who argued for equality before the law and at the polling place. If the Exposition provided the circumstance for activists to expand the notion of "woman's culture," it also provided the occasion for the different voices that enlivened women's reform efforts to be heard. Put another way, while the Chicago efforts in 1893 reflected Elizabeth Cady Stanton's concern for "social and civil evolution," those same efforts also reflected the "ideal of womanhood" that Frances Willard found personally and socially ennobling.

"That your children's children to many generations," Bertha Palmer told her colleagues on assuming office, "should cite their descent from lady managers of an exposition which served as a milestone to mark the world's grandest and swiftest progress, lies in your hands."[13] To accomplish this end, the Board of Lady Managers created a network of women's organizations that extended to Europe and parts of Asia. Prominent national and international associations and local women's clubs endorsed the Chicago program, including such prestigious groups as the International and the National Councils of Women, the Women's Christian Temperance Union, the National American Society of Women's Suffrage, and the Chicago Women's Club.

State and local committees were established across the United States to promote the gospel of involvement at Chicago, and on more than one occasion Bertha Palmer traveled to Europe to petition for involvement from established women's clubs and societies. Palmer held meetings with Queen Victoria's daughter, the wife of French President Carnot, and in Vienna, Princess Winderman extended hospitality to the American delegation. On her return from Europe, Bertha Palmer informed President Harrison that more than two dozen foreign countries had agreed to send exhibits to the Woman's Building at the Columbian Exposition.[14]

There were numerous practical problems to resolve as the Board of Lady Managers went about the business of organizing women's participation in the Columbian Exposition. In addition to overseeing the Woman's Building and coordinating exhibits for the department, the Lady Managers assumed responsibility for financing and staffing dormitories in and around Jackson Park for young women employed at the fair. Through private subscription the Lady Managers raised enough money to construct a Children's Building adjacent to the Woman's Building. The juxtaposition of the Children's Building with the Woman's Building reinforced the maternalist identification of women's issues with family and child-care issues at the end of the nineteenth century. The Children's Building, whose motto was "The Hope of the World Is in the Children," provided a nursery and recreational facilities, as well as exhibits and instruction on the most innovative methods of child raising and adolescent psychology.[15]

During the Palmer-Couzins turmoil, Mary Logan of the District of Columbia, wife of the famed soldier-senator John Logan, raised the issue of black participation in the fair. This had been a troublesome issue for some time, as African Americans had been deliberately excluded from all administrative agencies of the Exposition. Repulsed by the National Commission and the Exposition corporation, a delegation of black leaders approached Logan and requested that the Board of Lady Managers intercede on their behalf. On Monday, September 7, 1891, Logan went before the full board and stated, "I hold in my hands a petition and plan suggested by colored people of this city and state for their work and recognition. I want to present these documents and to ask you to appoint a committee, whichever you think is proper to do, that they may devise some plan by which these colored people of the state can be recognized."[16]

Logan's suggestion proved unsettling to the enlightened lady managers, all of whom were white and from what one observer called "the highest intellectual and social rank."[17] The awkward silence that first greeted Logan's petition gave way to a volatile debate on the proposition. The issue was at least momentarily resolved with Mary K. Eagle's motion to defer the matter to the individual state boards, which she said had sole jurisdiction over such questions. In a halfhearted effort to appease their critics, the lady managers eventually did accept the nomination of a black woman as an alternate to the Board. Though the lady managers had been willing, even anxious, to assume wide latitude over matters they wished to entertain, their refusal to support the cause of black participation in the White City contributed to one of the most striking anomalies of the Exposition season.[18]

When the Exposition opened on May 1, 1893, lavish ceremonies commissioned the Woman's Building. Women of national and international importance gathered to announce a new era of women's progress—declarations of sentiment that echoed the expectations of the larger enterprise. Bertha Palmer was accompanied on the speakers' platform in the Woman's Building's Hall of Honor by a cadre of guests that included the Duchess of Veragua; the Duchess of Sutherland; Lady Aberdeen, wife of the governor-general of Canada; Russia's Mary Schahovsky; and Frau Professor Kasetowsky of Germany. Among the Illinois women given a place of honor beside Bertha Palmer were the wives of the vice president (Mrs. Adlai Stevenson), the secretary of state (Mrs. Walter Gresham), and the governor (Mrs. John Altgeld). Theodore Thomas's Columbian Orchestra, fresh from performing at the morning opening ceremonies, provided the music for the occasion, which included a specially commissioned grand march composed by Frau Ingesborg von Bronsart. Bertha Palmer was the featured speaker, and in the words of the admiring *Chicago Daily Tribune*, she "never looked better" as her "clear, well modulated voice" carried the day.[19]

In her speech, Palmer addressed one of her pet concerns, the plight of women who had been forced by economic circumstances or abandonment to seek employment outside the home, especially in the factory. A familiar theme in Chicago and other industrializing cities, the story Palmer told went against the notion held by many that the city offered a reprieve from the tediousness of rural life. "Of all existing forms of injustice," Palmer said, "there is none so cruel and inconsistent as is the position in which women are placed with regard to self-maintenance, the calm ignoring of their rights and responsibilities which has gone on for centuries." "It is evident that women thrown upon their own resources have a frightful struggle to endure," she continued, "especially as they have always to contend against public sentiment which discountenances their seeking industrial employment as a means of livelihood."

Bertha Palmer's observation on the plight of abandoned women ill prepared to care for themselves in the marketplace touched a particularly sensitive nerve in a culture that revered marriage and motherhood as the ideal station for women. In the rapid reordering of life that attended the urban-industrial revolution, it was not only working-class women who found it necessary to work outside the home. The growing problem of abandonment left more women from seemingly secure middle-class backgrounds unable to care for themselves and the children left behind. It was a problem without simple solutions, though Palmer believed that with education and public enlightenment such unfortunate women did stand a chance of survival. "We advocate, therefore," the president of the Board of Lady Managers explained, "the thorough education and training of woman to fit her to meet whatever fate life may bring—not only to prepare her for the factory and workshop, for the professions and the arts, but more than all else, to prepare her for presiding over the home."[20]

Nothing in Palmer's address could be interpreted to deny the Victorian view of women's feminine and domestic nature or the enduring value of motherhood and marriage. The intention behind her remarks was not to undermine an ideal of womanhood, so much as to speak to the practical problems that a growing number of women would have to confront as a result of divorce and desertion. For Bertha Palmer, whose status among Chicago's social (and philanthropic) elites was unquestioned, it was only common sense—for their own good and for the good of society—that women be prepared to take all spheres of human labor as their own.

Numerous dignitaries followed Mrs. Palmer to the rostrum. Lady Aberdeen, head of the International Council of Women, observed that the Columbian Exposition would be the occasion for an awakening of immeasurable benefit for women and for society as a whole. Women of every walk of life would be moved by what she called "[a] common devotion and faith to serve their day and generation with a service with which past ages have never yet been blessed." In reflecting back on the day's program, Maude Howe Elliot echoed Lady Aberdeen's sentiments by stressing that the women never strayed far from "the unity of human interests" that made men and women partners in progress. What would emerge from their efforts would be a new era for women and a new woman for the era.

And it was to that end that the Woman's Building was dedicated. Once the speeches and musical program were concluded, visitors were invited inside to observe the material display of women's art and handicraft. The exhibits in the Woman's Building showcased what women could accomplish in all spheres of life if only given the opportunity. "Our building," Elliot wrote with pride, "is essentially feminine in character; it has the qualities of reserve, delicacy, and refinement. Its strength is veiled in grace," she continued as if writing of a woman herself, "its beauty is gently impressive; it does not take away the breath with a sudden passion like some of its neighbors."[21] There was a striking parallel between Elliot's characterization of the Woman's Building and Frances Willard's womanly ideal of "gentle seriousness."

The physical arrangement of exhibits in the Woman's Building implied a particular social message. The ordering of space within the structure was arranged to highlight the accomplishments of women in all spheres of human activities, from antiquity to the present day. (Like the Exposition itself, the Woman's Building gave a particular emphasis to the accomplishments of the nineteenth century.) Besides exhibiting the social, scientific, and commercial achievements of women, the Woman's Building offered a place for women to meet and to repose amid the hustle and bustle of the Exposition season.[22] In spirit it promoted a wider engagement in nondomestic labors; and at the same time it celebrated a "woman's culture" separate from men. While respecting the traditional role of women in western culture, its exhibits championed an equality of opportunity in the anticipated new era. In one of its more ironic twists, the Woman's Building was "gendered space," which sought to promote through separate exhibits the more complete inclusion of women in all walks of life.

The delicate ornateness of the exterior gave way to an interior whose central feature was a rotunda and Hall of Honor, around which were numerous works of art contributed by women. Plaster busts of Lucretia Mott, Susan B. Anthony, Lucy Stone, and Elizabeth Cady Stanton were clustered about the main hall. These early activists for women's rights in America not only enjoyed positions of prominence in the building, but each had made an important contribution to the organization of women's activities in the fair.

At either end of the Hall of Honor were large tympana with allegorical murals meant to symbolize women's social evolution. The first large mural, entitled *Primitive Woman*, was created by Mary Fairchild MacMonnies, wife of the sculptor and an accomplished artist in her own right. MacMonnies's allegorical scene depicted the focal figure of Motherhood, surrounded by lightly clothed women sowing seed and carrying water jars while carrying and caring for young children. Mary Cassatt, a leading American Impressionist painter, contributed the other mural entitled *Modern Woman*. In contrast to *Primitive Woman*, the panels of *Modern Woman* showed a group of women at work and play in an orchard, fully clothed in the habit of the day and unburdened by children.[23]

For those with a discerning eye, it was impossible to miss the contrast of ideals of womanhood implicit in the murals. Cassatt's work was better known than MacMonnies's, and her mural in the Woman's Building has been recognized as among the most important works of a nineteenth-century American female artist. Between these tympana at opposite ends of the building were rooms and galleries that, quite appropriately, presented a general and a retrospective view of what one critic called "the pervading influence of woman's hand, and heart, and brain" from primitive to modern times.[24]

The Woman's Building has been correctly labeled a "temple to her genius," and its galleries included exhibits from women's organizations in every state and territory and from over a dozen foreign countries. Tapestries, works of art, pottery and silverware, clothing and historical costumes, antique and contemporary furniture, needlework and the vestments of religious worship, all the products of women's labor, were found in the unprecedented collection of artwork and handicraft. Ornate Belgian fabric, Italian lace, Navajo blankets, drapery from Ceylon, Parisian millinery, Japanese and Russian tapestry, and samples of Queen Victoria's own needlework were among general items on display. Of particular interest to visitors was the display of elegant ball gowns and royal clothing, which included wax figures that modeled gowns from the court of Peter the Great and the dress worn by Mrs. Benjamin Harrison at her husband's inauguration.[25]

One of the busiest rooms in the building was the Organizations Room located in the second-floor gallery. More than fifty women's organizations and voluntary associations sponsored booths and exhibits devoted to industrial, social, and charitable causes championed by women. Among the numerous educational and philanthropic associations included in the displays were the Chicago Woman's Club, the Order of the Eastern Star (woman's auxiliary of the Freemasons), and the Young Women's Christian Association.

The largest of the association exhibits was presented by the Women's Christian Temperance Union (WCTU). Directed by Frances Willard and counting more than two hundred thousand members in 1893, the WCTU was perhaps the most influential women's organization in the country. Imbued with both Christian and republican values in the fight against alcohol abuse, the WCTU promoted through its exhibit in the Woman's Building a number of causes central to its advocacy of an expanded role for women in public life.[26] In the absence of Frances Willard, unable to attend the fair, the organization supplemented its program of lectures in the building with pamphlets, books, and other documents that promoted the association and women's issues.

One of the more intriguing features of the Organizations Room was the parlor sponsored by the Smithsonian Institution, which provided information on the philanthropic work of white women among the Indian tribes of

North and South America, though the government did not find it necessary to offer evidence of the accomplishments of Native American women. Nor was there a formal exhibit of the contribution of African-American women. However, the Lady Managers did allow the display of a private collection of West African jewelry crafted by tribal women.[27]

Following the dictum that education is the surest road to enlightenment (and empowerment), considerable space was devoted to an exposition of educational methods in women's academies and colleges. More than the physical, intellectual, or moral training of young women, the educational exhibits stressed the practical skills that women needed to meet the growing demands of modern living. From England and across the United States, institutions provided information on the curricula offered in the best business and professional schools that enrolled women. Nursing schools were especially well represented, and a large photographic exhibit depicted life in women's colleges in England and Ireland. Many visitors found the display of the British Training School for Nurses and its demonstration of the practical training of young women for hospital work especially interesting. Of the American institutions, Bryn Mawr College and its sister institutions provided ample evidence of the higher education available to young women in the United States. Like Bryn Mawr, the Pratt Institute and the School of Applied Design for Women stressed the intellectual and the physical culture of the working woman.

Several rooms were set aside to showcase the contributions of women inventors and scientists, as if to reinforce the important contributions women had always made beyond the household economy. But the exhibit that attracted the greatest interest was the "model American kitchen" nestled into the corner of the second floor, adjacent to the Assembly Room. At the Centennial Exhibition, visitors had inspected a replica colonial kitchen complete with an oversize hearth. The arrangement of the colonial kitchen served as a reminder of the virtues of familial and domestic order. In 1893, the Columbian kitchen was oriented toward "modern" home economics and what might be thought of as a science of domestic management.

In the Columbian kitchen, efficiency and mechanical production united to satisfy yearnings for an easier domestic life. In addition to the working exhibit, Sarah Rohrer of Philadelphia conducted daily clinics in which she demonstrated the new electric kitchen technology and answered questions about preparing and serving culinary delights. For women visitors who understood their roles as managers of a household and neighborhood economy, Mrs. Rohrer's morning seminars on domestic efficiency were particularly welcome.[28]

The satisfaction mothers and housewives found in Sarah Rohrer's sage advice was paralleled in the comfort found by professional women in the Records Room. A veritable mountain of statistical data had been collected to demonstrate the progress of women in the nineteenth century. Charts, graphs, tables, and ledgers demonstrated the extent of women's participation in industry and the professions, with ample evidence of the expanding opportunities for women beyond the hearth. Mortality rates for women were catalogued, as was the amount of money saved by women in different countries and other pertinent facts relating to women's material condition. One graph indicated that in the United States at least three million women could be classified as self-supporting, and at least fourteen thousand women were the heads of businesses or commercial concerns. According to this source, twenty-six thousand women were employed as clerks or bookkeepers, and another fifty-nine thousand women were engaged in farming and husbandry. To no one's surprise, the largest area of professional employment was in the field of education: an estimated one hundred and fifty-five thousand women taught in the elementary and secondary schools of the nation.[29]

Historically women had always been employed in a nondomestic economy, and their numbers had grown in the industrial era: that was the lesson of the Records Room. But the aggregate data betrayed a bias toward the status of white, middle-class women born in the United States. In the Records Room one found little descriptive information on the material condition of working-class women or on African-American and Native American women. The absence of such information reflected the preoccupations of the organizers, a shortsightedness apparent elsewhere in the Exposition scheme.

The Records Room celebrated the accomplishments of women beyond the household, and progress therefore was measured in terms of one's ability to choose from a widening range of opportunities beyond the household setting. Domesticity and maternalism were still the ideal, as other exhibits in the Woman's Building seemed to suggest, but in the Records Room at least, woman's progress was understood in terms of one's influence in the marketplace economy. Equality was measured in material terms, with an increasing emphasis on individual consumption. If, as the saying went, "more is better," then the Records Room with its statistics was perhaps the steadiest barometer of women's progress in the nineteenth century.

State and civic committee organizations sponsored their own parlors celebrating the accomplishments of women closer to home. The walls of the Cincinnati Room were adorned with photographs of famous women and the products of the Queen City's women's associations. New York State's women's groups sponsored a Woman's Library, which contained several thousand volumes of verse and prose written by or about women. Twenty-five nationalities and twenty foreign languages were represented in the collections, and among the more valuable pieces in the exhibit was a series of rare books loaned from the Biblioteca Nacional in Madrid. A collection of photographs and autographs of famous women in America, Europe, and Asia attracted great interest. A specially carved oak cabinet in the library contained forty-seven different translations of Harriet Beecher Stowe's *Uncle Tom's Cabin*. Some forty years after its publication, the novel remained immensely popular in the United States and Europe; and as adapted to the stage, *Uncle Tom's Cabin* was one of the most performed plays of the late nineteenth century.

One male visitor to the Woman's Library was particularly taken with the display of books for young children written by women. Betraying his unease over the attention directed at women's contributions outside the home, Daniel Shepp voiced relief when he came upon the children's books. "Many, we note," Shepp wrote, "are by women before whose name we see *Miss* placed, yet such are the true mothers of the race, taking the little ones by the hand, and leading them gently through the realms of beauty and delight; educating them by a process so gracious and easy that they do not feel the strain." "Thank God for such women," Shepp exclaimed, "and thank God for such books! . . . Many a woman will go away from this place prouder of her sex."[30]

But for all of Shepp's professed alarm, the Woman's Building celebrated the diversity of contributions that women had made in public and private life. Visitors had to look no further than Sarah Rohrer's kitchen or the exhibits in the adjacent Children's Building to find ample evidence of women's primary role as caregiver and guardian of domestic tranquility. Through the compilation of statistics and material evidence, the organizers sought to acknowledge and promote a diversity of opportunities for women within an expanded notion of the woman's sphere. While faithful to the "gentle seriousness" of which Frances Willard spoke as essential to woman's genuine nature, the Woman's Building sought a broader inclusion of women in all aspects of life—although it used a separate space reserved solely for the interests of women to advance its arguments.

The World's Congress of Representative Women was the intellectual counterpart to the material displays in the Woman's Building. Dubbed a "feast of intellect," the Congress brought leading women to the "banquet table of knowledge" to consider all aspects of the Woman's Question— indeed, the most important gathering of women in nineteenth-century America. The weeklong meeting in Chicago, which brought women's rights leaders together from around the world, was far broader in scope than the 1848 Seneca Falls Conference or the gathering of women at the 1876 Centennial Exhibition. Such were the expectations of the Columbian Congress that Susan B. Anthony confidently predicted, "It will advance woman's cause 100 years."[31]

The Woman's Congress met for six days, beginning on Monday, May 15. It had been organized by the World's Congress Auxiliary's Department of Woman's Progress, the first of the international conferences that would convene at the fair. The idea of a separate congress devoted exclusively to the Woman's Question (in all of its ramifications) was suggested by May Wright Sewall in February 1891. Sewall was the president of the National Council of Women, and she recommended to the officers of the parent International

Council of Women that its 1893 convention be held in Chicago, rather than London as was planned.[32] When the International Council gave its approval, Sewall and other American women petitioned Charles Bonney of the Congress Auxiliary for authorization to organize a separate Woman's Congress. Bonney supported the plan and appointed Sewall head of the Local Committee on Arrangements and, later, director of the congress.[33]

Women's clubs and voluntary associations seized on the Woman's Congress to bring attention to their work, and most of the major educational, religious, and reform organizations had a voice in planning the program. Besides May Wright Sewall, other prominent women from North America and Europe participated in organizing the program. Rachel Foster Avery of the International Council of Women; Frances Willard, president of the Women's Christian Temperance Union; Dr. Sarah Hackett Stevenson of the Chicago Woman's Club; and fellow Chicagoan Julia Holmes Smith were instrumental in coordinating the conference. In all, more than five hundred women lent their names to the Advisory Council of the World's Congress of Representative Women; some two hundred were official representatives of women's organizations and voluntary associations. Sixteen nations were represented on the council, along with fifty-six American societies, thirty British voluntary associations, and more than a dozen German and French women's organizations. As with the Board of Lady Managers, Chicago women took an important role in the organization of the conference. But, unlike the Lady Managers, the Woman's Congress was shaped by the influence of powerful women's rights activists, some of whom were allied with the Queen Isabella Society.[34]

No less impressive than the number of organizations that affiliated with the Woman's Congress were the individual women who actively promoted the Chicago gathering as central to women's interests. Clara Barton, Frances Willard, Susan B. Anthony, and Jane Addams joined May Wright Sewall on the Home Advisory Board. So too did Julia Ward Howe, Elizabeth Cady Stanton, Lucy Stone, the Reverends Antoinette Brown Blackwell and Ada Bowles, Dr. Emily Blackwell, and the actress Julia Marlowe. Numerous officers of women's denominational auxiliaries supported the meeting, as did leaders of voluntary associations and educational unions.[35]

Although women's rights pioneer Lucy Stone died shortly after the Woman's Congress convened, its program encouraged her by its "representative" character of the program, and she confided to Susan B. Anthony her faith that the Chicago meeting would reap great rewards for women. "The outlook is certainly good for our cause," Stone wrote to Anthony in the spring of 1893. "It will be lifted on a whole age by this effort in a new situation. The women themselves will learn so much. . . . Everything seems to be helping now," Stone concluded. "How good it is, after these long years of struggle."[36]

"Dawn of a New Age," the *Chicago Herald* headline proclaimed on Monday, May 15, as delegates filled Columbus Hall of the Memorial Arts Building. As women and men filled the main auditorium, the *Chicago Daily Inter-Ocean* reminded its readers that "in 1492 a woman sent Columbus to discover a new world; the opening of the Woman's Congress in this continent, 400 years later, is evidence that woman has since discovered herself." As the overflow crowd pushed its way into the room, a reporter for the *Chicago Times* observed the scene:

There sat Julia Ward Howe, whose eyes had seen "the glory of the coming of the Lord" and whose inspired voice had set the soul of the nation "marching on." Look well at her—the frail worn elderly woman in quiet black silk, a violet in her bonnet. . . . Over yonder one saw Susan B. Anthony's keen, intelligent face. Near her sat Elizabeth Cady Stanton, swarthy of skin and white and fluffy hair, wearing the quaintest of grey gowns, a voluminous cape and a sort of magnified baby's cap to match. A noticeable pair this.[37]

"Can we not feel today," Sewall observed in her official welcome, "that twenty centuries of aspiration lying behind us find some response in this event, and that twenty centuries of hope fulfilled lying before us, looking back shall find that this Congress dates the hour of a new march—not for divided womanhood as against separate manhood, but a new march for a unified, harmonious, onstepping humanity."[38] This imagery—that the struggle for equal rights had come to an end and a new beginning with the Chicago Congress—was entirely in keeping with the symbolism of the Exposition.

The Woman's Congress ran from Monday through Saturday and included more than six hundred speakers in sixty-seven formal sessions. One estimate placed more than one hundred and fifty thousand observers at the meetings, which ran simultaneously at the Memorial Arts Building on Michigan Avenue and at the Woman's Building on the fairgrounds. The official program listed eight departments in which women's progress was examined: Industry, Education, Literature and the Arts, Philanthropy and Charity, Moral and Social Reform, Civil Law and Government, and Philosophy and Science. In addition to the formal sessions, nearly two dozen associations held related meetings with the congress. The WCTU, the International Council of Women, the National American Woman Suffrage Association, and educational associations such as the National Kindergarten Union and the Emma Willard Association were the more important of these ancillary meetings. Women's patriotic groups such as the National Association of Loyal Women of American Liberty and the Daughters of the American Revolution also convened sessions in the congress.[39]

As one might imagine in a gathering of women from such diverse backgrounds and experiences, a unanimity of opinion on all issues was virtually impossible. Advocates of suffrage, those who affirmed a broader spectrum of reforms centering on the principle of equal rights, and women whose chief devotion was to family and child-care issues exchanged viewpoints and debated the proper sphere and role for women. Some delegates championed a political agenda, and others spoke to philanthropic and patriotic issues. In their deliberations, something akin to a process of self-definition emerged as congress participants labored to fashion an identity that allowed for the diverse experiences of modern urban life. Whether it was European women discussing problems peculiar to their own cultures or American women addressing the impediments to progress at home, certain shared convictions were sustained throughout the six days of deliberation and discourse.

Although advocates of equal rights played a more prominent role in the Woman's Congress than they had in the organization of the Woman's Building, the congress did not depart from an ideal of womanhood that stressed woman's primary obligations in relationship to family and child-care issues. In fact, traditional roles were deliberately reaffirmed even as women sought greater inclusion in public affairs. Several speakers expressed concern that in a pursuit of new opportunities in the marketplace some women might abdicate the role of moral guardian in the home and society. As custodians of the child's mental and spiritual development and protector of family values, these speakers averred, woman's chief duty was the preservation of that which was most noble in humanity. In such different presentations as Mrs. Arthur Phelam's "St. Catherine of Siena, 1347–1380" and Julia Ward Howe's "The Moral Initiative as Related to Women" the superiority of woman's moral charge to other callings was argued forcefully.

"We seem to see the fulfillment of the prophecy, 'The meek shall inherit the earth,'" Louise Thomas observed in response to remarks by Elizabeth Cady Stanton. "A victory has been won by patient, loving women, whose souls have stirred from the earliest days by suffering under inequality, while patiently bearing the limitations, and waiting for this hour."[40] In a presentation entitled "Woman's Awakening," Anna Green made much the same point. "Never before in the history of the world has the capacity of woman been more recognized than now," she told her audience. "It is her era of promise, a vivid reflection of exaltation. . . . Woman must wait, patience is golden, and in time will bring its reward."[41]

One important group of sessions analyzed the topic "Women in Religion," with representatives of Judaism, Catholicism, and the mainline Protestant denominations gathering to contemplate the contributions of women in religious bodies. One of these meetings brought together leading Protestant women clergy to discuss the changes of the last fifty years. Antoinette Blackwell, an ordained minister and a graduate of Oberlin College in Ohio, was the most famous member of the panel, joined by Methodist minister Eugenia St. John and Reverend Mary Stafford, ordained in the Unitarian Church. The session focused on the moral and intuitive powers that recommended women to the ordained ministry. They measured progress by the number of women ordained to the full ministry; according to one speaker, in 1893 no fewer than seven Protestant churches invited women to ordination. Of those seven, the most liberal denomination, the Universalist Church, had the greatest number of women clergy, with twenty-seven active female clerics. In a session considering the relationship of science and religion, the hope was expressed that as more women were accepted for ordination the likelihood of a reconciliation of science and religion would increase. This conviction rested on the oft-expressed assumption of women's natural ability as teacher and perfecter of the moral order.[42]

Some participants shared a general belief that the steady gait of progress sufficiently assured the rights and privileges of women in the century to come. While upholding the dignity of woman as wife and mother, as defender of morality and the civilizing force in society, they were confident that apparent expanding opportunities would only enhance the role of women as a force for good. "She [woman] needs, in my opinion, no additional powers or privileges—simply the opportunity, daily widening, to exert her manifold endowments," declared Mrs. W. D. Cabell of the District of Columbia. Such sentiments were designed to placate those who feared the expanding opportunities sought by middle-class women could irreparably harm the fabric of domestic relations. Though the remarks of Cabell and others expressed the optimism of the era, others in the Congress of Women were less content to counsel patience and accommodation. They instead advocated organization and collective action on the part of women to define their own destiny.

This disposition toward collective involvement was best represented by the leaders of women's clubs and voluntary associations and in the persons of Susan B. Anthony, Elizabeth Cady Stanton, and Lucy Stone. Less comfortable with the view of women as domestic managers, proponents of equal rights argued for a "new woman" capable of taking full advantage of the changed realities of modern life. For women like Anthony and Stanton and Stone, it was necessary to alter the institutional structure of society so that women could exercise a wider discernment and discrimination in political and economic affairs. Once again, the emphasis was on progress and opportunity, but now with a broader and more comprehensive approach to the barriers that stood against women's fulfillment.

For political activists, one issue transcended all others under consideration. Female suffrage, with its national and international implications, was more than a matter of political empowerment. In the culture of the 1890s, female suffrage had become the key to women's social and legal emancipation from the dictates of patriarchy. Drawing analogies to the status of African Americans after the Civil War, suffragettes had argued for a generation on the real and symbolic importance of voting rights. Suffrage brought all other dimensions of women's concerns into relationship, and it had a privileged place on the conference agenda.

Thursday, May 18—Illinois Day at the fairgrounds—was reserved for a full consideration of the historical and present efforts of women to secure the right to vote. A special afternoon session was organized by the National American Woman's Suffrage Association (NAWSA), the most important society of its kind in the United States. The association dated its origin to 1869, when Elizabeth Cady Stanton and Susan B. Anthony organized the National Women's Suffrage Association. That same year, Lucy Stone and Henry Ward Beecher established the rival American Women's Suffrage Association. Both groups sought the inclusion of women in the proposed Fifteenth Amendment, which would grant the right to vote to adult black men. It was a bitter defeat in 1870 when the states ratified the amendment without reference to women. Twenty years of common struggle led, in 1890, to the merger of the two associations into the NAWSA under the leadership of Elizabeth Cady Stanton. In 1892, while the Woman's Congress was in the planning stage, Susan B. Anthony succeeded Stanton as president of the association, and it was Anthony who promoted the role of the society in the Columbian Exposition. She was also the moving force behind the May 18 session on women's suffrage.[43]

Perhaps the most important address of the afternoon was delivered by Lucy Stone. Stone—"Mrs. Stone," as she was known—had shocked Harriet Beecher Stowe and most other Americans by entering into a highly publicized marriage covenant with Henry Blackwell that allowed her to retain her maiden name. One of the most controversial women in Victorian America, she was also one of the most ardent and consistent advocates of an expanding role for women in public life. Stone's half-century of involvement in the equal rights struggle made her especially qualified to address the subject of the day. There was more than a note of drama in Stone's remarks, as this would be the last public address of her life. Lucy Stone, gravely ill, would die in October of complications from a malignant stomach tumor.[44]

In a talk entitled "The Progress of Fifty Years," Stone chronicled the contributions made by women in a variety of reform movements in America. She paid respect to the courageous efforts of Sarah and Angelina Grimke and of Abby Kelly, whom Stone regarded as women of principle and conviction willing to endure personal hardship for the values they believed in. At the conclusion of her remarks, Lucy Stone paused and then closed with what might have been a fitting epitaph. She ended by reminding those present that women must "continue to speak the truth fearlessly," regardless of the consequences.[45]

The speakers who followed Stone to the podium asserted a common strategy best summed up in the words of Mary Frost Ormsby of the Democratic Influence Club. "Sisters," Ormsby announced to great applause, "take the ballot!" Susan B. Anthony, who had created a new stir just the day before the session when she met with Frederick Douglass, brought up the small membership and ineffectuality of women's suffrage organizations. "It is because women have been taught always to work for something else than their own personal freedom," she concluded. Lillie Devereux Blake of New

York agreed and went on to suggest two reasons why women were justified in seeking the vote. First, she proposed, it was important so women could have "industrial equality" with men, and it was even more important so women might have equality before the law and protection under it. This latter point touched on the sensitive issue of women's property rights. The vote, she argued, offered women the necessary means of self-protection while expanding the range of individual opportunities.[46]

In Blake's scheme, voting power said as much about the status of women in a democratic society as it did about the very nature of that society and its commitment to the principles of freedom and equality. As promoted in the suffrage session at Chicago, the right to vote was essential in women's struggle to secure social and economic justice, and in that sense voting could be thought of as a "natural" right. Or so said Elizabeth Cady Stanton in "The Ethics of Suffrage." "The right to vote," she explained, "is simply the right to govern one's self. Every human being is born into the world with this right, and the desire to exercise it comes naturally with the responsibilities of life." As a necessary step in women's economic and social evolution, the right to vote was fundamentally human, and when women achieved this goal, the participants agreed, society would have taken a bold step forward. At the conclusion of the session, participants were informed that the National American Woman's Suffrage Association planned a second meeting in August, a separate congress on voting rights under the direction of the World's Congress Auxiliary.[47]

In other sessions of the Woman's Congress a number of practical reform issues were discussed. Under a general consideration of women and education, several speakers addressed the issue of kindergarten education and its practical implications for children and society. Sponsored by the International Kindergarten Union, the session heard numerous proposals for the development of kindergarten education in American along the lines of well-established programs in Europe. The Union championed Friedrich Froebel's theories of early childhood learning as essential to the total formation of the person. The kindergarten, claimed its advocates, was a vital tool in the moral upbringing of young children; and, if properly instituted, the kindergarten was the first line of defense against juvenile delinquency and other social problems.

Dress reform was one of the most important issues of the period, with numerous practical and health implications attending modifications in women's wear. A spirited debate ensued in a session on dress reform over the relationship of dress to the expanding sphere of opportunity for women. The delegates were in general agreement that women's clothes were restrictive, unhealthy, and basically "ill-adapted" to such diverse tasks as factory labor and riding a bicycle. Elizabeth Krecher spoke for all women when she demanded fashions that did not interfere with convictions. Professor Ellen Hayes of Wellesley College reported the results of her research into the social aspects of women's dress. In a talk entitled "Woman's Dress from the Standpoint of Sociology," Hayes concluded that "it can not be doubted that her [woman's] present mode of dressing is a large retarding force in the civilization and progress of the whole race."[48] Among the resolutions that delegates to the session approved was one that advocated the use of science and a knowledge of human anatomy to develop a rational dress policy for the modern American woman.

In her discussion of social and moral reform, Congress President May Wright Sewall spoke of woman's growing "industrial freedom" and what it would allow her to become. What woman needed, Sewall argued, was to learn to discriminate among the conflicting demands and opportunities now open to her inspection.[49]

The social effects of industrialization were another concern for women reformers, with several speakers championing the factory system as a liberating force in the cause of women's progress. Their position might have appeared to contradict certain reform sentiments of the time; however, it was entirely in keeping with the principle of equal rights in all spheres of human endeavor. Although they were not blind to the abuses of the sweatshop, some women viewed industrialization as a benevolent giant that rescued the sex from the slavery and provincialism of the home. As the locus of manufacturing shifted from household production to the factory, their argument went, women were freed to venture out and seek new opportunities and new alternatives. For single, wage-earning women who lived apart from family and kin, the factory system provided an essential means to self-support and survival.[50] With hands and minds free to explore a world previously denied them, women owed the factory a certain debt of gratitude.

A concern for the condition and choices open to factory women carried over into a session on the impact of industrial work on a woman's chances of marriage. In a culture that still prized domesticity as commensurate with notions of "true womanhood," this issue was particularly relevant to single women from a working-class background. On this account, Jane Addams had much to say. In a talk entitled "Domestic Service and the Family Claim," the founder of Hull House reflected on the options open to working women, and she admitted that both domestic service and the factory had advantages and disadvantages worth considering. For those who contemplated factory labor, Addams advised that they take notice of the generally poor pay for unskilled women; those inclined toward household service, she reminded, must contend with the long hours demanded by some families. The overriding disadvantage of domestic service, Addams observed, was that a young woman was taken from her own family, her accustomed social routines were disrupted, and eventually she became isolated from her own kind. Those factors all worked against the possibility of a household servant's chances of a successful marriage with someone of similar station. Young men preferred factory girls to maids, Addams cautioned, and to secure a factory job would mean a better personal and social position for eligible working women, with the eventual goal of marriage more likely.[51]

Kaethe Schirmacker of Germany provided an international perspective to complement Addams's own experiences in Chicago. In any given country, Schirmacker noted in "The Effect of Modern Changes in Industrial and Social Life on Woman's Marriage Prospects," three variables influenced a woman's chances of marital bliss. The number of available men living in a country, the greater or lesser facility her countrymen found in establishing a household of their own, and the compatibility of views between partners all influenced the probability of wedlock. As an example of the third proposition, Schirmacher mentioned that in Germany the Church and the law required that a woman be obedient and submissive to her spouse. Technology, however, had intervened to rescue women and provide them with an option previously unavailable. The author's data suggested that industrialization had upset the equation by allowing the self-defined "modern woman" to remain single and self-supporting. Refusing the inevitability of marriage, the modern woman, with no small help from the industrial economy, could choose not to marry unless her mate accepted her on what Schirmacher called "equal footing with perfect equality."[52]

The formal sessions of the Woman's Congress concluded on Saturday, May 20. On Sunday, the historic convention was brought to a solemn end with the then-customary religious service. What was unusual about the service was that it was conducted entirely by ordained women ministers. The sermon of the day was written by Reverend Anna Howard Shaw and presented by her colleague, Reverend Mary L. Moreland. In the evening the women gathered in Columbus Hall of the Memorial Arts Building, the principal scene of their weeklong assembly, to enjoy an elaborate musical program performed by women under the direction of Chicagoan Lydia A. Coonley.[53]

In a closing address to the congress, Bertha Palmer returned to her ambivalence over modern life's tendency to remove women from the home. While the trend might have its advantages, Palmer felt it was imperative that the abandoned woman thrown to her own devices have the practical training that would allow her respectable employment. Evidence of a rising divorce rate—almost ten percent of all new marriages—had serious implications for family life at the dawn of the new era. Palmer felt that practical training was imperative for the abandoned woman and her children, and it was necessary for a society faced with growing problems of delinquency, desertion, and what was called social impurity.

"No attempt has been made," Palmer concluded of the Congress, "to demonstrate any theory, or to realize Utopian ideals which we would wish to see prevail. Our only desire has been to present the actual conditions existing, which will give us a basis to build upon for future improvements." As president of the Board of Lady Managers, Palmer's remark was not intended to be so much a criticism of the congress and a failure to come to terms with a pressing social problem, as it was a challenge to women not to rest with the present accomplishments of their assemblage in Chicago.[54]

The World's Congress of Representative Women and the Woman's Building were one in sympathy and spirit, each in its own way a testament to the unprecedented role of women in the largest world's fair of the century. Where the building (and its exhibits) was a material object lesson, a catalog of women's diverse contributions to civilizations past and present, the congress was a feast of intellect, a grand effort to hasten the social and civil evolution that Elizabeth Cady Stanton and others felt essential to the modern woman. Animated by a faith in progress, the women at Chicago sought through education to expose the impediments that stood in their way. With a moral and practical education in hand, the argument went, women would be prepared to claim their rightful place as partners with men in the vicissitudes of human progress. While not departing from the accustomed understanding and expectations of women's role in Victorian society, the efforts at Chicago focused on expanding opportunities in public culture. Despite ideological differences, the women who gathered at Chicago shared what Bertha Palmer called the "interchange of thought and sympathy" found in the Woman's Building and the congress.

During and after the Columbian Exposition there was much talk of a "New Woman," sometimes called the "Columbian Woman," who would emerge with the New Era. In the Woman's Congress, Amanda K. Lewis presented a poem extolling the virtues of "Columbia's Woman." "Columbia's women," she wrote,

> press on your bright way
> Rise higher in wisdom and art;
> But scatter about you wherever you go,
> Sweet blossoms from kindliest hearts.[55]

Visitors who toured the fairgrounds could not help noticing the repeated use of feminine imagery in defining the Court of Honor. Denoting national destiny buoyed by maternal strength and civic virtue, the *Statue of the Republic* looked west across the grand basin at the figure of *Columbia* steering the allegorical *Ship of State* on its "bright way." Abreast of the wave of progress, the Columbian Woman combined the best in traditional values with a knowledge of the world and its ways. The image conjured up the dream of women as equal to men, equally comfortable in the roles of nurturer and architect of social progress.

Mary Seymour Howell perhaps best captured the break with the past that many women thought imperative to their future. In a talk entitled "The Dawning of the Twentieth Century," she evoked the spirit of the Columbian Woman. "The destiny of the world lies today," Howell observed, "in the hearts and brains of women. . . . Hail, then, twentieth century, and hasten thy coming! Go to thy grave, oh nineteenth century!"[56] Although Bertha Palmer had steadfastly discounted "Utopian ideals," this New Woman was an ideal that the leading advocates of the Woman's Question hoped would be realized in the next generation. But this new woman need not come at the expense of the "gentle seriousness" that Frances Willard believed was essential to an ideal of womanhood.

A new vogue of womanhood did emerge from the Columbian Exposition, but it was different in character and form from the imagined Columbian Woman. Or rather, it was not so much the Columbian Woman as it was the Gibson Girl that found immediate favor in the years following the fair. As journalist Mark Sullivan saw it, it was a combination of the heightened interest in art and the popular attention directed toward women that created the environment in which illustrator Charles Dana Gibson found near-universal approval for his imagined ideal American woman.[57] Gibson's black-and-white sketches seemed to capture the qualities that the *New York World* associated with the "true American girl." The Gibson Girl, the closest approximation of an American Venus, was the epitome of the handsome woman of grace, intelligence, and sufficient resources to handle any situation that arose. For a chromo civilization prone to imitation and the commercial exploitation of beauty, Gibson's "girl" seemed made for the life of the country estate or the city parlor.

In many respects the Gibson Girl was the epitome of a middle-class conception of beauty, and her *look* was one that women from all classes sought to capture for their own. More than a bird in a gilded cage, as a popular song of the era put it, she was also less than a feminist in matters of public discourse. Displaying little interest in matters of social and civil evolution, the Gibson Girl exuded sensuous power that was equally captivating to men and women. Though she conformed to neither a feminist nor a maternalist outlook, the Gibson Girl had a tremendous appeal to those secretaries, schoolteachers, and housewives who dutifully read *Collier's Weekly* in the last years of the century. She was an immensely popular new conception of feminine beauty, one that Mark Sullivan noticed had the ability to "at once please the crowd and satisfy the critical."[58]

As a standard for women's beauty and decorum, the Gibson Girl owed much to the unprecedented attention devoted to women's interests at the Chicago world's fair. The heightened sense of expectancy that emerged from the Exposition season anticipated a new type of woman as symbol of a newfound freedom, the freedom to define her own identity and destiny. Within a generation's time women would receive the right to vote, and other reforms advocated at Chicago would come to the fore under the mantle of equal rights. For all of her powers of persuasion and her provocative charm, the Gibson Girl was suited neither for the domestic ideal some championed nor the cause of equal rights that surfaced in the decades after the Chicago fair. In this sense there was a striking ambiguity in this ideal of womanhood, an ambiguity central to the culture and the lives of many women in the new era.

Notes

1. Stanton's address reprinted in May Wright Sewall, ed., *The World's Congress of Representative Women*, 2 vols. (Chicago, 1894), p. 327. The most comprehensive accounts of the Woman's Congress are found in Sewall and in Mary K. Eagle, ed., *The Congress of Women* (Chicago, 1894); and Mrs. Rollin A. Edgerton, ed., *The Columbian Woman* (Chicago, 1893). A different but useful assessment of the role of women in the Columbian Exposition is Jean Madeline Weimann, *The Fair Women* (Chicago, 1981). Two important dissertations on the role of international exhibitions in the definition of woman's culture are Virginia Grant Darney, "Women and World's Fairs: American International Exhibitions, 1876–1904" (Ph.D. dissertation, Emory University, 1982); and Mary Frances Cordato, "Representing the Expansion of Woman's Sphere: Women's Work and Culture at the World's Fairs of 1876, 1893, and 1904" (Ph.D. dissertation, New York University, 1989).

2. Frances Willard, "A White Life for Two," reprinted in Walter R. Houghton, ed., *Neely's History of the Parliament of Religions* (Chicago, 1894), pp. 747–53.

3. On the international dimensions of the women's movement, see Leila J. Rupp, *Worlds of Women: The Making of an International Women's Movement* (Princeton, 1997); Nancy F. Cott, *The Grounding of Modern Feminism* (New Haven, 1987), esp. pp. 11–50.

4. On the divorce rate see William O'Neil, *Divorce in the Progressive Era* (New York, 1967); and on the world of single women wage-earners in Chicago, see Joanne J. Meyerowitz, *Women Adrift: Independent Wage Earners in Chicago, 1880–1930* (Chicago, 1988). For a succinct study of women's associations, see Anne Firor Scott, *Natural Allies: Women's Associations in American History* (Urbana, 1992).

5. On the definition of a maternalist ideology oriented to motherhood and family life, see Lynn Y. Weiner, "Reconstructing Motherhood: The La Leche League in Postwar America," *Journal of American History* 80 (March 1994): 1357–96.

6. Barbara Welter, "The Cult of True Womanhood, 1820–1860," *American Quarterly* 18 (Summer 1966): 151–74. On the issue of "woman's culture," see Kathleen D. McCarthy, *Women's Culture: American Philanthropy and Art, 1830–1930* (Chicago, 1991).

7. For a critique of the separatist strategy within the woman's movement, see Estelle Freedman, "Separatism as Strategy: Female Institution Building and American Feminism, 1870–1930," *Feminist Studies* 5 (Fall 1979): 512–29. On the issue of gendered space, see Daphne Spain, *Gendered Spaces* (Chapel Hill, 1992). For a summary of the debate over domesticity and autonomy, see Ruth M. Alexander, "'We Are Engaged as a Band of Sisters': Class and Domesticity in the Washingtonian Temperance Movement, 1840–1850," *Journal of American History* 75 (December 1988): 763–85.

8. Cordato, "Representing the Expansion of Woman's Sphere," p. 12.

9. James D. McCabe, *The Illustrated History of the Centennial Exhibition* (Philadelphia, 1975), pp. 218–20; *Official Catalogue of the U.S. International Exhibi-*

tion, 1876 (Philadelphia, 1876), 2:79–84; Dee Brown, *TheYear of the Century: 1876* (NewYork, 1966), pp. 139–66.

10. Bertha Palmer quoted in the *Chicago Daily Tribune* (hereafter *CDT*), 2 May 1893.

11. On this ideological distinction, see Nancy Cott, *The Grounding of Modern Feminism* (New Haven, 1987), esp. pp. 3–50; Cott, "What's in a Name?; or, Expanding the Vocabulary of Women's History," *Journal of American History* 76 (December 1989): 809–29; see also Rosalind Rosenberg, *Beyond Separate Spheres: Intellectual Roots of Modern Feminism* (New Haven, 1982).

12. Handy, *Official Directory*, pp. 178–79; Jeanne Madeline Weimann, "A Temple to Women's Genius: The Woman's Building of 1893," *Chicago History* 4 (Spring 1977): 23–33; Cordato, pp. 196–246. After she was forcibly removed from the Board of Lady Managers in a scenario orchestrated by Palmer, Phoebe Couzins sued in court to be reinstated. Her year-long feud with Palmer won her little sympathy within the Board of Lady Managers and among the male directors. Her legal challenge failed and the board members resolved their differences, but not without considerable agonizing.

13. "Minutes of the Board," 24 November 1890.

14. Bertha Palmer to President Benjamin Harrison, n.d., "Official Correspondence of Bertha Palmer," 9 vols., Chicago Historical Society.

15. *The Children's Building of the World's Columbian Exposition* (Chicago, [1893]).

16. "Minutes of the Board," 7 September 1891.

17. Cameron, *A World's Fair*, p. 449.

18. "Minutes of the Board," 7 September 1891.

19. *CDT*, 2 May 1893.

20. *CDT*, 2 May 1893.

21. Maude Howe Elliot, *Art and Handicraft in the Woman's Building* (Chicago, 1894), p. 35. Another interesting commentary on the Woman's Building can be found in Ellen Henrotin, "An Outsider's View of the Woman's Exhibit," *Cosmopolitan* 15 (September 1893): 560–66.

22. See Elliot, *Art and Handicraft in the Woman's Building* for a complete summary of the exhibits.

23. MacMonnies painted on her mural at the site, whereas Cassatt shipped her completed work from Europe in the spring of 1893. Unlike MacMonnies, who exhibited in the Fine Arts galleries, Cassatt eschewed repeated invitations to lend her work for exhibition at Chicago.

24. Hubert Bancroft, *The Book of the Fair* (NewYork, c.1894), pp. 263–65.

25. See Elliot, *Art and Handicraft*; Bancroft, *The Book of the Fair*, pp. 272–83.

26. Two important recent studies which offer different perspectives on the mission of the WCTU are Ruth Bordin, *Frances Willard: A Biography* (Chapel Hill, 1986); and Ian Tyrrell, *Woman's World, Woman's Empire: The Women's Christian Temperance Union in International Perspective, 1880–1930* (Chapel Hill, 1991).Where Bordin emphasizes a broader, secular agenda for Willard and the Association, Tyrrell stresses the evangelical Protestant and domestic character of temperance ideology.

27. Elliot, *Art and Handicraft*, p. 55; Bancroft, *The Book of the Fair*, pp. 271–78; Weimann, "A Temple to Women's Genius," pp. 23–33.

28. Elliot, *Art and Handicraft*, pp. 57–58.

29. Bancroft, *The Book of the Fair*, pp. 300–301.

30. James and Daniel Shepp, *Shepp's World's Fair Photographed* (Chicago, 1893), p. 284.

31. Anthony quoted in *Daily Columbian*, 15 May 1893.

32. Sewall, ed., *World's Congress* , pp. 46–48.

33. Sewall, *World's Congress*, pp. 46–48.

34. Sewall, ed., *World's Congress*, p. 5.

35. Sewall, *World's Congress*, pp. 932–34.

36. Quoted in Alice Stone Blackwell, *Lucy Stone: Pioneer Woman Suffragist* (Boston, 1930), p. 294.

37. All quotes were reprinted in the *Daily Columbian,* 16 May 1893.

38. Sewall, ed., *World's Congress*, p. 18.

39. *Daily Columbian*, 17 May 1893.

40. Sewall, ed., *World's Congress*, p. 331.

41. Quoted in Mary K. Eagle, ed., *The Congress of Women* (Chicago, 1894), p. 694.

42. Sewall, ed., *World's Congress*, pp. 224–38, 322.

43. "Susan B. Anthony," *Dictionary of American Biography* 1 (New York, 1964), pp. 318–20.

44. Blackwell, *Lucy Stone*, pp. 166–70, 276–77.

45. Sewall, ed., *World's Congress*, p. 448.

46. Sewall, ed. *World's Congress*, pp. 463–65.

47. Sewall, ed., *World's Congress*, pp. 482–63.

48. Sewall, ed., *World's Congress*, pp. 350–62.

49. Sewall, ed., *World's Congress*, p. 313.

50. On the growing reality of young women living in unconventional circumstances, in Chicago and elsewhere, see Joanne Meyerowitz, *Women Adrift: Independent Wage Earners in Chicago, 1880–1930* (Chicago, 1988).

51. Sewall, ed., *World's Congress*, pp. 626–31.

52. Sewall. ed., *World's Congress*, p. 592.

53. Johnson, *A History*, 4:80.

54. Eagle, ed., *The Congress of Women*, pp. 820–24.

55. See Mrs. Rollin A. Edgerton, ed., *The Columbian Woman* (Chicago, 1893), n.p.

56. Eagle, ed., *The Congress of Women*, p. 680.

57. Mark Sullivan, *Our Times: The Turn of the Century* (New York, 1926), pp. 193–96; see also Charles D. Gibson, *The Social Ladder* (New York, 1902); Fairfax Downey, *Portrait of an Era as Drawn by C. D. Gibson* (New York, 1936).

58. Sullivan, *Our Times*, pp. 194–95. On changing standards of female beauty, see Lois Banner, *American Beauty* (New York, 1983).

5

The Search for Equilibrium

Like many religious leaders in and around Chicago, Dwight Moody saw in the World's Columbian Exposition an occasion to bring new souls to Christ and new funds to the Tabernacle treasury. In early May, America's foremost evangelist returned from abroad to inaugurate a revival, a "six month campaign against sin," which would exceed anything in Chicago's memory. As usual, choirmaster Ira Sankey was at the shepherd's side, leading the congregation through the old familiar hymns, and his young lieutenant Billy Sunday helped minister to the crowd. Moody chose the parable of the prodigal son as the subject of his morning sermon that first Sunday of the Exposition season, and to an overflow evening crowd he drew from the text of *Isaiah*: "Let the wicked forsake his way, and the unrighteous man his thoughts."[1]

Dwight Moody parted company with his fellow clergymen's enthusiasm for the world's fair, judging the enterprise as nothing but the incarnation of secular evil with its appeal to the weakness of the flesh. As the architect of urban revivalism in America, Moody was not about to let such an opportunity slip away. Hurrying back to Chicago to preach against the Exposition, he told students at his Bible Institute, "We shall beat the World's Fair!"[2]

Lest Satan triumph in the "wicked city" at Jackson Park, Moody came home to Chicago to urge personal regeneration.[3] He saw the possibilities of a renewal of the spirit; convinced that personal atonement and the acceptance of Christ as Savior were the only valid answers to the darkness that clouded human destiny, Dwight Moody relished the opportunities afforded by the fair. His six-month revival, which coincided with the Exposition season, was conceived in those terms, and he was confident the large crowds would find his impassioned preaching as appealing as the Midway cabarets.

Moody's assault on the latter-day Babylon at Jackson Park was so successful that he was negotiating constantly for new meeting halls and churches.
Out of deference to Moody, the Chicago press gave ample coverage to the extended revival, as a part of its coverage of Exposition-related events. Alert
enough to recognize the growing cosmopolitanism of Chicago's immigrant
population, Moody had as many as a dozen services occurring on the same
night in different neighborhoods of the city. He employed ministers who
spoke the appropriate language of the local foreign-born residents. One of
the more popular sessions was held next to Buffalo Bill Cody's Wild West
Show, in a circus tent with a ten-thousand-seat capacity.

Before it was all over with a final rally on October 31 at the Central Music
Hall, Dwight Moody had claimed thousands of souls newly won to Christ
and a weekly attendance that had increased, by his count, from eight thousand in May to better than one hundred and fifty thousand in late October.
Chicago, and America, had never seen anything like Moody's extraordinary
revival tour.

At the close of the gospel campaign Moody told his audience by way of a
farewell, "I confess, dear friends, that there is always a tinge of sadness about
last meetings, and especially about our meeting tonight." "But it is a joy," he
assured the faithful, "to remember that we shall meet yonder, in the morning, where we shall see the face of our blessed Master and dwell in his presence forever."[4]

Few visitors to Chicago would have mistaken Moody's anxious homilet-
ics for the scholarly disquisition of a young Wisconsin historian. But in fact,
Dwight Lyman Moody and Frederick Jackson Turner stand in relationship
to each other, and each to a culture of renewal in the summer of 1893.
Where one might say Moody's central preoccupation was the "frontier of
the soul," Turner offered a more temporal meditation on the "soul of the
frontier." If Moody reflected a spiritual impulse for renewal, Turner's ambitions were more secular or nationalistic, but his concerns were no less ur-
gent. Beneath its scholarly dressing, Turner's "frontier thesis" was an
engaged examination of the course of national development and the contours of a national identity. Part historical analysis and part social criticism,
Turner's thesis, presented to the July Congress of Historians, reflected a
concern for American exceptionalism during decades of unprecedented
social and cultural adjustment.

"Up to our own day," Frederick Jackson Turner said in a paper entitled
"The Significance of the Frontier in American History," "American history
has been in large degree the history of colonization of the Great West. The
existence of an area of free land, its continuous recession, and the advance
of American settlement westward explains American history."[5] For Turner,
a midwesterner, Chicago's fair was the ideal setting to pronounce his conviction that the availability of free land—the West—had been the "distin-
guishing feature of American life." Though Turner's essay created little

controversy at the time, it would in time persuade historians to rethink the scope and direction of American history.

If Moody found the spreading pall of "irreligion" in nineteenth-century events, Turner found a continuous movement away from European influences and toward a new identity. The frontier nurtured democracy, Turner told this audience in Chicago, and democracy was the "salient" feature of America's national identity. Neither a simpleminded fatalist nor a false prophet of progress, Turner did not project a view of the future in his efforts to read the social and cultural landscape that Columbian season. Instead, he issued a strong cautionary note in his assessment of the present aspect of American social development.

Evidence from the recent (1890) federal census led to the conclusion that the frontier was for all practical purposes closed. With the end of the frontier, Turner said, there came "the closing of a great historical moment." "[T]he frontier is gone, and with its going has closed the first period of American history."[6] Implicit in Turner's trajectory was a belief that the very engines of material progress, those forces that settled the frontier, had brought America to an end and a new beginning in its brief history.

On a grander level, Turner's "frontier" functioned as a metaphor in an incisive work of social criticism. More than an academic exercise, "The Significance of the Frontier" was Turner's meditation on the course of national destiny and the troublesome origins of American distinctiveness. Turner had not only advocated the role of the West in the creation of a distinctive American identity, a position hospitable to Chicagoans and their fair, he also indirectly appropriated the imagery of a "new era" and of renewal, which was so much a part of the Exposition and the broader culture of the 1890s. In the lexicon of American folk culture, the frontier nurtured democracy and individualism, and it offered the possibilities of not only individual regeneration but also national renewal.

Commenting on the frontier's passing, Turner's geographic determinism took on the elements of a startling cultural critique. Beneath its veneer treatise lay a potent urgency for the possibilities of renewal found in the reform congresses. Turner was as concerned with the matter of social equilibrium as he was with the nomenclature of exceptionalism, and in his mind the two were entwined. Though his paper lacked the religious tone that informed public discourse in the late nineteenth century, Turner struck at the heart of the notion of America as a land perpetually blessed by divine sanction. For Turner, however, this dispensation was situated in the western landscape, which was receding in the face of what many understood as progress.

Like the Exposition itself, Turner's interest in the present aspect of American society was no less genuine than Dwight Moody's. Each sought to reconcile traditional mythologies with new social realities. In the end, however, both the evangelist and the professor were left with the question that burdened Henry Adams after visiting the fair, a question implicit in the enterprise's reform congresses and the society they examined: Did America know where it was tending?

In their separate ways, Dwight Lyman Moody and Frederick Jackson Turner embraced the theme of renewal and the possibilities of a new beginning that informed the Columbian Exposition's myriad reform congresses. Taken as a whole, the reform congresses sponsored by the Exposition's World's Congress Auxiliary attempted nothing less than a complete assessment of the social and spiritual condition of the nation. For a generation enamored of the certainty of evolutionary science but still clinging to the truths of Biblical orthodoxy, these convocations on the great social and moral issues of the day served as an enlightening barometer on sentiments and sensibilities at century's end. Ministers of the gospel and ministers of reform, one might say, engaged in a wide-ranging conversation that sought to clarify the source of social problems and their possible solutions.

Social critics and advocates of various causes gathered in Chicago to discuss and analyze and argue over the surest way to achieve and maintain what was called social "equilibrium." "Equilibrium" suggested that like a solution in a laboratory vessel, society was stable when competing elements were held in balance. Betraying a penchant to apply scientific terminology to social situations, the notion of equilibrium implied that social progress was possible as long as contesting groups were kept in harmonious accord; when social and economic groups clashed, social progress was jeopardized. Where reformers disagreed was not in their devotion to progress but in the origin of social problems—and therefore in their strategies for maintaining social equilibrium. But whether the causes of disequilibrium were in human nature or the nature of society, the social congresses offered a plentitude of solutions that demonstrated the variety of reform sentiments in late nineteenth-century America.

For this generation of Americans born in the shadow of the Civil War and raised in the belief in an ongoing "struggle for existence," an abiding faith in human progress made the tremendous social discord of the late nineteenth century more tolerable. No author expressed better this sustaining faith in the future than Edward Bellamy, whose utopian novel *Looking Backward* (1888), remained a popular work of fiction in 1893. "*Looking Backward* was written in the belief that the Golden Age lies before us and not behind us," Bellamy confessed by way of explanation, "and it is not far away. Our children will surely see it, and we, too, who are already men and women, if we deserve it by our faith and by our works."[7] This was very much the spirit of the "new era" and of the reform congresses at Chicago during the Columbian season.

In many respects the Congress Auxiliary was a grand-scale Chautauqua campground brought to the shores of Lake Michigan (see Table 5.1). Embracing the urgency and the optimism, if not the cooperative ideology, of Bellamy's Nationalism, the various reform congresses engaged the salient issues of the day. In this sense, the Exposition's reform congresses offer the clearest

**TABLE 5.1   The World's Congress Auxiliary:
General Departments**

May
Woman's Progress
Public Press
Medicine and Surgery

June
Temperance
Moral and Social Reform
Commerce and Finance

July
Music
Literature
Education

August
Engineering
Art and Architecture
Government, Law Reform, and Political Science
Science and Philosophy

September
Labor
Religion
Sunday Rest

October
Public Health
Agriculture

---

evidence that the fair was not simply a "grand illusion," an escapist retreat from present-day problems, as some critics have suggested.[8] Through the multifaceted social congresses, artists and activists, vegetarians and theosophists, suffragettes and single taxers—activists across a broad spectrum of concerns—promoted their prescriptions for the ills that plagued society.

Through their common deliberation that Columbian season, a dramatic cultural conversation emerged, not only on the varieties of reform sentiment in Victorian America but also on what Peter Conn has described as a "divided mind" in American thought. Both progressive and nostalgic—modernist and Victorian, some would say—tendencies in social discourse were evident in the social congresses, reflecting broader tensions in the culture. Whether it was Eugene Field and Hamlin Garland debating the merits of Romanticism and Realism in the Literary Congress or Josiah Royce and John Dewey debating Pragmatism and Thomism with Catholic clerics in the Philosophical Congress, the social and intellectual congresses of the Columbian Exposition engaged the social politics of the era. Cultural brokers from across the ideological spectrum sought a middle ground to maintain the social equilibrium necessary to assure progress amid an accelerated reordering of everyday life and values.[9] Whether blame was placed on the moral collapse of the individual or the structures of political economy, even the harshest critics shared a confidence in the possibilities of renewal that was not unlike the spirit of a Moody revival.

When the World's Congress Auxiliary convened on May 15, President Charles Bonney announced the theme that would animate the reform congresses under his direction. "The new age has dawned," he told the assembled leaders of world opinion. "A new leader has taken command. The name of this leader is Peace. . . . In the service of this new commander we proclaim a Universal Fraternity of Learning and Virtue as the best means by which ignorance, misunderstanding, prejudice, and animosity can be removed, and intelligence, charity, productive industry, and happiness promoted." Bonney observed that the outcome of the meetings would be "To make the whole world one in sympathy/ To make the whole world one in mental aim/ To make the whole world one in moral power/ Learning and Virtue passports to all lands."

To advance the lofty aims of this "important epoch in the history of the human mind," the leading critics and custodians of culture were petitioned to act as advisors. Charles Eliot of Harvard, Richard T. Ely, Carl Schurz, Carroll D. Wright, Frances Willard, Jane Addams, Thomas Wentworth Higginson, and Seth Jones were but a few of the important architects of the reform congresses, and John Greenleaf Whittier was an early enthusiast. Committee members solicited advice from Frederick Douglass and Booker T. Washington; and Susan B. Anthony, Frances Willard, and Lucy Stone offered their counsel on topics pertinent to the Woman's Question. An ecumenical committee of religious leaders also cooperated with the Auxiliary, including James Cardinal Gibbons and Archbishop John Ireland, Rabbi Isaac Wise, and Social Gospel ministers Josiah Strong and Washington Gladden.[11]

Although controversy was to be avoided, to its credit the Congress Auxiliary was more "inclusive" in its program of speakers. There seems to have been a deliberate effort to assure that women reformers and African-American leaders were included in the hundreds of sessions under the Auxiliary's direction. Booker T. Washington and Frederick Douglass contributed papers and spoke before several different meetings, and Jane Addams, Susan B. Anthony, and Elizabeth Cady Stanton reflected the routine involvement of women throughout the several hundred sessions. Leaders of America's immigrant communities frequently were included on appropriate subjects. American Indians, however, were not invited to participate in the planning sessions; and though several congresses addressed the status and future needs of American Indians, Native Americans were not given a voice in the debate. Usually it was some government official or the member of a charitable association who spoke on behalf of the "forgotten Americans."

Similarly, in the effort to be inclusive on the wide range of social issues addressed by congress delegates, one issue of searing immediacy did not receive its due. Weeklong congresses were devoted to the Woman's Question, the Labor Question, the Temperance crusade, Social Purity matters, and an array of less prominent issues, but there was no separate congress devoted to the so-called Race Question. At best, incidental attention was given to matters of civil rights (in isolated sessions), which reinforced the marginal status of African Americans in social life. In this era of racial lynching and state-sanctioned segregation, in this nascent period of the Black Migration northward to places such as Chicago, the official silence of the Congress Auxiliary on the deteriorating condition of race relations is particularly instructive.

With the exception of the Congress on Representative Women, whose scope exceeded every other meeting except the Parliament of Religions, the first of the important reform congresses convened the week of June 5. Under the direction of the Auxiliary's Department of Temperance, a wide array of meetings addressed the social implications of alcohol abuse. Temperance was one of the most resilient reform issues of the nineteenth century; with the exception of the antebellum abolitionist movement, no other movement rivaled the enthusiasm of temperance advocates. The temperance crusade in the United States actually dated from the era of the Revolutionary War; and as there arrived successive waves of foreign immigrants with different attitudes toward imbibing, an unhealthy xenophobia fueled the impassioned speeches and tracts of those who believed alcohol was the root of all personal and social misfortune.[11] For American women, the temperance movement was an important agency for promoting not only abstinence from alcohol but also a broader range of social and political reforms aligned with the Woman's Question.

Though the religious zeal of the early temperance crusade remained, by 1893 the spiritual motivations of groups like the American Society for the Promotion of Temperance and the American Temperance Society had given way to a campaign for abstinence as a means of social control. The moralistic dimensions of the movement were sustained in the efforts of Frances Willard's Women's Christian Temperance Union (WCTU) and in church-affiliated societies, but increasingly in the nativist climate of the 1890s the call for voluntary abstinence was succumbing to pressure for mandatory state prohibition aimed at curbing social vices associated with the burgeoning foreign-born populations. By the summer of 1893, though, the temperance movement in the United States was at a crossroads, and the

Anti-Saloon League's politicization of the temperance question contributed to the movement's split personality as the Columbian congress convened.[13]

The stated purpose of the Auxiliary's Department of Temperance was to explore the "most efficient and advisable means of preventing or decreasing pauperism, insanity, and crime; and of increasing productive ability, prosperity and virtue throughout the world."[14] Whether one saw alcohol abuse as a personal tragedy or as a social problem, none in the congress doubted intemperance was a formidable obstacle to individual improvement and social progress. Catholic archbishop John Ireland of St. Paul, Minnesota, himself a staunch advocate of abstinence, played an active role in the debate as general chairman of the conference. He presided over a program that considered the relationship of temperance reform to such diverse issues as prison reform, social purity, charitable work, and the care of the feebleminded and impoverished. These sessions were run in conjunction with the Auxiliary's Department of Social Purity. A host of groups, including the Sons of Temperance, the Catholic Temperance Society, and the Royal Templars of Temperance, joined the WCTU in sponsoring the forum.[15]

Because of poor health, America's most famous advocate of temperance reform could not attend the congress. Frances Willard, president of the WCTU, did send an enthusiastic letter to the organizers encouraging her colleagues to join ranks in common cause. "Humanity has called a halt at last to its Bacchanal procession," she observed with a sense of confidence. "The great revolt is fast growing. Science with her pure torch pilots the way out of the wilderness, and Faith marches beside her fearless sister, with calm eyes turned to heaven."[16]

At the opening of the Temperance convention on June 5, Charles Bonney echoed Willard's sentiments when he noted the dual aspects of a movement joined in a single aim. "The temperance movement as it exists in the world today is of a twofold character," Bonney explained. "It is a moral movement, advancing by moral means; and it is a legal movement, proceeding against admitted evils by the enforcement of coercive legislation." (This contrast of strategies paralleled the disagreement over philanthropic and political activism that surfaced in the Woman's Congress the preceding month.) "The greatest evil the Church has to contend with is intemperance," Bonney declared. A Chicago clergyman, Bonney ended with an indictment of politicians who "worshipped at the throne of vile whiskey," a situation not unfamiliar to reformers in a city reviled for its "wide-open" manners.

Ministers, medical doctors, lawyers, and the presidents of colleges and public health agencies—women and men who had a personal and professional acquaintance with abuse—spoke at the Temperance congress. Scientific and anecdotal evidence was brought to bear on what many believed the great social problem of the era. Convinced that alcohol was the root of all other social vices—the saloon and the brothel were partners in the ruin of humankind—they saw temperance reform as essential to the maintenance of social equilibrium. Although the organizers had agreed that partisan interests would be shelved in favor of a common front, controversy did surface during the weeklong congress. On Tuesday, June 6, a spirited exchange occurred in a session devoted to temperance legislation. Participants included B. W. Richardson, a physician, who delivered "The Physical Benefits of Abstinence," and the Reverend O. P. Gifford, who spoke on "The Effects of Intoxication upon Politics and Government." A third paper by Edward Bellamy, entitled "Nationalizing the Liquor Trade," was read in absentia.

According to the *Chicago Daily Tribune* report on the meeting, the argument boiled down to the question of which approach to ridding society of intemperance was the wisest. Participants and members of the audience split over whether alcohol abuse was primarily a social problem best resolved by prohibition legislation or a moral dilemma addressed through education. The *Tribune* article informed readers that the delegates could not reach agreement on which strategy was wisest and concluded that a combination of both approaches was most prudent.[17]

Archbishop Ireland's session on "Temperance and Christianity" drew one of the largest crowds of the congress. To advocates of personal abstinence—taking the pledge—the rising tide of intemperance was intimately bound up with the spread of "irreligion." As such, alcohol not only threatened the stability of the home and factory; it jeopardized the foundations of a Christian commonwealth. Ireland, as one of the most liberal leaders of an essentially immigrant Church, was especially sensitive to the association of intemperance with newly arrived immigrants, the greater percentage of whom were Catholic. Mandatory prohibition was suspect in some circles because it threatened the free exercise of choice, which many Americans at least loosely affirmed. But temperance leaders such as Ireland believed that if voluntarism failed, the rewards of prohibition would outweigh the risks. In Ireland's talk entitled "Total Abstinence" and in the Reverend Hugh Price Hughes's "Abstinence an Essential Element of Aggressive Christian Effort," the relationship of Christian ethics to the problem of intemperance was explored. The two agreed that where the churches failed, the law was free to proscribe remedies. Such a concession did not mean to put legal above religious authority; rather, the instruments of government were a cooperative gesture in the mutual crusade to preserve the moral fiber of society.[18]

Meeting the same week, the Department of Social Purity was closely aligned to Department of Temperance. This linkage reflected popular associations of alcohol with criminal vice. "Social Purity" was an all-encompassing phrase, which included any behavior that seemed to undermine public and private morality. Closely allied with the work of numerous charitable and philanthropic organizations, social purity campaigns were usually infused with a strong dose of Evangelical Christianity and Victorian self-control. Under its mantle, temperance advocates, opponents of obscenity and prostitution, and leaders of charitable and philanthropic associations joined ranks in defense of civilization.[19] The weeklong Chicago conference considered such diverse topics as obscene literature, the problem of prostitution, dress reform, and the contribution of public vice to national decay. The Reverend W. T. Sabine, who addressed "Social Vice and National Decay," and Elizabeth Cady Stanton, who spoke on "Woman's Suffrage and the Moral Question," were among the more recognized discussants, but by far the most celebrated advocate to appear on the Chicago agenda was Anthony Comstock.[20]

Anthony Comstock was the ambitious young reformer and guardian of public morality who had taken on the likes of Ezra Heywood and George Francis Train. His most celebrated feud occurred in 1872, when Comstock battled with Victoria Woodhull and Tennessee Claflin over the sisters' publication of Henry Ward Beecher's affair with Elizabeth Tilton. The subsequent arrest and prosecution of the Claflin sisters for public obscenity made Comstock a national celebrity. As chief spokesman for the New York Society for the Suppression of Vice, his appearance in the Social Purity congress created quite a stir. Comstock spoke at length on "Impure Literature," a subject he knew well from his years as America's chief proponent of censorship. Each of Chicago's daily newspapers, as well as the fair's *Daily Columbian*, gave Comstock star treatment and carried his remarks at length.

A third and related reform congress met in June, reflecting the Auxiliary's ambitious program. The Congress on Social and Moral Reform's progressive agenda included the causes and prevention of idiocy and feeblemindedness, the role of institutions in their care, and the training of health officials to deal with what was now becoming recognized as a public policy issue. In its broader scope the Congress on Moral and Social Reform examined the charitable and philanthropic work of those judged to be "deficient" or "defective," including hospital care for the insane, prison reform and aid to paupers, and the proper punishment for children and juvenile delinquents.

Once again, women took an active role in the meeting, reflecting both the role of women in the campaign for decency and the close association of social purity reform with women's benevolent activities. Evidence of the growing professionalization of health care was also apparent throughout the sessions. Among those expected to attend a session on nursing and public health issues was Florence Nightingale. The *Tribune* acknowledged the "great disappointment" of the audience when informed that "Miss Nightingale" would not be attending after all. Her paper, "The Principles of Nurse Training," had not arrived in time to be included in the program.[21]

Washington Gladden, author of "Applied Christianity" and a leader of the emerging Social Gospel movement, was one of the principal speakers in the Congress on Social and Moral Reform. On the Sunday preceding the congress, Gladden preached a sermon at a religious service sponsored by the International Congress of Charities and Corrections. Joined by Graham Taylor, a Chicago university professor and champion of settlement-house

work, Gladden took as his inspiration a verse from Paul's letter to the Gala-
tians: "Bear ye one another's burdens and so fulfill the law of Christ." This
became the central theme of the Congress on Social and Moral Reform, a
melding of Christian humanitarianism and social reform in contrast to the
"rugged individualism" of the day. In a talk delivered later in the week,
Gladden championed the role of the churches in eradicating injustice and
inequity from society, thereby speeding the realization of what Gladden and
his disciples called the "Kingdom of God on Earth."[22]

A changing perception of the tie between individual moral regeneration and
the reconstruction of society lay behind these several June congresses devoted
to important aspects of the Social Question. Whether or not one adopted the
religious dimensions of reform expressed in Chicago, a growing number of activists were clearly no longer persuaded that individual conviction was sufficient to solve an increasing number of social problems. Ministers of the
Gospel and "ministers of reform," to quote Robert Crunden, joined hands in
the early reform congresses to advocate institutional solutions where appeals
to character and conscience failed.[23] In this sense, the reform congresses evidenced a significant ideological shift in the history of nineteenth-century reform movements. Reformers who expressed a humanitarian concern for the
welfare of fellow human beings were rapidly surrendering to apostles of reform as a mechanism of social control. The end result was the same, a pursuit
of equilibrium, but the object of their attention was shifting from the character of the individual to the character of society at large.

Under the auspices of the Congress Auxiliary's Department of Education, a spirited session focused on the relationship of the settlement-house
movement to the Social Question. Beginning with London's Toynbee House
at mid-century, urban centers committed to "social work" had sprung up on
both sides of the Atlantic. Its purpose was to address in a personal and immediate way the pressing problems of the urban poor in the industrial age.
Not content with dispensing aid, these community centers were also important clearinghouses for political and economic reform initiatives. Several of
the best-known settlement houses were in Chicago, including Hull House
and the Chicago Commons.

Jane Addams of Chicago's Hull House and Charles Zueblin of the University of Chicago coordinated an Exposition program devoted to the work
of settlement houses in the United States and Europe. Addams used her
many personal connections to bring together the leading figures of the
movement. Joining Addams and Zueblin on the program were Graham Taylor and Florence Kelley, Robert Woods of Boston's Andover House, Patrick
Geddes of the University of Edinburgh, and the Chicago journalist and reformer Henry Demarest Lloyd. Much in the way settlement houses sponsored open-ended roundtable discussions, the several presentations evolved
into a free-flowing dialogue on the relationship of settlement work to the
poor and unemployed, as well as a consideration of industrial conditions in

the United States and Europe. Addams and her colleagues concluded, not surprisingly, that the settlement house was central to the maintenance of social harmony in large cities.[24]

Government's role in addressing obstacles to social progress did not escape reformers in the Congress Auxiliary. Sessions of the Department of Government, Law Reform, and Political Science attracted a host of government officials, municipal reformers, and social activists. Their deliberations touched on such issues as the need for continuous civil service reform, problems of government management and accountability, and the pursuit of arbitration and peace as an alternative to armament. In this age of farmers' unrest and the burgeoning Populist revolt, the highly emotional issue of the free coinage of silver was reserved for the consideration of bankers and financiers in the sessions of the Department of Commerce. No debate in the Department of Government matched the spirited one in the U.S. Congress over the repeal of the 1890 Silver Purchase Act, a contest of wills over the "battle of the standards," which dominated the headlines for much of the summer.

Reflecting the growing concern for efficiency and accountability in government, the Congress on Civil Service Reform convened on Tuesday, August 8, with a panel that included Seth Low of Columbia College.[25] The retired mayor of Brooklyn, Low was a politician widely admired for instituting a merit system in city government, and his success in expanding municipal services to new areas had won him general acclaim as a new breed of politician. His participation as chief organizer of the Civil Service Congress brought considerable credibility to the consideration of an ambiguous though widely supported reform issue of the day. Low spoke on the subject "Civil Service from the Point of View of City Government." No one objected to Low's advocacy of good government and the need to restrain the "boodlers" and special interests. It was not recorded whether members of Chicago's City Council attended the session.[26]

Seth Low returned to the stage of the Congress Auxiliary in early August, part of a session on City Government that debated such topics as the need for law and order in metropolitan areas, financial management and city government, and the exigencies of municipal reform. Florence Kelley and Jane Addams participated in the forum. Kelley, Illinois's first state factory inspector, was an associate of Addams in Hull House, and she drew on her experiences in settlement work and factory inspection to discuss "The Relationship of the Municipality to the Sweating System."[27]

Assistant Secretary of State Josiah Quincy was lured from his desk in Washington to officiate at the Congress on Arbitration and Peace, which began August 16. With the Exposition itself associated with a new era of international harmony, it was fitting that the congress evoked the optimism of such noble sentiments. To a century that had witnessed the most violent political upheavals in memory, the condemnation of international discord and the rush to armament seemed enlightened, if a touch naive. Among the specific topics discussed throughout the week were the origin and development of peace societies, the economic aspects of war, woman and war, the appeals of ecclesiastical bodies for arbitration, and the future convention of peace congresses.[28]

In contrast to the sharply polished steel of the military technology displayed throughout the fairgrounds, the Congress on Peace reaffirmed the Enlightenment supposition of an international order premised on the law and a dutiful respect for the sovereignty of fellow nations. Klemens von Metternich had expressed such views earlier in the century, and Woodrow Wilson would do the same a generation later, but in Chicago that August twenty-one years before the Great War, delegates seemed convinced arbitration would in fact replace armament as the only viable option for hostile nations in the new era. Harmony in international relations could not come at the expense of individual rights. Somewhat ironically, a consideration of the "moral aspects of war" was reserved for the concluding session, a general peace vigil held on August 20.[29] Two weeks after the Congress on Arbitration and Peace proclaimed its faith in a new era of international order and friendship, the Exposition played host to Franz Ferdinand d'Este, the Crown Prince of the Austro-Hungarian Empire.

Although the Exposition proper venerated the changing world order brought by industrial capitalism, it was appropriate that its most portentous reform congress was reserved for the era's greatest social conflict, the so-called Labor Question. Chicago was a thriving industrial center, which boasted not only a diverse cosmopolitan working-class population but also a strong organized labor movement. As the 1886 Haymarket Riot showed, there was an influential if controversial radical element within the city's labor leadership. The decade preceding the Exposition had included over eleven thousand labor strikes; and since the May 4, 1886, Haymarket Square incident, Chicago had been identified with the perils and the possibilities of the labor movement.

Once again, in the summer of 1893, Chicago was engulfed in labor turmoil, owing chiefly to the early warning signs of the burgeoning economic panic. As the Labor Congress prepared to meet, the *Tribune* carried daily denunciations of the several thousand unemployed men and women—the paper called them "loafers"—who gathered along the lakefront. On Saturday, August 26, four thousand protesters marched on City Hall and clashed with police; nine men were wounded in the skirmish, which evoked Mayor Carter Harrison's personal plea for restraint on both sides.[30]

In such a climate the Exposition's Department of Labor convened its congress on Monday, August 28. With few exceptions, every significant leader of organized labor in the United States and many interested reformers and journalists participated in the weeklong assembly dedicated to the consideration of the relationship of labor and capital in all spheres of American life.

Henry Demarest Lloyd and Jane Addams were two members of the program committee, and they shared the belief that the Chicago meetings would mark a watershed in the history of organized labor in America. Lloyd's biographer credited the Congress on Labor with bringing Lloyd to the forefront of the labor movement and brought him into contact with numerous important reformers and union activists.[31] Those who wished that the socialist and anarchist elements of Chicago's and America's labor movement be given a voice in the proceedings would be disappointed. With the issue of collective bargaining controversial in its own right, a middle ground of activism was the order of the day.

Although rain and strong winds discouraged some from attending the opening session on the 28th, those present observed an unprecedented gathering of activists, labor organizers, and reformers committed to the rights of working men and women. The weeklong assembly included most of the important leaders of the day and those sympathetic to their cause: Terence Powderly of the Knights of Labor and Samuel Gompers of the rival American Federation of Labor, economists John R. Commons and Richard T. Ely, attorney Clarence Darrow, Carroll D. Wright of the U.S. Bureau of Labor, and Catholic archbishop John Ireland.

Though different in personality and approach, the delegates shared misgivings about the concentrations of economic wealth in monopoly capitalism. While favoring the rights of workers to join unions, they were critical of the disproportionate political influence of corporations in state and federal governments. Collectively, they recited a litany of abuses heaped on working men and women, as they engaged in a spirited debate on the worsening economic conditions registered in the anxious crowds daily milling on the pavement outside the Michigan Avenue meeting hall. Although the congress was formally organized around several major themes—The Condition of Labor, Work and Wages of Women and Children, Statistics of Labor, Literature and Philosophy of the Labor Movement, Arbitration and Other Remedies, and Living Questions and Means to Progress—what ensued the last week of August was unexpected and in some respects unplanned. Owing to its topic and the nature of the times, the Labor Congress was the most contentious of all the Congress Auxiliary's sessions.[32]

Eugene Debs, president of the recently organized American Railway Union, Terence Powderly of the Knights of Labor, and Samuel Gompers of the American Federation of Labor were all active supporters of the Congress on Labor. Powderly's influence in labor circles had waned since his denunciation of the Haymarket anarchists in 1886, but he was still a powerful presence in the Chicago meetings. Gompers was the best known of the three among Chicago trade unionists. If Debs was least known to Chicagoans in the summer of 1893, within a year his name would be intimately linked with labor unrest through his leadership in the Pullman Strike during the summer of 1894.

Other public figures who addressed the congress included General James B. Weaver, the Populist leader and 1892 presidential candidate of the People's Party; Henry George of Single Tax fame; Father Edward McGlynn; Booker T. Washington of Tuskegee Institute, the most influential black leader in the country; and Felix Adler of the New York Ethical Culture Society. Edward Bellamy declined Henry Demarest Lloyd's repeated solicitations to address the conference, upset with Lloyd's refusal to grant Bellamy a separate session to discuss his program of reform.[33]

Nowhere was the partisan spirit of the Labor Congress more visible than in a Wednesday morning talk by George E. McNeill of the Federal Labor Union, cofounder of the AFL. "The labor movement is God's movement through the ages," proclaimed McNeill, whose personal appearance reminded Samuel Gompers of Henry Wadsworth Longfellow. "God gave the command over all the things of the earth to man, not to a man or a class of men, but to all men."[34] A denunciation of the unequal distribution of wealth in American society, coupled with strong antimonopoly sentiments, pervaded the assembly. Delegates argued and debated the growing class tension that characterized industrial associations. Most delegates worried that the tendency toward monopolistic consolidation of wealth and power was the great threat to republican values and personal liberty. While paying homage to worker solidarity, few paused to consider why factory workers had failed to join farmers in the Populist vision of an alternative economic order. A fissure between skilled and unskilled labor was largely glossed over.

Large crowds gathered on August 28 to hear Samuel Gompers' address "What Does Labor Want?" a talk subsequently reprinted by the AFL Gompers observed that the mounting tension between workers and managers in the 1890s resulted from "the practical separation of the capitalistic class from the great mass of the industrious." "This distinction [between classes]," he said,

scarcely noticeable in the United States before the previous generation, rapidly became more and more marked, increasing day by day, until at length, it has widened into a veritable chasm; economic, social, and moral. On each side of this seemingly impassable chasm, we see the hostile camps of the rich and the poor . . . the arrogance of the rich ever mounting in proportion to the debasement of the poor.

Arguing that the capitalist class has "its origins in force and fraud, shameless fraud, stooping so low in its abject meanness," Gompers saw that the only solution to the Labor Question was the organization of workers for self-protection. Denouncing capitalists as "wealthy social parasites," Gompers proclaimed, "Today, modern society is beginning to regard the Trade Unions as the only hope of civilization; to regard them as the only power capable of evolving order out of the social-chaos." Capital and labor must reach a new accommodation that guarantees working people justice and harmony in the factory and in family life, Gompers concluded. After reciting a litany of worker rights and management abuses, Gompers concluded with a plea for more jobs, shorter hours and better wages, more books and fewer armaments, more learning and less vice, and what he described as "more opportunities to cultivate our better natures, to make manhood more noble and womanhood more beautiful, and children more happy and bright."[35]

Samuel Gompers's address was one of the most important of the Labor Congress, but his words were not universally supported. Within the congress's ranks were those who opposed the exclusionary features of the AFL and trade unionism.[36] One the most articulate and controversial delegates to dissent from Gompers's strategy was Father Edward McGlynn, a Roman Catholic priest and ardent supporter of the Single Tax. McGlynn's advocacy of Henry George's theory of wealth redistribution through shifting the burdens of taxation from the poor to the wealthy—a "single tax" on the resources of land—brought criticism from his superiors and his excommunication from the Catholic Church in 1887.

The Single Tax, perhaps the most popular reform measure of the late nineteenth century, was a widely misunderstood theory that appeared to some to undermine the dignity of private property. In accordance with its tradition and teachings of the subject of wealth, the Catholic Church affirmed the legitimacy of private ownership of property. When McGlynn refused to moderate his support of Henry George or to go to Rome to explain his position, he was stripped of his pastorate and then barred from receiving Church sacraments. The long-drawn-out affair was resolved only through the intervention of James Cardinal Gibbons, the American Primate and Archbishop of Baltimore. After protracted negotiations with the Vatican, McGlynn was restored to the priesthood and full communion in the Church in 1892, just in time to appear on the rostrum of the Labor Congress in Chicago.[37]

Although a bit ruffled by recent experiences, Edward McGlynn countered Samuel Gompers's gospel of trade unionism with a vigorous defense of the Single Tax as the solution to labor's woes. In remarks entitled "The Destiny of Labor," McGlynn invested the modern labor movement with a divine calling, but he cautioned that unless the Labor Question was addressed in relation to George's theory, the movement would fail to secure justice. Once the nation adopted the Single Tax, the reigning social and economic dislocation, made more troublesome by the worsening financial panic of the year, would be resolved and unfettered progress realized. "In reaching for the good," McGlynn told the Labor Congress, "true and beautiful labor is but fulfilling the Father's task, for the workman was placed here by the Master Workman."[38]

Trade unionism and the Single Tax were not the only cure-alls prescribed to alleviate the discordance of capital and labor. William Clark, leader of the English utopian-minded Fabian Society, offered his own remedy in "The Philosophy of the Labor Movement." "We shall not permit the public to be insulted, plundered, and outraged by rings of millionaires," Clark boasted. "Indeed, we shall not allow millionaires at all. They are diseased human products," he announced in the emotion of the moment, "and we intend to take away their power of acquiring millions for their own good as well as ours." A paper written by Eugene Debs, who was prevented from attending the meeting by other commitments, offered a more sober examination of labor's future. Speaking through his surrogate, Debs advocated unionization of all workers as the only way to preserve justice and freedom in the marketplace.[39]

Fiery oratory was not reserved for the Memorial Arts Building; on Wednesday afternoon it swept across the lawns of the lakefront as conferees affected solidarity with Chicago's jobless and homeless. Formal sessions of the Labor Congress were canceled in favor of a mass rally where speakers addressed the unemployed workers who kept a daily vigil on Michigan Avenue. An air of frustration was apparent, fueled by the newest *Tribune* denunciation of "loafers" on the lakefront and by a morning article that reported that city relief stations were running short of food and clothing.[40]

As was the custom of the day, invited speakers arrived with escort and preached their particular sermon from atop horse-drawn wagons assembled for the occasion. Approximately twenty-five thousand people turned out to hear Samuel Gompers of the AFL and Terence Powderly of the rival Knights of Labor, as well as Henry George and Edward McGlynn. Chicago socialist and labor organizer Thomas J. Morgan had a strong following among the workers on the lawn, and Florence Kelley and Jane Addams were among the several women who spoke. Although organizers hoped he might attend, Eugene Debs remained away from the rally because of business outside Chicago.

Reporters first noticed Father McGlynn, who had attracted a crowd of several thousand men and women to his side. "It is unfortunate in the economy of this Commonwealth," the labor priest intoned over the noise, "that there are two great classes of people—those who work for a living and those who do not." Refusing to accept the then-popular Malthusian explanation for the job shortage (overpopulation), McGlynn reaffirmed the Single Tax as the only solution to economic inequities. "Make the holders of property pay in taxes what the right of its use is worth. Make the monopolist mill and land owners disgorge," he counseled to great cheers. McGlynn concluded with an appeal to Christian virtue and the petition that no worker should ever pray "Father, give us this day our daily bread" in vain.[41]

From wagon four came an echo of what Father McGlynn had said, only now it was from the prophet himself. "Let land be opened and there will be no idleness," Henry George assured his audience. "Adding to the growth of rent and increasing the valuation of land is the cause of the decline of wages and is filling our cities with unemployed men and our roads with tramps. There is but one remedy." This, of course, was the Single Tax, which George had fashioned into the great equalizer for industrial discontents.[42]

By far the largest crowd gathered about wagon five to hear Samuel Gompers. Gompers proposed less an explanation for existing conditions than an immediate plan of action to help the jobless. (A morning article in the *Chicago Daily Inter-Ocean* quoted Gompers as stating, "Hungry people can neither reason nor work.") Aware of the worsening economic circumstances across the country and the estimated twenty-five thousand out of work in Chicago, Gompers proclaimed that "As a representative of organized labor I declare that such a condition is unnatural." Not surprisingly, the leader of the AFL suggested, "The organized labor movement offers the only practical solution to this question." Gompers called for an immediate government-funded program of public works jobs to resolve the employment crisis. His proposal foreshadowed Jacob Coxey's controversial program put forth in 1894, though it lacked the religious inspiration of Coxey's "Commonweal of Christ." Gompers mentioned several worthwhile projects, including the improvement of the Mississippi River, the completion of the then-bankrupt Nicaraguan canal, and the repair of impassable rural roads. Like Henry George, Samuel Gompers found opening up unsettled lands to public use a safety valve for urban discontent. "Keep up this labor movement," he advised his colleagues. "It may require a long time to properly solve this [labor] question, but it can be done with patience and perseverance."[43]

With the lakefront rally over, the Labor Congress continued through the week toward its conclusion with a mass march and oration by Gompers on September 4, Labor Day. Other sessions of the congress included talks by Booker T. Washington on "The Progress of Negroes as Free Laborers" and a similar discussion of Native American progress by Charles C. Painter of the Indian Rights League. Washington's comments foreshadowed his more famous address two summers later at the Atlanta Cotton Exposition, where he argued that black Southerners accept social inequality as they struggle for economic self-sufficiency. In a separate address, Populist James Weaver lamented that the Declaration of Independence had become, in his words, an "iridescent dream" destroyed by the monopolists.

In other sessions, Richard Ely and Henry George collaborated in a discussion focused on labor's relation to the public economy. Like Weaver, they concentrated on the injurious effects of monopoly and its threat to democratic freedoms. Though clearly sympathetic to the Populist campaign for an alternative economy, Ely embraced state ownership of the railroads and other "natural monopolies" as an essential reform measure. In a well-attended evening session, Samuel Gompers joined with Beatrice Webb and Florence Kelley in a free-flowing discussion of ways to eliminate the "sweating system" in modern factories. Felix Adler of the Ethical Culture Society and William Salter were among those who offered observations on morality as a force in labor-management disputes, and Kansas Populist Mary E. Lease boldly suggested that if the men could not solve the Labor Question they should stay at home with the children and leave the task to women.[44]

Many of the speakers were involved in meetings held in conjunction with the Department of Labor, including the Congress on the Single Tax. Ever since the publication of *Progress and Poverty* in 1879, Henry George and his theory of taxation had been widely praised and criticized. By 1893 George had a trans-Atlantic following that rivaled Edward Bellamy's movement. Perhaps it was Henry Demarest Lloyd's decision to grant George's views special consideration in the Congress Auxiliary, while denying a similar privilege to the prophet of Nationalism, which led Bellamy to decline any direct participation in the program. In any event, the Congress on the Single Tax drew large audiences who heard George, Edward McGlynn, and other supporters discuss the relationship of the tax to every conceivable social issue of the day, including farm problems, industrial workers, immigration, public morality and private religion, social purity, and financial monopoly, as well as to intemperance and the most recent scientific discoveries. There were more than thirty sessions to the Single Tax Congress, climaxed by a mass rally on August 27 in which George himself occupied center stage.[45]

Perhaps the most important session of the Congress on Labor came toward its conclusion on Sunday evening, September 3. More than twenty-five hundred people packed the Hall of Washington in the Memorial Arts Building to hear clerics and labor leaders confer on "The Church and Labor." Henry Demarest Lloyd presided over the gathering, and Catholic Archbishop John Ireland presented the keynote address.[46]

"The Church and the Labor Question" was a defense of Pope Leo XIII's 1891 encyclical on the working class, *Rerum Novarum*. Consonant with its spiritual and social mission, Ireland asserted, the Catholic Church had the responsibility of "proclaiming the great principles of truth and moral duty which underlie the whole region of human thought and doing, and without which humanity, in its search for rights and purposes, is a ship sailing without compass or rudder."

In contrast to what other speakers had said throughout the week, Ireland argued that social relations should not be seen through the narrow prism of class conflict. The Labor Question was intimately bound up in all other questions of moral and social importance; it was a profoundly human struggle, which engaged a full view of human nature. "At the very foundation of the labor question," Ireland explained of Pope Leo and the Church's approach, "lies the proper appreciation of the individual man." "Labor in man is honorable," he said, echoing St. Benedict. "But labor is no longer honorable when the worker is no longer treated like a man."

Ireland deemed it "shameful" that employers looked upon workers as only "so much muscle to make money by." Labor, the creative impulse, was a gift from God, Ireland concluded, and any resolution of the Labor Question must ultimately be in human, not structural terms.[47] Less than a year later, as federal army troops entered Chicago to end the Pullman Strike, the radical potential of Ireland's message was lost amid the clash of rifles and bayonets.

The Congress on Labor concluded the next day (September 4) with a Labor Day filled with speeches, picnics, and athletic contests between the city's rival unions. That morning, more than fifteen thousand men and women marched through Chicago's Loop, accompanied by thirty marching bands; the same enthusiasm carried over to the afternoon picnics in the city's parks. As Samuel Gompers, Mayor Carter Harrison, and Illinois Governor John Altgeld made the rounds of the various gatherings in the parks, the immediacy of labor troubles could not escape their attention.

Archbishop Ireland's remarks the previous evening did nothing to mollify the partisan spirits of the Labor Congress, and in his own way Ireland demonstrated the complexity of the problem to a generation given over to the pursuit of institutional solutions to social problems. Ireland's talk, like the great social encyclical *Rerum Novarum*, did not only embrace the continued relevance of religion to the pressing problems of the day. It also engaged a particular understanding of human nature as the basis of social relations that had fallen out of favor in an age of market capitalism and scientific certitude. Even as the Labor Congress ended, however, what was regarded as the greatest of the Exposition's social congresses was already underway.

The World's Parliament of Religions, the "crowning glory" of the Exposition's intellectual congresses, was the most ambitious assemblage of religious leaders and reformers in modern times. The idea dated from the spring of 1891 when Reverend John Henry Barrows was appointed chairman of the Congress Auxiliary's Department of Religion. In a more general sense, however, the plan for a series of interdenominational meetings capped by a great interfaith Parliament of Religions reflected a growing concern for "irreligion," the spreading pall of disbelief and religious indifference at the end of the century. To arrest this trend and reestablish the central role of religious faith in the modern age, Barrows and his planning committee agreed with Auxiliary President Charles Bonney that a religious assembly should be preeminent among all other concerns taken up by the World's Congress Auxiliary. In the words of an early circular from the Department of Religion:

It [the Parliament of Religions] is proposed to consider the Foundations of religious Faith; to review the triumphs of Religion in all ages; to set forth the present state of Religion among the Nations, and its influence over Literature, Art, Commerce, Government and Family Life; to indicate its powers in promotion of temperance, and social purity, and its harmony with true Science; to show its dominance in the higher institutions of learning; to make prominent the values of the weekly-rest-day on religious and other grounds; and to contribute to those forces which shall bring about the unity of the race in the worship of God and the service of man.[48]

If not a latter-day Pentecost on American soil, as one writer has suggested, the Parliament of Religions enshrined an unprecedented discussion on the relationship of religion to the changing circumstances of everyday life.[49] Combining the spiritual with the social in a clarion call for individual and collective renewal, the Parliament aptly summarized the impulse of the larger Congress Auxiliary. On more than one occasion Dr. Barrows expressed the hope that in bringing together the great religious leaders of the Orient and the Occident in an atmosphere unencumbered by denominational strife, the forces of Religion could triumph over secularism. If this were not ambitious enough, Barrows hoped the Parliament might reunite Christendom and advance the moral progress of the race.

To accomplish this ambitious agenda, Barrows and his interfaith planning committee organized a series of denominational congresses held between August 27 and October 15 in general sessions at the Memorial Arts Building on Michigan Avenue. In all, more than twenty-five separate religious bodies held their own denominational congresses, including each of the mainstream Protestant denominations, the Catholic Church and disciples of Judaism, and numerous sects and traditions not so familiar to the largely American audience. Denominational congresses ran from two days to one week each, with the premise that enlightenment was the surest means to correct the ignorance and prejudices that stood in the way of universal brotherhood and civilization's advance.

In addition to the denominational congresses, a number of religious societies and missionary associations met under the auspices of the Auxiliary's Department of Religion. They included the Young Men's Christian Association, the Evangelical Alliance, the Theosophists and Free Religionists, Ethical Culture societies, and a Congress on Evolution. The highlight of the Evolution Congress was the presentation of a paper written by Thomas Huxley. While the denominational congresses were underway, the Philosophical Congress also met for two days in Memorial Hall. Several of America's leading academic philosophers were on hand to debate the nature of knowledge and the merits of Thomistic and Pragmatic inquiry.[50]

The third and largest element of the Department of Religion was by unanimous opinion the most important, the magisterial Parliament of Religions, which opened with solemn ceremonies on September 11 and continued for seventeen days in what John Barrows called "a great school of comparative theology." Where the denominational congresses focused attention on the particular beliefs of individual faith traditions, the Parliament brought together religious leaders in a common forum to "unite all Religion against Irreligion; to make the Golden Rule the basis of this union."[51]

Although the denominational congresses and the Parliament of Religions were celebrated for being "higher and nobler" than any other part of the Exposition ensemble, they were not without their critics. Its ecumenical spirit also had noticeable limits. The Catholic denominational congress in particular became the subject of lingering controversy within the Church hierarchy. Claims of fraternity, tolerance, and goodwill notwithstanding, other religious groups were noticeably absent from the program. Chief among these denominations was the Church of Jesus Christ of Latter-Day Saints—the Mormons. Despite the church's official ban, in 1890, on the practice of polygamy, a concession to statehood, the disciples of Joseph Smith seem to have been unwelcome at Chicago. There is no evidence that the planning committee extended an invitation for their participation in any form, and members of the church did not take part in the meetings.

Unlike the Mormons, the members of the Church of Christ, Scientist, were extended an invitation, but Mary Baker Eddy was reluctant to accept it. As founder of the Christian Scientists, Eddy was fearful that the Parliament might misinterpret her teachings, and she did not cooperate in the organization of a Christian Science denominational congress. In fact, Mrs. Eddy looked upon the entire Exposition with suspicion, dubbing the enterprise the "Vanity Fair." When the paper she had written was read by a disciple to the Parliament of Religions and inaccurately quoted in the newspapers, Eddy, her worst fears now realized, lashed out in public and demanded that her words not appear in the Parliament's commemorative volume.[52] For Mormons by their absence, as for Christian Scientists in their presence, the Parliament of Religions proved to be less than the festival of Christian unity its organizers claimed.

Reflecting the Parliament's primary attention to mainline and historic denominations, another group received but scant attention in the meeting. Except for a gathering of the Evangelical Alliance, conservative Christianity received little consideration in the Parliament of Religions. The emerging Holiness and Pentecostal congregations and what would soon be called the Fundamentalist movement had no place in the religious gatherings. In their preference for mainstream denominations, organizers made no gesture to what was already one of the most dynamic movements in American Christianity. Within a generation's time, evangelical and fundamentalist congregations would radically transform the landscape of American Christianity, in a manner the Parliament's planners never imagined.[53]

Despite these breaches of etiquette, several faith traditions recognized in the denominational congresses an opportunity to answer the prejudices and attacks against them that were endemic in the nativist climate of the decade. Especially for American Jews and Catholics, the denominational congresses and the Parliament of Religions offered a chance to demonstrate that the claims of the American Protective Association and other anti-immigrant agencies were unfounded. Catholic and Jewish leaders viewed participation in the religious meetings in Chicago as essential to winning a wider acceptance in American life. For each it was a chance to dispel religious misconceptions that branded them as outsiders in American progress.

Jewish participation was organized by the Union of American Hebrew Congregations (UAHC) and by the Central Conference of American Rabbis (CCAR). Under the direction of Rabbi Isaac Mayer Wise and his followers, the UAHC and the CCAR were essential organizations in the promotion of Reform Judaism in the United States.[54] Wise was perhaps the most prominent Judaic scholar in America, as well as the founder of the Hebrew Union College in Cincinnati. In fact, proponents of Reform Judaism followed Wise's example in actively supporting the Jewish Congress and participating in its sessions. Prominent Reform rabbis who joined Wise included Kaufmann Kholer, Emil Hirsch, Gustav Gettheil and H. P. Mendes. Although illness prevented his attending the conference, two papers written by Alexander Kohut were presented in absentia.[55]

Organizers of the denominational congress sent invitations to prominent Jewish organizations, announcing that the Chicago meeting provided the opportunity to "state clearly and emphatically the great aim and the objects of Judaism before the entire world and to substantially refute all the slanderous charges made against it through the successive ages by its declared foes." The president of the organizing committee declared it would be "criminal negligence" not to embrace the opportunity the Columbian Exposition afforded American Jews. For reasons that went unexplained, European Jewish organizations chose not to accept the organizers' offers of inclusion in the proceedings.[56]

The Jewish Congress was the first of the several dozen denominational meetings to convene, opening for four days on Sunday, August 27. (A separate Congress of Jewish Women met on September 5.) "It seemed meet that the oldest faith, the forerunner of Christianity, should usher in a series of world's religious congresses designed to promote the spiritual welfare of mankind," observed one chronicle of the congress.[57] The chief meeting stressed an open examination of the history and theology of Judaism, with a special emphasis on its contribution to world and American civilization. Among the key topics discussed in the four-day congress were "The Doctrine of Immortality in Judaism," "Ethics of the Talmud," "Synagogue and Church in their Mutual Relation," "Orthodox or Historical Judaism," "Judaism and the Modern State," "Jewish Contributions to Civilization," and "The Outlook of Judaism." Clearly reflecting the theological and social agenda of Isaac Wise, the congress demonstrated the strong influence of Reform thought in contemporary Judaism. Giving a comparative dimension to the deliberations, several speakers commented on the relationship of Judaism to other Western religious traditions.

The acknowledged leader of Reform Judaism, Isaac Mayer Wise delivered several presentations to the Jewish Congress, including a public lecture on "Ethics of Judaism" and the more scholarly "An Introduction to the Theology of Judaism." In the latter presentation, Wise spoke of the "four postulates" that Judaism shares with other authentic religions: the existence of God; the validity of revelation and worship; conscience, ethics, and aesthetics; and immortality, reward, and punishment. For all that divides "various systems of theology," Wise argued that Judaism has much in common with Christianity and the other great world religions.[58]

Equally important was the relationship of Judaism to current social conditions in the United States. If some scholars detected a strong assimilationist component in the conference's vision for American Jewry, they were not mistaken. Perhaps Professor D. G. Lyon of Harvard University best explained the message of the congress when he observed that Jewish dreams—for a home, prosperity, and universal brotherhood—were really American dreams, as seen in the noble ambitions of the Columbian year. "The Jew ... is in our midst an American," he said, as if to suggest Judaism and Americanism were complementary facets of the same personality—a republican personality that prized freedom and brotherhood above all else.[59] This was a message with powerful social and cultural ramifications in an era of heightened East European Jewish immigration to the United States.

Wise and other organizers seemed pleased with the reception accorded them in Chicago, and in 1894 they published a commemorative volume of speeches to celebrate the triumph of their acceptance. In his introduction to the volume, Isaac Wise summarized the sentiments of his colleagues, claiming that the religious congresses had "made warm friends for it [Judaism] in hitherto hostile or at least coldly indifferent circles, and the seed has been sown that will undoubtedly bring forth a harvest of esteem and good fellowship."[60]

The challenge faced by the Jewish Congress—winning a greater measure of tolerance in what was perceived as the foreign territory of Protestant America—also confronted supporters of the Catholic denominational congress. The Columbian Catholic Congress opened with much pageantry and a solemn high Mass on September 4, but even before it closed, the gathering became the subject of great and enduring controversy within the Church hierarchy.[61] Organized under lay initiative with support from liberal American bishops, the Catholic Congress became an important issue in the so-called Americanist controversy, which engulfed the Church at the end of the century. In an effort to win Catholicism's wider acceptance in America and to demonstrate effectively the Church's support of republican principles, liberal bishops such as John Ireland; John Keane, rector of the Catholic University of America; and even James Cardinal Gibbons backed William J. Onahan's plan for a great lay congress. The unprecedented conference would be, in Onahan's words, "an *object lesson*, demonstrating how woefully and how unfairly the Catholic Church has been misjudged and misrepresented by her enemies."[62] Its apologetics betraying a note of defensiveness, the Catholic denominational congress ran afoul of more conservative bishops, who complained to the Vatican that in their pursuit of acceptance the liberals had devised a strategy that ran perilously close to compromising Church teachings and traditions.

Irish-American bishops were among the most important participants in the denominational congress, which also attracted a large number of prominent lay leaders. In addition to the direct participation of Gibbons and Ireland, Patrick Feehan, John Spalding, and John Keane cooperated in the planning sessions and delivered addresses to the congress. The Reverend Walter Elliot, author of a controversial biography of Paulist Fathers founder Isaac Hecker, joined Maurice F. Egan of the University of Notre Dame, Terence Powderly of the Knights of Labor, and converts George and Rose Hawthorne Lathrop, the daughter of Nathaniel Hawthorne. The substantive issues considered in the Catholic Congress ranged from a discussion of the Labor Question (with special attention to the 1891 encyclical *Rerum Novarum*) and the role of Catholic education in the United States to the matter of the independence of the Holy See. Immigration, the Church and the Social Question, and the present condition of Native Americans and African Americans were also explored. One unscheduled issue that divided the congress was a debate over Irish Home Rule legislation then before the British Parliament. This proved to be a particularly delicate issue for people like Onahan, Ireland, and Feehan—all of Irish heritage.[63]

In an attempt to counteract the mounting nativist campaigns against immigrant Catholics, William Onahan had the halls of the congress adorned with patriotic banners, the papal flag hanging conspicuously beside the American flag. Pictures of Pope Leo XIII and the American Catholic hierarchy were arranged alongside the heroes of American history. William Onahan, John Ireland, and the other supporters of the Catholic Congress made no apology for the fraternity of religious faith and patriotic fervor that animated the proceedings, as sentiments of faith and patriotism's "holy partnership" in American life reverberated through the sessions.

For an immigrant church, the Columbian Catholic Congress was an unprecedented opportunity to gain wider approval in Protestant America. None other than Archbishop Francesco Satolli, America's first Apostolic Delegate, expanded on the theme in his greetings to the delegates. In words he later regretted, Satolli encouraged the participants, "Go forward, in one hand bearing the book of Christian truth and in the other the Constitution of the United States. Christian truth and American liberty will make you free, happy and prosperous. They will put you on the road to progress. May your steps ever persevere on that road."[64]

After several days of deliberations, the Catholic Congress closed amid a storm of controversy. Among the resolutions approved by delegates in their final session were those that praised the American hierarchy for the "wonderful growth" of the Church and proclaimed without equivocation that no antagonism existed between Church and State. Most agreed hopefully with the final assessment given by Cardinal Gibbons: "The voice of the Congress has succeeded in dissipating prejudices and in removing many misunderstandings in regard to the teachings of God and practices of the Church of God." Gibbons developed his defense of Catholicism and American republican values in an address to the general Parliament of Religions, which received wide circulation in Catholic circles shortly after the Exposition season ended.[65]

Despite the optimism of Cardinal Gibbons's remarks, opponents within the American Church mounted a vigorous campaign intended to dispel the celebratory mood of the lay congress's supporters. Conservative bishops attacked the congress and its organizers for what they thought was a betrayal of Church doctrine to appease the adversaries of Catholicism in America. In their view, the denominational congress was another step in an ongoing effort by "Americanists" to compromise Church traditions to secure wider acceptance. Though no breach of orthodoxy was uncovered, critics assumed that, especially in the interdenominational Parliament of Religions, fraternizing with other religious traditions must inevitably undermine the Catholic Church's integrity.

In 1895, Pope Leo XIII issued the encyclical *Longinqua oceani*, which prohibited further lay congresses. The pontiff's criticism of the Columbian Catholic Congress was fueled by Francesco Satolli's about-face denunciation of what he had earlier praised. Four years later, in 1899, the Columbian Catholic Congress figured prominently in the encyclical *Testem benevolentiae*, which condemned errors loosely associated with what had come to be called "Americanism." William Onahan and John Ireland defended the Chicago congress, but as the controversy grew they chose not to pursue the matter and further antagonize their critics in Rome and the states. A bold and hopeful effort engulfed in the tensions within the emerging American Catholic Church, the Columbian Catholic Congress was the last gathering of its kind.

Though each of the several dozen denominational congresses had its own story to tell, all served as a preamble to the much larger and more ceremonial World's Parliament of Religions. Through the Parliament of Religions, the leaders of the world's historic religions came together to advance religion's cause and clarify its relationship to the great social and moral issues of the day. As befit this first and largest gathering of religious leaders, no fewer than four thousand people representing twenty nations assembled at noon on September 11 for the inaugural ceremonies in Columbus Hall. The multitude sat "wonderfully quiet" as the facsimile Liberty Bell tolled ten times—one stroke for each of the commandments—and the organist played "Jerusalem the Golden" to commemorate the occasion. On the platform sat nearly one hundred religious leaders from around the world, brought together from diverse countries and continents to celebrate this unprecedented moment.

In his opening remarks, Charles Bonney captured the spirit of the new era and made an explicit linkage to the august religious ceremonies he oversaw. His words also invoked the culture of renewal that ran throughout the Exposition, here lending an explicit spiritual meaning to the theme. "This day," an excited Bonney observed in his opening remarks, "the sun of a new era of religious peace and progress rises over the world, dispelling the dark clouds of sectarian strife. This day a new flower blooms in the garden of religious thought, filling the air with its exquisite perfume."[66] Bonney's exuberance set the tone for the seventeen-day Parliament, reflecting the confidence and optimism with which the ecumenical assembly had been conceived.

Charles Bonney's profession of faith in the Parliament engaged an eschatological vision of the "Beloved Community" that animated liberal Protestant social thought in the late nineteenth century. "This day a new fraternity is born into the world of human progress, to aid in the upbuilding of the Kingdom of God in the hearts of men. Era and flower and fraternity bear one name. It is a name which will gladden the hearts of those who worship God and love man in every clime. Those who hear its music joyfully echo it back to sun and flower. It is the brotherhood of religions." Reverend John Barrows, chairman of the Parliament of Religions, was less ethereal in his claims for the program, but not less enthusiastic: "It seems to me that the spirits of all just and good men hover over this assembly."[67]

On September 25, American diplomat and reformer Frederick Douglass echoed Barrows's assessment when asked to offer a few words to the delegates assembled. "I have only to say to all those who have the spirit of liberty within them," Douglass told them in unprepared remarks, "that I hold them as countrymen, classmen, kinsmen, and brothers beloved. . . . It is very hard for an Englishman, for instance, to do justice to an Irishman. It is hard, perhaps, for an Irishman to do justice to an Englishman. It is very hard for a Christian to do justice to a Jew, and it is hard for a Jew to do justice to a Christian. But we are reconciling them all to-day." "We are bringing them all into unity," Douglass conceded, "and it is a delightful thing to see brethren dwelling together in unity."[68]

The formal program of the Parliament ran for seventeen days, and in its sessions nearly every variety of religious belief was afforded the opportunity to play out the great drama of interdenominational brotherhood that Bonney extolled in his opening remarks. Protestant; Catholic; and Jew; Evangelicals and Evolutionists; the followers of Buddha and Shinto, Ethical Culturalists and Theosophists, the disciples of Confucius, Swedenborg, and Zoroaster; and the growing number of Americans who advocated a Social Gospel had their say as the assembly worked its way through an exposition of the world's sacred teachings. As might have been expected, for all of the ecumenism, the sessions exhibited a decided preference for Christianity. The program also betrayed Bonney and Barrows's preoccupation with the application of Christian teachings to the social problems of the era.

For many Americans, the Parliament of Religions was as exotic as the Midway haunts. It was their first meaningful introduction to creeds, sects, and beliefs as foreign as the names and appearances of the advocates who had crossed ocean and continent to explain them. Greek Orthodox Archbishop Dionysius of Zante and Swami Vivekananda of Calcutta were among the more distinguished international religious figures to participate in the Parliament. Vivekananda, a devoted disciple of Sri Ramakrishna, at the age of thirty was already considered a Hindu saint-philosopher. Delighted by his invitation to come to Chicago and ready to use the occasion to advance his cause in America, Vivekananda willingly participated in many of the public ceremonies attending the Parliament. He contributed a well-received paper entitled "Hinduism Is a Religion" to the general session of the teachings of Hindu.[69]

Dressed in a saffron-colored robe and his traditional turban, Vivekananda's presence was easily noticed in the several sessions he attended. His disquisition on the traditions of Hinduism was greeted with generous applause from an appreciative audience. Keeping with the spirit of the assembly, the holy man told one session, "Sectarianism, bigotry and its horrible descendant, fanaticism . . . have filled the earth with violence, drenched it often and often with human blood, destroyed civilization and sent whole nations to despair." "I fervently hope that the bell which tolled this morning [referring to the opening ceremonies] in honour of this convention may be the death knell of fanaticism, of all persecutions with the sword or the pen and all uncharitable feelings between people."[70]

Vivekananda was so touched by the enthusiasm that greeted his remarks throughout the Parliament that he chose to remain in the United States after the close of the Exposition. He traveled around the country for several years, lecturing to sympathetic audiences and helping to open Hindu missions and temples for a small but growing number of people drawn to his message.

Swami Vivekananda was not the only foreign religious leader to seize upon the Parliament of Religions to introduce his teachings to the United States. The Right Reverend Reuchi Shibata, president of Japan's Thikko sect, spoke on conventions of Shinto piety; Jinanji Jamshedji Modi of India delivered a paper on "Belief and Ceremonies of the Followers of Zoroaster"; and another Indian, Virchand Gandhi, lectured on "The Ethics and History of the Jains." Protap Chunder Mozoomdar participated in a panel discussing the Indian reform society, Brahmo-Somaj. Kung Hsien Ho of Shanghai lent his expertise to a session of Confucian traditions and teachings, and the Reverend Doctor George Washburn of Constantinople offered a comparative analysis of Christianity and Islam.

The international session that received perhaps the greatest attention in the press was one devoted to Buddhism. In his talk on "The World's Debt to Buddha," A. Dharmapala defined Gautama's moral and social code; and in a talk on "Buddhism and Christianity," he offered a lengthy analysis of the similarities between the social teachings of Buddha and Jesus. He stressed the common salvation they offered and the spiritual deliverance open to all through each tradition. Shaku Soyen, a Japanese student of the Rinzai school of Zen, spoke at length on the more esoteric subject of "The Law of Cause and Effect as Taught by Buddha." Like Swami Vivekananda, Soyen remained in America after the close of the Exposition and traveled the country spreading the teachings of Buddha to all who would listen. Soyen's efforts have been credited with establishing Buddhism's foothold in North America.[71]

In many respects the Parliament of Religions was the great "school of comparative theology" that John Barrows claimed it to be, but its major thrust was toward the applicability of Christianity to the current conditions of American life. Religious leaders were not only concerned about the growing authority of Science, against the validity of Scripture, but they also had to contend with the great uncertainties of the times. For many, the forces of modernization presented new challenges to the certainty of orthodox beliefs. To an age enamored of material progress and preoccupied with the notion that a golden age was imminent, the Parliament's message was unabashedly optimistic. Christianity, particularly in its mainstream Protestant version, was more than an outworn husk; it was vital to the social and spiritual renewal in the new era.

The applicability of Protestant Christianity to the temper of social reform was put forth in a series of meetings that evidenced religion's enduring place in the culture. In addition to Thomas Wentworth Higginson, an early enthusiast for the Parliament of Religions, some of the most important social critics and religious leaders of the era participated in the assemblage. They included Russell Conwell, author of the popular "Acres of Diamonds" speech; Edward Everett Hale of the "Lend a Hand Movement"; economist Richard T. Ely; and the leading exponents of what was then called a Social Gospel. In addition to Washington Gladden and Josiah Strong, English reformers Henry Drummond and William T. Stead contributed to the program.

Washington Gladden and Richard Ely each made forceful presentations on the relationship between the spiritual and the social as the foundation of a just commonwealth. Gladden was best known for his essay "Applied Christianity," in which he argued that the churches had a social as well as a spiritual mission in industrial society and that the salvation of the individual was intimately bound up in the renewal of society. In a talk entitled "Religion and Wealth," Gladden argued that the Christian ethic of love and not socialism was the key to discernment. "That wealth should exist," he told the Parliament, "plainly [is] in accordance with the will of God, but in whose hands?" With the possession of wealth came an obligation to assist the less fortunate, Gladden insisted, and the church was essential in the formation of a proper social conscience. "And religion, which seeks to discern and follow the divine plan, must teach that the wealth of the world will be rightly distributed, only when every man shall have as much as he can wisely use to make himself a better man, and the community in which he lives a better community, so much and no more." "It is obvious," Gladden observed of current social and economic conditions, "that the divine plan is yet far from realization."[72]

Richard Ely made much the same point in his principal address, "Christianity as a Social Force." A professional economist infused with the zeal of a religious crusader, Ely was one of the most thoughtful American advocates of social Christianity. He observed to his audience that Christianity's distinction was as "a social force above everything else." As far back as the Hebrew prophets, Ely said, private property was known to exist for social purposes, and the responsibility of the holder to the community was an integral feature of the Christian heritage. Individualism and materialism were hostile to the Kingdom of God, he asserted, as they divided women and men and thwarted human destiny. "Christianity as a social force makes not only for progress," Ely concluded, "but for peaceful progress, which in the end is the most rapid and secure progress."[73]

Both Gladden and Ely addressed social Christianity's potential to transform the individual as the basis for a comprehensive reconstruction of society. In their critique of the present aspect of American social development, advocates of the Social Gospel promoted a sense of community—"Beloved Community"—and communality in place of the rugged individualism of the day. Individual salvation was intimately bound to the renewal of society in accord with the Sermon on the Mount. The moral and the social order were indivisible in Social Gospel theology, and by uniting religion and reform its proponents hoped to infuse the moral authority of the church into social relations.

Other religious leaders from differing denominations offered their own considerations of Christianity's relationship to social and economic turmoil. In separate addresses Catholic archbishop John Ireland and Professor F. G. Putnam agreed that Christianity's respect for the individual must be the basis for any solution to social problems. A.M.E. Bishop B. W. Arnett spoke on the subject of "Christianity and the Negro" and reminded his listeners of the historic friendship between the Christian Church and his race. "It was a black man," Arnett said, "a native of an African city, who became the cross-bearer of the Son of God on his way to Calvary."

Edward Everett Hale and Lyman Abbott, two of the more liberal Protestant ministers of the Gilded Age, gave startling testimony to the confidence of the age. Hale, a Unitarian minister and author, rejected the unbending individualism of social evolutionists like William Graham Sumner and Andrew Carnegie. Acknowledging the existence of serious social problems in America, Hale claimed evidence of greater forces for good in the present aspect of society. In a speech entitled "Spiritual Forces in Human Progress," Hale predicted the banishment in the next generation of the evil and suffering that had in the past afflicted humankind. A great tribunal, which a hopeful Hale called the "sign of life with God," would assure the rights of every person in the years to come. "The twentieth century, for instance, is going to establish peace among all nations of the world," Hale said in words reminiscent of Edward Bellamy's *Looking Backward*. Hale not only embraced the spirit of the "new era" but also clearly articulated the vision of the coming "Kingdom of God on Earth," which his fellow social gospel advocates confidently awaited. Lyman Abbott's remarks on "Religion Essentially a Characteristic of Humanity" echoed Hale's acceptance of the role of religion in reforming social relations in anticipation of the coming golden age.[74]

Perhaps the clearest evocation of the churches' role in a program of social renewal came in a paper that was read in absentia. Pressing business problems in London kept William Thomas Stead, the controversial English reformer and editor of the *Review of Reviews*, from attending the Parliament of Religions; he did send a paper entitled "The Civic Church." "The fundamental idea of the Civic Church," the paper explained, "is that of the intelligent and fraternal co-operation of all those who are in earnest about making men and things somewhat better than they are today." The aim of the Civic Church was the regeneration of society, and its basis was simply a willingness to serve others. "The Civic Church is the spiritual counterpart of the town council . . . ," Stead said. "It is an attempt to organize the conscience of the community so as to bring the collective moral sentiment of the whole community to bear upon the problems which can only be solved by collective action."[75]

William Stead affirmed social Christianity as the only complete answer to the myriad forces working against social regeneration in the industrial age. The pivotal doctrine was the Sermon on the Mount, and the congregation was the entire human community. In Stead's formula, religious institutions were vital to redressing the social and economic injustices of the age, speeding the progress of the race, and realizing a triumphant "Kingdom of God" in the new era.

Though he was absent when his speech was read to an appreciative audience in Columbus Hall, word of its positive reception encouraged Stead to travel to Chicago at the earliest opportunity. This latter-day Jeremiah's arrival in the city several weeks after the Exposition closed and his efforts to establish the Civic Church in a city known for its wide-open character led to one of the era's most important if comical urban reform crusades in late nineteenth-century America.[76]

The World's Parliament of Religions was perhaps the greatest of the reform congresses sponsored by the Exposition, and its conclusion on the evening of September 27 was an occasion of mixed emotions for many of the participants. "This closing hour of this parliament is one of congratulations, of tender sorrow, of triumphant hopefulness," said John Barrows. True to the spirit of the revival format, Barrows then shared a personal experience with the delegates that summed up the meaning of the occasion. "While floating one evening over the illuminated waters of the 'White City,' Mr. Dharmapala said, with that smile which has won our hearts, 'All the joys of heaven are in Chicago,' and Dr. Momerie, with his characteristic mingling of enthusiasm and skepticism, replied, 'I wish I were sure that all the joys of Chicago are to be in heaven.'"[77]

In his remarks, Charles Bonney thanked the several thousand participants for their contribution to the Parliament and its ancillary sessions, as well as the advancement of civilization. Their combined efforts, Bonney said, "will exert on the peace and prosperity of the world . . . [a force] beyond the power of human language to describe." Rabbi Dr. Emil Hirsch followed Bonney to the podium and offered a nondenominational prayer for the welfare of all the delegates assembled. Brotherhood noted and human progress extolled, it remained for Catholic Bishop John Keane to offer the final petition for divine guidance and protection as the Parliament's delegates carried the message forth into the light of a new day. The similarities to the biblical Pentecost were too obvious to mention in words. With God thanked and Keane's brief supplication concluded, the entire audience in Columbus Hall rose from their seats and sang in unison "America, the Beautiful."

Even before the Exposition season ended in late October, criticism of the Parliament of Religions mounted around the country. As editor William Stead made plans to come to Chicago and test his Civic Church plan in the city's red-light district and as women delegates to the WCTU convention at the fair journeyed into the Levee to investigate residents "lost to every consideration of purity," editorialists and church leaders began debunking the spirit of the Parliament. Though most religious leaders praised the meeting's idealism and optimism and its effort to bring religion into the debate on great social questions of the time, others were less certain of what had been accomplished. The editors of the *New York Sun* spoke out most emphatically, labeling the Parliament a "polytheistic symposium," which propagated an "agnostic indifference" to truth by bringing Christianity down to the level of lesser faiths.[78]

The Parliament of Religions was faithful to the essence of the World's Congress Auxiliary and to the careful blending of sacred and civil images in the Exposition itself. In its confidence and devotion to the spirit of renewal, the Parliament brought religion to the center of the cultural conversation that informed the Columbian Exposition. Within a comparative setting the Parliament fused religion to a broader program of social regeneration and renewal. In staking a claim for Christianity's relevance to individual and social progress, the Parliament embodied the search for equilibrium that animated all of the reform congresses. Although Dwight Moody measured the enterprise with suspicion, the Parliament's aims and enthusiasms—its faith, one might say—were not so far removed from his own longings for renewal.

Notes

1. *Chicago Daily Tribune* (hereafter *CDT*), 8 May 1893.

2. Henry B. Hartzler, *Moody in Chicago, or the World's Fair Gospel Campaign* (New York, 1894), p. 63.

3. Hartzler, p. 15; James F. Findlay, "Dwight L. Moody, Evangelist of the Gilded Age" (Ph.D. dissertation, Northwestern University, 1961), pp. 334–35; Findlay gives only brief mention to the Chicago revival in his published work, *Dwight L. Moody: American Evangelist, 1837–1899* (Chicago, 1969), p. 401. In his recent book

on Chicago in 1893, James Gilbert devotes considerable attention to Moody's efforts in Chicago. See James Gilbert, *Perfect Cities: Chicago's Utopias of 1893* (Chicago, 1991), pp. 169–207.

4. Findlay, pp. 334; Hartzler, pp. 40–59, quoted on p. 209.

5. *Annual Report of the American Historical Association*, 1893 (Washington, 1894), p. 12; Frederick Jackson Turner, "The Significance of the Frontier in American History," in *Early Writings of Frederick Jackson Turner* (Freeport, N.Y., 1938), pp. 185–229.

6. Turner, pp. 185–229.

7. Edward Bellamy, "Postscript" to *Looking Backward* (1888; New York, 1960), pp. 220–22.

8. For the most recent statement of this theme, see Neil Harris, et al., *Grand Illusions: Chicago's World's Fair of 1893* (Chicago, 1993), a catalog to accompany an anniversary exhibition at the Chicago Historical Society, which lends the Society's imprimatur to the fantasy interpretation. See especially Wym de Wit's "Building an Illusion," pp. 41–98, and Robert W. Rydell's "A Cultural Frankenstein?" pp. 141–70.

9. On the ambivalent or divided allegiances in social thought see Peter Conn, *The Divided Mind: Ideology and Imagination in America, 1898–1917* (New York, 1983); on anti-modernism and nostalgia in social thought see T. J. Jackson Lears, *No Place of Grace: Anti-Modernism and the Transformation of American Culture, 1880–1920* (New York, 1981).

10. Rossiter Johnson, ed., *A History of the World's Columbian Exposition*, 4 vols. (New York, 1898), 4: 8–9, 12.

11. Rossiter Johnson, ed., *A History of the World's Columbian Exposition*, 4:6–7; *World's Congress Auxiliary Organization*, 5 vols. (Chicago, 1890–1893), 1:34–42, 55–56, World's Columbian Exposition Collection, Special Collections Division, Chicago Public Library (hereafter *WCAO*); *Preliminary Publication, Department of Religion* (Chicago, c.1892), Pamphlet File, World's Columbian Exposition Collection, Special Collections Division, Chicago Public Library.

12. For a general consideration of the temperance movement in the nineteenth century, see William Rorabaugh, *The Alcoholic Republic: An American Tradition* (New York, 1979); and on Prohibition, see Joseph R. Gusfield, *Symbolic Crusade* (Urbana, 1956); and James W. Timberlake, *Prohibition and the Progressive Movement* (Cambridge, Mass., 1956).

13. K. Austin Kerr, "Organizing for Reform: The Anti-Saloon League and Innovation in Politics," *American Quarterly* 32 (Spring 1980): 37–53; Kerr, *Organized for Prohibition* (New Haven, 1982); Ruth Bordin, *Women and Temperance: The Quest for Power and Liberty, 1873–1900* (Philadelphia, 1981); Bordin, *Frances Willard: A Biography* (Chapel Hill, 1986); Ian Tyrrell, *Woman's World, Woman's Empire: The Women's Christian Temperance Union in International Perspective, 1880–1930* (Chapel Hill, 1991).

14. *Preliminary Publication, Department of Temperance* (Chicago, c.1892), Pamphlet File, Chicago Public Library.

15. *Daily Columbian*, 5 June 1893; *Chicago Daily Tribune*, 8 June 1893.

16. Willard's letter is reprinted in *Preliminary Addresses, Department of Temperance*, in *WCAO*, 1:364.

17. *CDT*, 7 June 1893.

18. *CDT*, 7 June 1893.

19. Martin Henry Blatt, *Free Love and Anarchism: The Biography of Ezra Heywood* (Champaign, 1989), see esp. pp. 67–99, 111–12.

20. *Programme of the Congress on Social Purity*, in *WCAO*, 5:240; CDT, 7 June 1893.

21. *CDT*, 14 June 1893.

22. *CDT*, 12 June 1893.

23. Robert Crunden, *Ministers of Reform* (New York, 1982).

24. *Preliminary Addresses, Department of Education*, in *WCAO*, 1:667.

25. *Programme of the Civil Service Congress* (Chicago, 1893), Pamphlet File, CPL.

26. *Programme of the Civil Service Congress*.

27. *Programme of the Congress on City Government* (Chicago, 1893), Pamphlet File, CPL; Jane Addams, *Twenty Years at Hull House* (New York, 1960), pp. 150–55.

28. *Programme of the Congress on Peace and Arbitration* (Chicago, 1893), Pamphlet File, CPL.

29. *Programme of the Congress on Peace and Arbitration*.

30. *CDT*, 27 June 1893; see my "The 1893 Labor Congress at the World's Columbian Exposition," *Journal of the Illinois State Historical Society* (Summer 1983): 131–8.

31. Chester McArthur Destler, *Henry Demarest Lloyd and the Empire of Reform* (Philadelphia, 1963), pp. 258–60. Lloyd's own correspondence in the spring of 1893 attests to his growing association with national labor leaders through his role in the Labor Congress. See Microfilm Roll 5, "Correspondence, 1893–1894," The Papers of Henry Demarest Lloyd, State Historical Society of Wisconsin, Madison, Wisconsin.

32. *Preliminary Address, Department of Labor*, in *WCAO*, 2:1045–46; *Programme of the Department on Labor* (Chicago, 1893), Pamphlet File, C.P.L. Several English labor supporters also lent their names to the congress, including William Gladstone, editor William T. Stead, and Henry Cardinal Manning.

33. *Programme of the Department of Labor*; Chester Destler, p. 258; Henry Demarest Lloyd to Samuel Bowles [editor of the Springfield, Mass., *Record*], 13 March 1893; Lloyd to Eltweed [?] Pomeroy, 26 May 1893; Pomeroy to Lloyd, 31 May 1893, Henry Demarest Lloyd Papers.

34. *CDT*, 31 August 1893; "Excepts from News Accounts of the 1891 Convention of the AFL in Birmingham," in Stuart B. Kaufman and Peter J. Albert, *The Samuel Gompers Papers*; vol. 3 (Urbana, 1989), pp. 125–28.

35. *CDT*, 29 August 1893; Samuel Gompers, "What Does Labor Want?" in Kaufman and Albert, eds. *The Samuel Gompers Papers*, 3: 388–96.

36. In 1893, the AFL championed the cause of skilled workers to the exclusion of the mass of nonskilled workers, many of whom were foreign-born. The AFL also denied membership to women and blacks, and in time it would become one of the principal champions of national immigration restriction legislation.

37. For the best accounts of the so-called McGlynn Affair, see Robert Emmett Curran, *Michael Augustine Corrigan and the Shaping of Conservative Catholicism in America, 1878–1902* (New York, 1978); Gerald P. Fogarty, *The Vatican and the Americanist Crisis: Denis J. O'Connell, American Agent in Rome*, vol. 36 of Miscellanea Historiae Pontificiae (Rome, 1974); Fogarty, *The Vatican and the American Hierarchy, From 1870 to 1965* (Stuttgart, 1982), esp. pp. 93–114; John Tracy Ellis, ed., *Documents of American Catholic History* (Milwaukee, 1956), pp. 453–56.

38. *Programme of the Labor Congress; CDT*, 29 August 1893.

39. *CDT*, 30 August 1893; Ray Ginger, *The Bending Cross* (New Brunswick, N.J., 1949), p. 98; Nick Salvatore, *Eugene V. Debs, Citizen and Socialist* (Urbana 1982).

40. *CDT*, 30 August 1893; 31 August 1893.

41. *CDT*, 31 August 1893.

42. *CDT*, 31 August 1893; Anna George deMille, *Henry George, Citizen of the World*, ed. by Don C. Shoemaker (Chapel Hill, 1950), pp. 440–61.

43. *CDT*,31 August 1893; "How to Lend Aid," *Inter-Ocean*, 30 August 1893, in Kaufman and Albert, eds. *The Samuel Gompers Papers*, 3:396–97.

44. *Programme of the Labor Congress; CDT*, 31 August–3 September, 1893.

45. *Programme of the Single Tax Congress* (Chicago, 1893).

46. *CDT*, 4 September 1893. A copy of Ireland's address is in the William J. Onahan Papers, Archives of the University of Notre Dame, Notre Dame, Indiana.

47. Ireland, "The Catholic Church and Labor," Onahan Papers.

48. *Preliminary Publication, Department of Religion* (Chicago, n.d.) in Pamphlet File, C.P.L. In addition to the detailed *Programme of the World's Religious Congresses* (Chicago, 1893) and the *General Programme, World's Religious Congresses of 1893* (Chicago, 1893), the most complete source for the proceedings is *Neely's History of the Parliament of Religions and Religious Congresses of the World's Columbian Exposition*, ed. by Walter R. Houghton, et al. (Chicago, 1894).

49. The most complete recent discussion of the Parliament of Religions is found in Richard Hughes Seager, *The World's Parliament of Religions: The East/West Encounter, Chicago, 1893* (Bloomington, 1995).

50. *Programme of the World's Religious Congresses; Preliminary Publication, Department of Science and Philosophy*, in *WCAO*, 2:935–39.

51. John H. Barrows, *The Results of the Parliament of Religions*, Pamphlet File, C.P.L. Barrows' remarks originally appeared in the September 1894 issue of *The Forum*. See also the *General Programme, World's Religious Congresses of 1893*, p. 19.

52. Robert Peel, *Mary Baker Eddy*, vol. 3: *Years of Authority* (New York, 1977), pp. 48–49.

53. See James R. Gross, Jr., *Fields White unto Harvest: Charles F. Parham and the Missionary Origins of Pentecostalism* (Fayetteville, Ark., 1988); Martin E. Marty, *Modern American Religion: The Irony of It All, 1893–1919* (Chicago, 1986), esp. pp. 208–47; George M. Marsden *Understanding Fundamentalism and Evangelicalism* (Grand Rapids, 1991), pp. 9–61.

54. Michael A. Meyer, *Response to Modernity: A History of the Reform Movement in Judaism* (New York, 1988), p. 276.

55. *Judaism in the World's Parliament of Religions* (Cincinnati, 1894); Meyer, pp. 272–84.

56. *Judaism in the World's Parliament of Religions*, p. v.

57. *Neely's History of the Parliament of Religions*, p. 871.

58. Wise, "An Introduction to the Theology of Judaism," in *Neely's History of the Parliament of Religions*, pp. 96–100.

59. *Judaism in the World's Parliament of Religions*, pp. 1–407; *Neely's History of the Parliament of Religions*, pp. 373–78.

60. Wise, Introduction to *Judaism in the World's Parliament of Religions*, p. viii.

61. For a complete discussion of the Columbian Catholic Congress and Catholic participation in the Columbian Exposition see my article, "Tradition and Accep-

tance: American Catholics and the Columbian Exposition," *Mid-America* 63 (April–July 1981): 79–92.

62. William J. Onahan, "The Columbian Catholic Congress at Chicago," *Catholic World* 57 (April–September 1893): 607. The William J. Onahan Papers in the Archives of the University of Notre Dame contain important information on the planning and execution of the congress; also included are many of the speeches presented by distinguished guests.

63. *The Columbian Catholic Congress of the United States: Daily Programme, Order of Proceedings, Papers, Etc.* (Chicago, 1893), in the Onahan Papers.

64. *CDT*, 6 September 1893; Gerald Fogarty, *The Vatican and the Americanist Crisis: Denis J. O'Connell, Americanist Agent in Rome, 1885–1903*, Miscellanea Historiae Pontificiae, vol. 36 (Rome, 1974), p. 242; Fogarty, *The Vatican and the American Hierarchy From 1870 to 1965* (Stuttgart, 1982), pp. 130–31; *The World's Columbian Catholic Congress and Educational Exhibit*, 3 vols. (Chicago, 1893), 1:44–45.

65. *The World's Columbian Catholic Congress and Educational Exhibit*, 1:105; Gibbons, "The Needs of Humanity Supplied by the *Catholic Religion*," *Catholic World* 58 (October 1893): 1–9.

66. Walter F. Houghton, ed., *Neely's History of the Parliament of Religions and Religious Congresses at the World's Columbian Exposition* (Chicago, 1894), pp. 33–36; Bonney quoted in J. W. Hanson, ed., *World's Congress of Religions: Addresses and Papers* (Chicago, 1894), p. 19.

67. Hanson, p. 19; Houghton, p. 40–41.

68. Douglass's remarks are reprinted in *Neely's History of the Parliament of Religions*, p. 703.

69. Houghton, pp. 438–45; C. B. Tripathi, "Swami Vivekananda, 1863–1894," in *Abroad in America: Visitors to the New Nation, 1776–1914*, ed. by Marc Pachter and Frances Wein (Washington, D.C., 1976), pp. 238–46.

70. Quoted in Tripathi, p. 242.

71. Hanson, pp. 341–535; Charles Prebish, *American Buddhism* (North Scituate, Mass., 1979), pp. 5–6.

72. Quoted in Hanson, pp. 838–39.

73. Quoted in Hanson, pp. 863–67.

74. Hanson, pp. 739–803, 191.

75. Quoted in Hanson, pp. 763–65.

76. Dennis B. Downey, "William Stead and Chicago: A Victorian Jeremiah in the Windy City," *Mid-America* 68 (October 1987): 153–66.

77. Quoted in Hanson, pp. 979.

78. This editorial was reprinted in *Ave Maria Magazine* 37 (July–December 1893): 380.

6

Indian Summer

For an aspiring attorney and erstwhile romantic, the Columbian Exposition was a charmed season by the lake. "When the westering sun set back of the Court of Honor," Edgar Lee Masters wrote four decades later, "gilding with brighter gold the statue of the Republic, or when the sickle moon shone above it, and the air was full of music as the gondoliers pushed their gondolas about its waters, all that was wonderful in life seemed to be realized."[1] Masters recalled sitting for hours at the Midway's Old Vienna cafe, sipping wine and watching the parade of people. For much of the summer his usual companion was a "Minnesota girl" of rare beauty and sophistication named Gertrude. In contrast to his own provincialism, Masters remembers, "She knew Paris and even Constantinople, and in fact she looked foreign, something like a Persian beauty with her tan-colored skin and her tiger eyes." Listening to his poems as her eyes wandered among the passing crowds, she would smile and respond politely, "You are an interesting boy." Though he lost Gertrude to the pectoral splendor of James Corbett, the heavyweight boxing champion who gave daily exhibitions on the Midway, Masters remembered those days as perhaps the "most glorious of my life."[2]

For Hilda Satt, an immigrant Jewish girl who had settled with her family in Chicago during the previous year, the Exposition brought new wonders and excitement. She remembered that after the season began, "Many relatives descended on us at that time. They all came to see the world's fair. Mother improvised beds for us children on chairs so that our guests could have the beds." Her father was able to take one day off work and accompanied family members to Jackson Park. "The wonders of America are as wonderful as the stars," he told his daughter of the nighttime electrical display in the Court of

Honor. "He seemed to take a personal pride in the fair," she wrote years later of her father, "as if he had helped in the planning." "Father kept telling us that the great fair would never be forgotten by those who were fortunate enough to see it."[3]

Edgar Lee Masters and Hilda Satt were not alone in remembering the Columbian season as a time of enchantment and innocence. Despite the harshness of the times, the Chicago fair left on its visitors a remarkably unblemished impression that brought back fond memories years after that Indian Summer of the late nineteenth century had passed. The six-month season not only insulated Chicago from the debilitating effects of a national economic panic—the Depression of 1893—that began with a series of bank failures the very week the Exposition opened, it also instilled a self-congratulatory buoyancy in the city and the nation.

Like all great public attractions, the world's fair became something of a sanctuary, a safe haven from the tumult and contentiousness of a world increasingly assaulted by social and economic problems that summer. Within the friendly confines of Jackson Park, Congress's debate over the Silver Question, the commonplace reports on lynching, and the growing problems of the poor and unemployed seemed, if only for a moment, to belong to another place and time. Perhaps it was the overpowering impression of buildings and statuary, a ride on Ferris's Great Wheel, or the effect of John Philip Sousa's band playing a Stephen Foster melody on the promenade, as fireworks christened the evening sky. In the end, the Columbian Exposition was more than the sum of buildings and exhibits—it was a great festive occasion to experience, an experience that visitors remembered long after the world had moved into another season.

For all of its pretensions to high culture and progress, the Columbian Exposition was also a revealing benediction of popular amusements and distractions. Throughout its six-month season the Chicago fair offered a wide variety of programs and attractions to lure visitors to Jackson Park and then bring them back again. As the numbers show, people did come back time and again during the season to drink in the atmosphere. As the worsening economy took its toll on admission receipts, the Exposition management modified its calendar of events to address financial realities. Recognizing it was imperative to get paying customers through the gates, management adjusted the program of concerts, performances, and what were called special fete days to draw in larger crowds. By August, matters had reached a critical stage, as reports of slackening admissions and potential losses circulated freely in the national press. But by mid-month attendance was on the rise, and the fair seemed rescued from financial calamity. Whether this success was due to strategic planning, good luck, or the arrival of one of the age's most eccentric practitioners of psychic energy was a matter open to debate.

As could be expected of such enormous and widely publicized extravaganzas as the Columbian Exposition, the parade of personalities drawn to the limelight of the enterprise could be as intriguing as the new wonders found in the exhibition halls. The fair played host to royalty and diplomats, celebrities and commonfolk, and in the process served as something of a sideshow melting pot of the curious and the captivating. Among the more than twenty-seven million customers who entered the turnstiles between May and October were some of the most privileged and most peculiar people of the era.

Strolling the broad avenues of Jackson Park or lounging in one of the cafes along the Midway, one might observe a person of note passing by. The arrival of visiting heads of state or members of a royal family was announced in advance, to arouse public interest. In this sense, the fair created its own cult of personality by exploiting the popular interest in celebrities of one kind or another. Newspapers, of course, played an important role in this consuming self-promotion throughout the Columbian season.

After the opening ceremonies, the Duke and Duchess of Veragua stayed for several days of touring, as did members of the U.S. Congress and the Supreme Court. The Austrian Archduke Franz Ferdinand came for two weeks in August, but he generally shunned the limelight. That same month the Rajai of Kapurthala enjoyed the company of Director-General George Davis on a boat tour of the park. Much ado was made over the arrival of His Imperial Highness, Prince Komatsu Yoharito of Japan. Lord and Lady Aberdeen, who had helped sponsor a concession on the Midway, were treated as special guests during their visit, as were the Sultan of Johore and the Greek Patriarch Dionysius Latas. But the greatest attention given a visiting dignitary was reserved for the Spanish Infanta, Princess Maria Eulalia.

Thursday, June 8, was officially declared "Princess Eulalia Day" at Jackson Park, in honor of the visit of the Spanish princess and her husband Prince Antoine. The Infanta and her party had arrived in Chicago the day before and planned to spend a week visiting the city and the fair. To great fanfare, Mayor Carter Harrison escorted Eulalia—Mr. Dooley called her "Princess Oo-la-la"—and her entourage to the park, where she was greeted in a lavish ceremony by Director-General George Davis and other officials. Reporters and sightseers followed her every move as she toured the great halls and the Midway villages. Eulalia seemed especially interested in the exhibits in the Woman's Building, and she made an extensive study of the Spanish parlor. At the Libbey Glass Works on the Midway, a seamstress fitted Eulalia for a special glass-fiber dress. That night the princess and her companions were honored at a private banquet in the Administration Building, attended by Exposition executives and Chicago's leading citizens. Framed against the nighttime illumination of the Court of Honor, a dazzling display of fireworks entranced Eulalia and her friends, as they watched from behind the statue of the *Republic*. After several more days of sightseeing and receptions, Eulalia left Chicago on Wednesday evening, June 15. Bertha Palmer, who hosted a gala reception at the family mansion on Prairie Avenue, recalled that Princess Eulalia's visit was the "social high-light" of the season.[4]

Many a famous personality paid a visit to Jackson Park during the Columbian season. Buffalo Bill, whose "Wild West and Congress of Rough Riders of the World" was situated just west of the park, frequently toured the grounds or appeared at public ceremonies. Bat Masterson and heavy-weight boxing champion Jim Corbett were regulars on the Midway, and Frederick Douglass often was found in the Haitian Building, which he su-pervised. Notables in Chicago theaters also ventured to Jackson Park. Julia Marlowe, Lillian Russell, and the English actors Henry Irving and Ellen Terry toured the grounds while in the city. Literary types such as William Dean Howells, Richard Watson Gilder, and Henry Adams visited more than once, and Hamlin Garland and Henry Blake Fuller were regular pa-trons. Mark Twain apparently got as far as a Chicago hotel before illness forced him to cancel his intended family visit. Thomas Edison, Elihu Thompson, Alexander Graham Bell, Nikola Tesla, and their colleagues in the science congresses willingly surrendered their time to inspect the tech-nological exhibits and the Midway sideshows.

The great and the near-great and the not-so-great of the late nineteenth century found their way to Jackson Park. Herr Pollack, billed as the world's fastest talker, came and stayed, as did George Francis Train, the "great Amer-ican humbug" who served as the model for Phileas Fogg in H. G. Wells's *Around the World in Eighty Days.* The marriage of a "donkey boy" in the Street in Cairo concession merited a wedding announcement in the local papers. Antoine Breasseau (and his dog "Pete") received a hero's welcome for pad-dling a canoe one thousand miles from the Canadian wilderness to the Jack-son Park pier. The chance to see somebody famous, or infamous as the case might be, was but one of the allures of the Columbian Exposition. Chicago's fair was a place to see, and for some it was the place to be seen.

Throughout its six-month season, the Columbian Exposition had more than its share of controversies and conundrums, and it had its lighter mo-ments. Like the time "Lilly," an elephant in Hagenbeck's Animal Menagerie on the Midway, imbibed a pail of beer and got loose on the Avenue of Na-tions. As her handlers pleaded with her and as several young men standing nearby sang "We Won't Go Home Until Morning," Lilly sat down and re-fused to budge for much of the afternoon.[5] In June, the Exposition spon-sored the "Chadron Race," a nine-hundred-mile-long horse-and-rider contest from Chadron, Nebraska, to Buffalo Bill's arena near the fair-grounds. A fantastic publicity stunt, which involved such colorful characters as "Rattlesnake Pete" and "Doc Middleton," the contest dissolved into chaos amid complaints from the humane leagues, condemnation by Gover-nor John Altgeld, and cheating by several of the riders. By the time John Berry arrived atop "Poison" on June 27 to win the race, several riders had been disqualified and officials wondered if anyone had abided by the rules.

The Chadron Race was front-page news for nearly two weeks, rivaling Altgeld's decision to pardon the remaining Haymarket anarchists and news of Lizzie Borden's murder trial in Massachusetts.[6]

More serious was Lucy Guffin's experience on the Movable Sidewalk in August. A native of Rushville, Indiana, Guffin apparently was pushed by the rush of the crowd off the pier platform and into the rough waters of the lake. No one saw her fall or heard her cries for help above the noise of the electric engines. She clung to a pylon for what seemed hours until a longshoreman spotted her and dove to her rescue. The *Chicago Daily Tribune* said she was "nearly dead" when retrieved and taken to a local hospital, where she was revived.

Criminal mischief was a concern throughout the season, and the nearly four thousand Columbian guardsmen hired for crowd control were also to be on the lookout for any suspicious activities. At one point during the season, three hundred men were employed in a Secret Service Bureau to clear the grounds of "criminals and bad characters." The bureau's final report showed they had identified 135 ex-convicts on the grounds, and 400 persons had been "put off" the grounds for petty crimes and vandalism. Throughout the season, agents had "shadowed" some 539 suspicious persons, and there was one case of a "Zulu acting improperly." Thirteen hundred children were reported lost or missing while visiting Jackson Park. The Medical Bureau reported that thirty-six people had died, most often from skull fractures, at Jackson Park during the season, as compared to the thirty-two laborers who were killed by accidents during the construction of the fair.[7]

Perhaps the Exposition's greatest tragedy occurred at mid-season, on July 10, when the Cold Storage Building near the Court of Honor burned to the ground. Twenty-four city fire companies joined the Exposition's force in battling the flames, which leaped twenty feet above the roof line and engulfed the large tower, trapping at least two men inside. Within minutes of the first alarm's sound, the building appeared to one spectator as a "seething furnace," and before the conflagration was extinguished a dozen firefighters and one civilian had lost their lives. Insurance companies covered only half the $250,000 loss, and another $100,000 was raised in a private subscription to aid survivors and their families.[8]

Early speculation suggested faulty electrical wiring was the problem, but an official investigation quickly focused on more sinister motives. In August the *Tribune* reported that a local Chicago gang had deliberately set the blaze to disguise their routine pilfering of Exposition food supplies. Members of the Blue Island gang, who were employed on the fairgrounds, apparently had been stealing for months, and fearing their mischief would be discovered they ignited the building to destroy all evidence of their crime.[9]

Matters of public health and hygiene were never far removed from management's scrutiny. Cholera and typhoid fever scares were common in large cities in the late nineteenth century, and Chicago was not alone in its continuous battle for clean drinking water. To avoid a public health crisis,

Exposition directors shunned the municipal water supply and contracted with Hygeia Mineral Springs Company to pipe in pure water from springs near Waukesha, Wisconsin, to more than five hundred taps and booths in the park. Patrons willingly paid a penny a glass for the privilege of drinking safe water, or they could receive free filtered water from the one hundred fountains placed in the park by the Pasteur-Chamberland Filter Company of Ohio. The Exposition relied on city water for all other needs.[10]

Similar concerns about smallpox attended the arrival of the Midway villagers, and throughout the season Exposition directors routinely tested the inhabitants for fear of the deadly pox. Almost coincidental with the onslaught of the economic depression, an outbreak of smallpox, which some associated with the fair, swept through the city and over a year's time claimed twelve hundred lives.[11] Exposition officials were astute enough to realize that real or rumored outbreaks of epidemics would have an adverse effect on ticket sales, which were already sluggish because of the worsening economy.

The Exposition was not immune to the labor troubles that gripped the nation in the summer of 1893. During the first week in May, amid accusations of ticket scalping by Columbian guardsmen and price gouging in some cafes and restaurants—the White Horse Inn was accused of selling ten-cent beers for thirty-five cents, and pieces of pie for a half-dollar—labor disputes threatened to shut down several concessions.[12] Hundreds of Columbian guardsmen threatened a walkout over what they thought were less-than-generous wages: $60 a month in May, which was reduced in August by $10 because of the depressed economy. The Union of White Waiters engaged in a short-lived job action to protest low wages and what it judged to be unfair labor practices, and American women hired as cashiers and barmaids in the Turkish Village objected to the style of uniform required by the restaurant management. Some found the bloomer-style pants "horrible and hideous" and unbecoming to a proper lady, and the women insisted that unless the uniform was changed they would go out on strike.[13] Such disputes clearly did not rival news of instability on Wall Street, or even the failure of branch banks in the Exposition's Administration Building, but one controversy in the first week did have significant repercussions.

Another tussle that erupted before the Exposition opened was the "Sunday Rest" issue. Some Christian denominational leaders joined a group called the Sunday Association in protesting management's decision to open the fair on Sundays. Sunday was the day of Christian rest, but it was also the one day of the week on which many laborers did not have to report for work. Especially when the national economy began to weaken, management sought to exploit every opportunity to increase revenues.

While some ministers saw the fair as a sign of God's presence, others worried that if given a choice congregants would elect to go to the fair rather than to morning church services. The clash between cultural and commercial values seemed inevitable, and compromise seemed fruitless. Newspapers, magazines, and national organizations of every persuasion got into the fray, and eventually the entire matter wound up in federal court.

May 28 was the first Sunday the fair stayed open, with John Philip Sousa's band and an evening fireworks display the featured attractions; one newspaper headline read "Softly Did Sousa's Band Play 'Nearer My God, To Thee.'" Debate continued throughout May, as litigants went to court and ministers delivered Sunday sermons for and against the opening.[14] On Saturday, June 10, the Supreme Court suspended a Circuit Court order that closed the gates on Sundays, and the following Saturday the federal Court of Appeals issued a unanimous decision that since the fair was not a "charitable trust," opponents could not prevent its opening seven days a week.[15] Although the arguments persisted into August, the court ruling effectively decided the issue, but not without hard feelings on both sides and a lingering suspicion that commerce had won out over Christian piety.

Another public controversy had far-reaching consequences for the fair and for its ambitious program of orchestral and choral concerts. It was also the first act in a larger drama that led to the resignation of Theodore Thomas as the fair's Director of Music. The "piano wars," as the incident became known, was more than a contest of wills over musical tastes. Behind the scenes, commentators saw anew the tension between the cultural and commercial agendas that resurfaced throughout the Exposition's program.

In addition to serving as the Director of Music, Theodore Thomas was the nation's preeminent orchestral conductor and head of the recently formed Chicago Symphony Orchestra. It is useful to know that the same civic leaders who brought Thomas to Chicago to lead the fledgling symphony also recruited him to oversee the Exposition's music program. For his labors with the fair, Thomas received $1,000 per month.

Theodore Thomas was given a free hand to recruit the most famous and most appropriate soloists, bands, and orchestras to perform at Jackson Park. His professional mission for several decades had been to bring "serious" European classical music to an American audience, and with Daniel Burnham's blessing he conceived of the Exposition as an excellent opportunity to advance the cause. Assisted by W. L. Tomlins, the director of Choral Music, and George Wilson, the secretary of the Music Bureau, Thomas was remarkably successful in bringing under contract some of the finest national and international musicians and singers to perform at Jackson Park.

Unfortunately, financial constraints and public indifference to what Thomas called "good music" undermined his ambitious educational program, forcing the Bureau of Music to adopt a series of more popular musical concerts. As the season advanced, rousing marches and sentimental ballads became the order of the day, much to Thomas's disappointment. Although classical music concerts were still presented, under financial pressure the Exposition bowed to popular tastes.

Adolph Liesegang's Chicago Military Band, Michael Brand's Cincinnati Band, and John Philip Sousa's band were given the most lucrative contracts of the nearly two dozen orchestras and bands that performed at the fair. Before the series of concerts was severely curtailed in August, the Columbian Exposition spent more than $250,000 on its musical program, half of which went to pay the expenses of Thomas's Columbian Orchestra and its soloists. Owing to the enormous difficulty of coordinating the ambitious schedule and the public disinterest in highbrow music, the Bureau lost approximately $90,000 on its series of nearly two hundred concerts and recitals.[16]

To inaugurate the Exposition's concert series, Theodore Thomas retained the renowned international pianist Ignace Jan Paderewski. Paderewski, who would later serve Poland as prime minister, was the closest approximation to a matinee idol to appear on the Exposition stage. In their world's fair editions, *Puck* and *Halligan's Illustrated Weekly* enjoyed lampooning Paderewski, with his youthful appearance and long, stylish hair, and the crowd of young women who seemed ever present. "In an age worshiping the virtuoso," one historian of the piano has written, "Paderewski was the virtuoso extraordinaire." The *Tribune* spoke admiringly of Paderewski and the "tenderest melodies drawn from the soul of the piano of the long-haired wizard" during the May 2 concert in the as yet unfinished Music Hall.[17]

Paderewski had been well received during a performance two years earlier at Chicago's Central Music Hall, and Thomas was aware of his tremendous following among the city's Polish and East European communities. It was not Paderewski's presence that created the problem during the first week of the Exposition; it was the brand of piano he elected to use in his concerts that created a serious rift. Reflecting the at-times uneasy relationship between artistic and commercial interests in Victorian culture, the "piano war" brought unwelcome attention to one of the Exposition's more evident dualisms. What for Theodore Thomas and Jan Paderewski was a matter of artistic freedom was for certain exhibitors a horrendous breach of etiquette. When politicians and editorialists entered the fray, it was a prescription for certain disaster.

During his 1893 American tour, which included his performances at the Exposition, Paderewski had a licensing agreement with the Steinway Company that obliged the artist to use only that manufacturer's piano. What complicated the arrangement was the decision by Steinway and other eastern manufacturers not to exhibit at the Columbian Exposition, believing that western firms had rigged the judging to favor themselves. When Paderewski took the stage for the inaugural concert, Kimball of Chicago and other exhibitors immediately protested the pianist's use of a Steinway on the Music Hall stage. No matter that at the age of thirty-two Paderewski was generally regarded as the world's most accomplished pianist, and quite a catch for the Exposition. There were business principles at stake.

In the showdown, Thomas sided with his soloist and claimed artistic discretion, while exhibitors mounted a compelling brief to the National Commission. By the time the issue was settled against Paderewski and Thomas, the soloist had left Chicago in a huff and canceled a benefit concert in New York due to exhaustion. Theodore Thomas was dispirited and embarrassed amid calls for his resignation from hostile Commissioners; Kimball and other exhibiting manufacturers were ebullient. Cartoonists found much to satirize about the episode, and for the next month the Chicago newspapers continued to harp on problems within the Bureau of Music. Joseph Keppler inked one of the more famous caricatures for the cover of *Puck*. It showed the likeness of Paderewski playing no fewer than a half-dozen pianos at once. The caption to Keppler's sketch read: "A Peaceful Solution—at the next World's Fair Paderewski will play on all the pianos at once."[18]

Throughout June and July, Thomas and his assistants continued to spar with the National Commission, which routinely interfered with Thomas's authority as Music Director. Incident upon incident further distanced Thomas from the management of the Bureau of Music, and the decision to cut short the full program of classical concerts in favor of lighter fare was the last straw. In June, the National Commission demanded Thomas's resignation, a move that the Board of Directors opposed, but by mid-July Thomas had left Chicago for his home at Fairhaven in Massachusetts. Several weeks later he forwarded an official letter of resignation as Director of Music. Thomas's most recent biographer has suggested that the great conductor never quite recovered from the "debacle" of the fair, and though he returned in the autumn to resume his duties with the Chicago Symphony Orchestra, he refused several invitations to return to the Exposition.[19]

In September, Thomas wrote a frank letter to one of the directors, acknowledging the unfortunate consequences of the previous three months. "It is a great pity," Thomas told James Ellsworth, "that the plans of the Music Bureau could not have been carried out—I fear the outcome, and the untimely end will do much harm to the cause of good music in this country, and encourage vulgarity . . . all because of low and small politicians and vulgar newspapers [which] influenced the Directors against the [bureau?]."[20]

Charles McKim echoed Thomas's sentiments in a letter to Daniel Burnham. "As for this row about Theodore Thomas," McKim said in criticism of the Commission, "it is simply disgusting and an eternal reflection upon the selfishness and narrowness of some men. . . . It is a blot on our civilization that such men as he do not receive the recognition to which their genius and efforts of a lifetime entitle them."[21] Thomas and McKim each thought this episode another example of commercialism's triumph over artistic sensibilities in America.

Despite the Music Bureau's trials and tribulations, Thomas and his associates promoted a wide spectrum of musical tastes and traditions to their Exposition audience.[22] The Bureau sponsored nearly two hundred concerts and performances. In addition, several dozen dramatic plays and operettas were staged in the outdoor theater and in Festival Hall. Nothing exotic was included in the Exposition's program of musical and dramatic performances; the shift from classical to popular music suggested the caution that governed the Bureau's decisions. There were European and American vernacular influences, and patriotic and military music was a regular feature of the concert program. As one might expect, nostalgic ballads and to a lesser extent religious hymns seemed to be the order of the day, reflecting the period's popular tastes. Similarly, in the several theatrical productions at the outdoor theater, nothing more adventuresome than Shakespeare was performed.

In accommodating popular musical tastes, the Exposition also made a conscious appeal to the burgeoning ethnic communities around the city. Thomas solicited the best American bands and orchestras and prominent European orchestras. There is no evidence, however, that the Bureau of Music made any gesture to include African-American ensembles, continuing the pattern of racial discrimination pervading the so-called White City. By including the growing ethnic populations, albeit to serve the fair's bottom line, while excluding talented black bands and orchestras, the musical program reflected important cultural barriers in American life. Perhaps unknowingly the musical program, like other features of the Exposition, reflected the growing if begrudging respectability of foreign-born white inhabitants in the social compact and the continuing marginalization of African Americans.

Of all the music groups retained for the season, none proved more popular than John Philip Sousa's band. Sousa's ensemble, the stepchild of his years with the Marine Corps Band, could play a spectrum of arrangements and styles from military marches and classical suites to Stephen Foster folk melodies and current popular tunes. Sousa was a natural for the Exposition program, and the Exposition was a natural venue for the band.

Throughout June, Sousa presided over a series of evening concerts that drew thousands of enthusiastic fans to the Court of Honor pavilion. People enjoyed the marches, and they tolerated the classical pieces intermixed with more contemporary offerings. But as Sousa recalled in his autobiography, the Exposition audiences took greatest pleasure in singing along to the popular songs of the era. "After the Ball" and "Old Folks At Home" and "Suwanee River" were frequent requests, indicating the appeal of sentimental ballads in public programs of the period. Traditional Protestant hymns also struck a responsive chord. Romantic innocence and religious longings, one might say, still resonated through the culture as a basis for community. One new song that Sousa was regularly asked to perform was "America, the Beautiful." Evoking images of pastoral abundance and providential reward, "America, the Beautiful" became in Sousa's hands the unofficial anthem of the Exposition.[23] It would appear that John Philip Sousa was more in touch with popular tastes than Theodore Thomas.

"The night air was cool and still," wrote the *Chicago Herald* of Sousa's farewell concert on the evening of June 27, "and when the leader mounted the stand to open the closing concert, he was met with loud cheering." For several hours the band went through its regular fare, interspersed with requests from an audience estimated at more than twenty thousand fans. Sousa seemed as willing as the crowd to let the concert continue past the appointed hour, and it was not until 10:30 P.M. that he raised his baton for the final encore. With the audience joining in, Sousa's band bid farewell to the Exposition with a rousing rendition of the tested folk melody "Auld Lang Syne."[24]

The bureau was more successful in engaging American bands and choral groups than it was at attracting prominent European orchestras, which balked at the expense of traveling to Chicago. The Russian Orchestra was paid $2,700 for its performance in the Music Hall, seven hundred dollars more than either the Boston Symphony Orchestra or the New York Symphony Orchestra received. Although Thomas was unable to persuade Brahms, Rubinstein, or Tchaikovsky to perform at the Exposition, he did manage to secure the talents of other European artists. There was, of course, Paderewski; there was also the great Czech composer Antonin Dvorak.

In 1893, Chicago had more people of Czech (or "Bohemian") descent than another city in the world except Prague. According to the *Tribune*, an estimated ten thousand people turned out to greet Dvorak when he visited the Exposition on Saturday, August 12, the featured artist on what was called "Bohemian Day." Born near Prague in 1841, Dvorak only recently had come to the United States as Director of the National Conservatory of Music in New York. "In disposition he is modest and retiring," said the *Tribune* in announcing Dvorak's arrival in Chicago, "and does not look near as fierce as would be supposed from his picture. . . . His genius is of the heroic order—bold and venturesome." The paper regretted that Dvorak would not meet Theodore Thomas, who was at Fairhaven preparing his resignation letter. Despite the fact that they did not meet, Thomas has been credited with having done more than anyone else to popularize Dvorak's work in the states.[25]

Dvorak, who had not yet completed his *Symphony from the New World* (1894), was the principal conductor in an afternoon program in Festival Hall. A crowd of eight thousand fans applauded for more than two minutes when the composer entered the hall and stepped before the Columbian Orchestra. The concert included several of Dvorak's *Slavonic Dances* and his Symphony no. 4 in G Major, which the *Tribune* said was "considered a severe test of technical writing as well as playing." Professor V. I. Hlavac followed Dvorak to the podium and led the orchestra through several spirited folk pieces popular with what the paper called "Bohemian-Americans." Hlavac also accompanied on the organ the United Bohemian Singers of Chicago as they sang the "Bohemian Chorale" and the "Star-Spangled

Banner." Late in the afternoon, thousands of people gathered in the open-air Live Stock Pavilion to watch a series of athletic contests among various fraternal clubs,[26] the conclusion of the day's program.

Following his duties as conductor, Dvorak met with leaders of the Chicago ethnic community, then toured the fairgrounds before returning to New York. At some point, he gave an interview to the *Tribune* that caused a stir in highbrow circles. In a column titled "For National Music," the paper quoted Dvorak as stating that "in the negro melodies we find a sure foundation for a national school of American music." He suggested that the roots of an authentic American musical tradition were to be found in the Negro spirituals and, to a lesser extent, in American Indian chants. Dvorak explained to the *Tribune* how much he had been influenced by a young pupil, presumably black, from St. Louis, who had written a number of "Creole Dances" (in the spirit of Dvorak's own nationalist works). Unaware of any controversy his words might create, Dvorak spoke candidly of the influence on his work of these lesser-known musical elements. He also hinted that a new work in progress—what would become the "New World" Symphony—would reflect his growing appreciation for an American folk idiom.[27]

Perhaps unintentionally, Antonin Dvorak's comments transgressed the boundaries between elite and folk culture. But his more cosmopolitan sensibilities also ran contrary to the *educational* philosophy of the fair's own music department, which traced America's musical heritage to West European antecedents. Furthermore, and most controversial, Dvorak's statement contradicted reigning racial stereotypes of the day, ones firmly embedded in the cultural symbolism of the "White City" itself.

"Bohemia Day," as the newspaper termed it, was not unusual in its celebration of one of the country's many ethnic communities. Despite the designers' devotion to the theme of unity in the Exposition ensemble, the proliferation of "nationality days" reflected the growing ethnic and cultural diversity of the nation. The challenge, of course, was to successfully incorporate elements of pluralism into the larger patriotic and celebratory themes of the Exposition program. While advancing assimilationist interests—not only in the Exposition but in the wider culture it represented—the schedule of nationality days also unwittingly gave voice to divergent forms of expression that coexisted within the Exposition ensemble. By promoting a degree of inclusiveness that might otherwise have been absent in the Exposition, the fete days acknowledged the reshaping (or redefinition) of national identity at century's end. More than a sideshow melting pot, the Exposition came to reflect the increasingly cosmopolitan nature of society in an age of unprecedented immigration.

The most ambitious ploy to draw more paying customers to Jackson Park was to expand a limited program of special events to include a wide variety of nationality, state, and city days. In addition to a celebration of Czech and Slovak cultures, days were reserved for Italians, Swedes, Austrians, the Irish,

Germans, the Polish, Russians, and other European ethnic groups. Twenty-five thousand Poles turned out for "Polish Day" on October 7, a day marked by parades and floats, musical concerts and speeches, and even a wedding at Jackson Park.[28] Costa Rica, Brazil, and several other non-European countries were also accorded the special status on the Exposition calendar. African and Asian peoples were less prominent in the schedule of fete days.

Every state in the union had its own day at the fair, as did major American cities. More than 280,000 paying customers visited the fair on July 4, "United States Day," and on August 24 over 240,000 came out for "Illinois Day." But the day that surpassed all other days at the Columbian Exposition and drew more paying customers than any other single day at any previous international exhibition was "Chicago Day" on October 9. Coinciding with the anniversary of the 1871 Great Fire, Chicago Day drew a staggering 756,000 people (40,000 complimentary passes were issued) to Jackson Park. Over the following days nearly one million additional people paid a visit to the Exposition. By comparison, throughout the entire month of May, the Exposition had attracted only 1,050,000 paying customers. City schools and businesses closed for the day, and several hundred thousand people turned out for a grand civic parade celebrating Chicago's meteoric rise over a generation's time. At the fairgrounds, the Mormon Tabernacle Choir headlined an afternoon concert in Festival Hall. The day ended with a brilliant nighttime fireworks display in the Court of Honor.[29]

Engineers, Odd Fellows, Sportsmen, Foresters, Railwaymen, Catholics, and even some visiting dignitaries had their special days at the fair. "Grand Army of the Republic Day" (September 9) saw thirty thousand veterans of the Union Army gather in the Court of Honor for the first ringing of the facsimile Columbian Liberty Bell. (A similar courtesy was not extended to veterans of the Confederate Army.) For August 30, "Poet's Day," Shakespeare's *As You Like It* was staged in the Sylvan Dell.[30] When the Spanish Caravels arrived from Barcelona on July 7, followed by the docking of the Viking Ship five days later, the fair rolled out the red carpet with extravagant ceremonies. Management continued to expand its list, including multiple celebrations on the same day, trying to be as inclusive as possible and leave no potential paying customer out.

No one, that is, except Native Americans and African Americans, who were initially denied their own day in the schedule of events. There was never even a consideration of whether the native peoples of North America should have a special day to acknowledge their contributions to the development of the nation. Three years after the massacre at Pine Ridge, the failure even to think of recognizing the culture and talents of Native Americans in the program of the Columbian Exposition reinforced the "invisible" character of America's most marginal group.

It was only after a stinging protest organized by Ida B. Wells that management relented and designated Friday, August 25, as "Colored Americans

Day" at Jackson Park. When it became apparent that black Americans would be denied even the most minor role at the Columbian Exposition—no black person served as a waiter or waitress or a member of the Columbian guardsmen—Wells, the noted antilynching crusader from Memphis, enlisted the cooperation of Frederick Douglass and other prominent African Americans to protest the "lily-white" ambiance of the White City. With Douglass contributing the introduction, Wells published a biting assault on the racism of the management entitled *The Reasons Why the Colored American Is Not in the World's Columbian Exposition*. Twenty thousand copies were printed for distribution in August, and she advocated a boycott of "Colored Americans Day" when it was added to the schedule.[31]

"The exhibit of the progress made by a race in twenty-five years of freedom," Wells wrote in her pamphlet, "as against two hundred and fifty years of slavery, would have been the greatest tribute to the greatness and progressiveness of American institutions which could have been shown to the world." While denouncing racism and the commonplace occurrence of lynching, the pamphlet castigated the Exposition management for refusing to appoint one black person to any position of influence in the fair. Of the Exposition, Wells wrote that African Americans "saw in this great event their first opportunity to show what freedom and citizenship can do for a slave," but instead they were treated as "personae non grata" by every executive officer and the Board of Lady Managers. "Theoretically open to all Americans," Wells concluded, "the Exposition practically is, literally and figuratively, a 'White City,' in the building of which the Colored American was allowed no helping hand, and in its glorious success he has no share."[32]

The proposed special day to acknowledge the accomplishments of African Americans divided the nation's black leadership, with some favoring Wells's call for a boycott and others arguing this opportunity should not be squandered.[33] Though he wrote an eloquent introduction to Wells's pamphlet, Frederick Douglass did not join in her call for a boycott of "Colored Americans Day," which some white editorialists ridiculed as "Darkies' Day." Colored Americans Day enjoyed none of the fanfare accorded other ethnic celebrations, and the local press showed little enthusiasm for the modest program of events. On the appointed day, the *Tribune* gave no special notice to upcoming festivities at the fairgrounds, and its article summarizing what occurred was buried on page three of the Saturday edition. Douglass later concluded that Wells had been correct in her assessment, as Colored Americans Day failed to elevate the stature of the race. It did lead, however, to one of the most passionate if little-known speeches of Frederick Douglass's brilliant career.

At 2:30 P.M., the only formal feature of the day's celebration began in Festival Hall. An interracial audience of some twenty-five hundred persons gathered for a program of music, literary recitations, and public orations. The Fiske Jubilee Singers entertained the audience with a medley of plantation songs and spirituals. Prominent black vocalists Madame Deseria Plate and J. Arthur Freeman performed a selection of classical and popular works. Paul Laurence Dunbar, a young and as yet unknown poet from Dayton, Ohio, read several of his poems, including "Colored Americans." Joseph Douglass, an accomplished classical violinist and a descendant of the most famous African American in the world, performed several classical pieces. But most everyone had come to hear Joseph's grandfather, and as Frederick Douglass emerged onto the stage at three o'clock, the crowd burst into spontaneous applause.[34]

As the applause quieted and Douglass began his prepared address on "The Race Problem in America," several white youths in the hall began to heckle the aging crusader. Douglass departed from his prepared text and for more than half an hour spoke eloquently of the burdens of slavery and the tragedy of inequality in America. "Men talk of the Negro problem," Douglass thundered. "There is no Negro problem. The problem is whether the American people have loyalty enough, honor enough, patriotism enough, to live up to their own Constitution." Douglass silenced his critics while cutting to the heart of the issue that tarnished American society and its great world's fair.[35]

Ida Wells praised Douglass for his speech and begged his forgiveness for her criticism of his lack of support for the boycott. But Colored Americans Day came and went with no lasting effect on race relations, and Frederick Douglass's observations were soon forgotten, to be replaced in time by the more deferential pleas of Booker T. Washington. Two years later at the Atlanta Cotton States Exposition, Washington's counsel that blacks "cast down their buckets" while acknowledging their secondary status was more in keeping with the emerging system of Jim Crow social segregation, which the Supreme Court would find permissible the next year in *Plessy v. Ferguson* (1896).

Frederick Douglass had died several months earlier in 1895. Washington's words were a betrayal of everything Douglass had fought for since he fled slavery on Maryland's Eastern Shore in 1838. Washington's philosophy of race improvement also contradicted Douglass's courageous oration at the White City in the summer of 1893. Some fairgoers remembered that there were more than the usual number of Jackson Park vendors who sold watermelons on August 25 (*Puck* printed a cartoon to that effect), and few black people seemed to have entered the turnstile on Colored Americans Day. Had observers stopped to think about it, they might have found a relationship in the juxtaposition of the two developments.

In many respects August was a make-or-break month for the Exposition. Management was still beleaguered with litigation over the Sunday Closing issue, and the worsening economy had discouraged millions from attending the fair. By late July, the *Chicago Times* was estimating that unless daily paid admissions averaged 184,000 for the rest of the season, the fair would be a financial failure. Given that combined daily attendance in the first three months had averaged less than 99,000, this seemed an impossible task. By early August, Theodore Thomas had had his fill of the National Commission and submitted his formal resignation from Fairhaven. When concertmaster Max Bendix took over the orchestra, he—contrary to Thomas's wishes— supervised a program of popular music concerts for another month, until the effort was abandoned. To the Board of Directors it must have appeared that everything was happening at once, and much of it at the Exposition's expense. If these irritants were not enough, in early August what had been a nuisance since opening day erupted into an enormous public altercation.

"War has at last begun on the disreputable dives in Midway Plaisance masquerading under the names of 'dancing theaters,'" the *Chicago Herald* reported in its August 5 edition. In a development carried in newspapers all over the country, the Board of Lady Managers had lodged a protest the previous day with Director-General George Davis and Director of Works Daniel Burnham, demanding that the Persian Theater complex be shut down. The *New York Times* informed its readers that the Lady Managers were incensed by the "immorality of the performances," but the *Herald* went further, explaining how these Midway theaters appealed to the "depraved of both sexes." In response to complaints from the Board of Lady Managers, the WCTU, and other groups, the Exposition ordered the Persian Theater closed to the public "until such time as the dancing part of the programme should be revised and approved by the censor."[36]

At issue were the several Midway theater concessions—the Turkish Village, the Street in Cairo, and the Persian and Algerian Theaters—that featured scantily clad young women performing provocative dances to exotic music and ever more enthusiastic crowds. Complaints about the establishments had circulated since mid-May. Marietta Holley's fictional "Samantha" said "them Persian dancin' girls carry dancin' clear to the very verge of indecency, and drop way off over the verge. . . . I see lots of wimmen comin' out with their fan held before their blushin' face." "Mildred Berry," a character in the novel *Sweet Clover*, said of the "naked savages" in the Midway theaters: "to listen to them yell, and see 'em dance, is a mighty queer thing for Christians to seek for entertainment."[37]

What complicated the Midway theater controversy was that many people, Christian or not, did seek out and enjoy such entertainment. The theaters represented a pleasure principle, a suspension of reality, that was at the heart of the Midway's appeal. On the Plaisance, cultural restraints were loosened, if only temporarily, and what was judged impermissible elsewhere was suddenly brought to life with startling immediacy. In years to come, Dream Land, Steeplechase, and Luna Parks on Coney Island, as well as less well established traveling carnivals and circus sideshows, would remind cultural critics why sightseers had flocked to the humbug, irreverence, and license of the Midway. The Persian Theater's manager understood the attraction and asked reporters following the order to close, "If my place is indecent, why do they [lady managers] come here in parties one, two, three—yes, six times—and sit for one, two and sometimes three hours to see my girls—my pretty girls—dance?"[38]

Were the Midway performances good-natured fun or portents of some darker rhythms in culture? Were they liberating or licentious, harmless or deviant? No one denied the appeal of exotic foreign dancers on the Avenue of Nations, but there was growing concern about the propriety of the shows within the context of Victorian conventions and sexual mores. Temperance women who visited the theaters and left aghast made note of the close proximity of alcohol to the Midway dives. Both the Street in Cairo complex and the Persian Theater were directly across from the German Village and its beer garden. Beyond the Midway, reformers warned repeatedly that the saloon and the dance hall were cooperating in the ruination of Christian society. Eventually no man, and especially no woman, would be safe from the devil and the nefarious "Pit." The "lure of the dance," as one popular account of social impurity phrased it, would lead participants "from the Ball Room to Hell!"[39]

While Davis and Burnham accepted responsibility for curbing the excesses, they were aware that along with the Ferris Wheel these theaters brought in greater concession revenues than all other Midway venues combined. By the Exposition's own count, the Street in Cairo exhibit generated more than $150,000 for the fair coffer on total receipts of nearly $800,000. By comparison, the Ferris Wheel, which ran for only two-thirds of the season, gave the Exposition over $200,000 on receipts of $733,000.[40]

Even though the early August theater controversy overshadowed life on the Midway, it did not cast a pall on other happenings along the Plaisance. Crowds continued to flock to the Ferris Wheel, where long lines of patrons waited for their chance to touch the sky. What Denton Snider called the great wheel's "deep suggestiveness" was best captured by the fictional "Samantha," who remembered:

Wall, my feelin's when I wuz a-bein' histed up through the air wuz about half and half—half sublimity and aw as I looked on the hull glory of the world spread at my feet, and Lake Michigan, and everythin'—that part wuz clear riz up and noble, and then the other half wuz a skittish feelin' and a-wonderin' whether the tacklin' would give way, and we should descend with a smash.[41]

No other amusement or concession challenged the majesty of "the Wheel," and its wonder was replicated at county fairs and amusement parks for generations to come. George Ferris's technological novelty succeeded beyond expectations once opened in late June, with more than a million and a half passengers riding the wheel by season's end. Visitors enjoyed rummaging through the Blarney Castle and Sitting Bull's log cabin, and the International

Beauty Contest at the eastern end of the Plaisance regularly attracted large crowds. Many, like Edgar Lee Masters's friend Gertrude, enjoyed the pugilistic performances of Gentleman Jim Corbett in the Midway boxing arena. Children and adults delighted in the unusual menagerie of intelligent beasts corralled in Professor Hagenbeck's zoo. "Darling Lilly," the elephant with an affection for hops, was neighbor to donkeys who played baseball, tropical birds that enjoyed a game of poker or progressive euchre, and an assortment of animals that performed tricks for the amused audience. The Ice Railway, the Captive Balloon ride, and the Electric Theater each enjoyed healthy business, but none came close to the financial rewards or popular enthusiasm showered on the Midway's great wheel.

If the Ferris Wheel was the most profitable Midway concession, without a doubt the greatest objects of curiosity were its semipermanent residents in the international villages. Donkey boys in the Street in Cairo, Bedouin horseman in the "Wild East Show," Samoan warriors and American Indians, supposed cannibals from Dahomey, and the dancing girls in the Oriental theater—the "Midway types" as they were known in the popular press—evoked to the fictional "Clara Bryant" a "babel of tongues, a baffling concatenation of noises and odors, a dizzying throng of sensations and emotions" unlike anything one might imagine.[42] When the financial picture looked so bleak, the management exploited the lure of the Midway's "polyglot peoples" and invited one of the great eccentrics of the day to preside over the occasion.

On the very day the Lady Managers "declared war" on the Midway theaters, the *Chicago Record* announced in a bold headline: "Train to the Rescue."[43] George Francis Train, known to a generation as "Citizen Train," was one of the most unusual individuals to walk the face of the earth. Variously hailed as a financial wizard, champion of human rights, defender of women and children, and a declared lunatic bent on self-aggrandizement, Train had enjoyed a long public career in which fact and fiction blended to the point where no one, not even Train, could tell the difference. He came to Chicago in August 1893, with a convoluted scheme to save the fair that relied on innovative financing, aggressive marketing, and the application of his own psychic energy.

In the late nineteenth century, a growing number of Americans were convinced electricity (mechanical and mental) had a curative power and that under proper conditions a well-regulated voltage could "renew" the body and the spirit. Citizen Train believed that he possessed a reservoir of mental electricity that, if properly applied, could produce a desired effect. He explained to a reporter that he never shook hands with anyone, for fear that it would deplete his reserve.

Few took the self-defined "globe trotter and magnificent prophet" seriously, but Train told reporters he had consented to go to Jackson Park and do his part to turn around the fair. On the surface, Train had been asked to host two weeks of athletic contests and social events involving the residents of the Midway. This was the cover for a more serious responsibility—the exertion of psychic energy to reverse sluggish ticket sales. George Francis Train seemed the ideal match for the exotic villagers, who were ripe for further exploitation.[44]

With Citizen Train as chief judge, the Exposition management promoted a series of events billed as primitive confrontations among the uncivilized races of the world. Loaded with racial and ethnic stereotypes, these contests were promoted for their amusement value. Train presided over a kite-flying competition between Japanese and Javanese villagers, an international tug-of-war, ceremonial dances by American Indians and South Sea Islanders, the first-ever international swim race at a world's fair, and an international canoe regatta. There was also a contest among "fat men," who walked across a greased pole suspended thirty feet above the basin for the prize of a large bologna sausage.

At the north lagoon regatta held on the afternoon of August 15, Train sat in a launch with Director-General George Davis and Jat Jat Jit Sing, the Rajai of Kapurthala. Kayaks, birch canoes, seal boats, and sampans lumbered toward the finish line as Midway residents and other spectators on shore cheered for their favorites. The *New York Times* said the Rajai and the estimated seventy-five thousand other onlookers enjoyed watching the Midway "savages" in what amounted to the most unusual scene ever to grace the waters at an international exhibition.[45]

The crowning event of the exploitation of Midway types came the next evening, in the form of an International Ball in the Natatorium Building on the Midway. What the *Tribune* lampooned as the "Ball of Midway Freaks" gave the Exposition's cosmopolitan pretense new meaning. Promptly at 9:15 P.M., a Mexican band struck up a march tune. Suddenly from atop the staircase Citizen Train appeared in a white duck coat and an armful of sweet peas to proclaim, "All men are brothers!" His companion for the evening was a "dusky" ten-year-old Mexican girl named Donna Nita, who was dressed as a ballet dancer.[46] "Psycho at the Front," reported the *Chicago Times*. With Exposition officials and invited guests watching from balcony seats, more than seven hundred Midway residents followed Train down the staircase and about the hall in a grand international march. Participants were dressed in colorful native attire, and over the next several hours they feasted on an exotic fare: "Roast Missionary" from Dahomey, "Monkey Stew" from Hagenbeck's zoological menagerie, and "Fried Snowballs" courtesy of the Ice Railway. An evening of dancing followed the sumptuous banquet, complete with music from the assembled countries and a Christopher Columbus waltz, a Lady Commissioner's schottische, and a Caravel reel. Spectators were charged twenty-five cents to watch what the *Tribune* dubbed "the strangest gathering since the destruction of the Tower of Babel."[47]

In many respects, the International Ball of Midway Types was Citizen Train's swan song. He seems not to have participated in the Psychic Congress, which met in the Memorial Arts Building during his stay, but he managed to drop in on the Midway's impromptu "Congress of Incongruous Men," which convened beneath a shade tree to debate the Silver Issue, causes of poverty, and the worsening economy.[48] In the afterglow of his ceremonial visit, Train departed the Columbian Exposition in late August and faded into obscurity. He died in 1904 from complications brought on by nephritis. Few took seriously Citizen Train's faith in psychic energy and his imaginative scheme to rescue the fair. For most people who bothered to pay attention, he was, like his Midway compatriots, an object of curiosity and amusement.

But almost coincidentally with Train's arrival at Jackson Park, things began to improve. By the end of August, Exposition officials had a renewed confidence that the fair might see a profit (eventually more than $400,000), and admission rates improved steadily from early August into October. More than twice as many people visited the fair in the period of August through October than had attended in the first three months of the season, and in October alone almost eight million customers entered the turnstiles.[49] (See Table 6.1.)

This marked improvement can be dated from the first week in August, the week George Francis Train arrived with his grand schemes and simple faith in the power of the mind. In a manner that would not have surprised him, Citizen Train was given no credit for this remarkable turnaround. Was Train the foolish eccentric tolerated for the humor he provoked, or was there something to this gentle soul who walked the avenues of Jackson Park rubbing his hands together, his balding forehead slightly aglow? Was he but one of the many humbugs and confidence men drawn to the glitter of an international exhibition, or did he single-handedly save the century's greatest world's fair from certain disaster? This was the stuff of which legends, and lunatics, were made.

After the controversies and uncertainties of August had passed, the Exposition settled into its final months with renewed vigor. With admissions improving and greater revenues coming in from increased ticket sales and brisk business in the Midway concessions, it appeared that the Chicago fair would escape the financial losses that had plagued almost every other world's fair since the 1851 Crystal Palace Exhibition in London. Even as the national economy faltered, the fair flourished. There were rumors the management might extend the Exposition season by several months, perhaps another year, if public interest could be sustained. Congress's original charter for a six-month season, however, and opposition from the South Park Board that supervised Jackson Park persuaded the Board of Directors to close in late October, as originally planned.[50]

One indication of the late-season success of the Columbian Exposition was the tremendous turnout for Chicago Day on Monday, October 9. Im-

TABLE 6.1 World's Fair Balance Sheet

TOTAL RECEIPTS	$28,787,532.80
TOTAL DISBURSEMENTS	$28,340,770.44
BALANCE	$ 446,832.36

MONTHLY ADMISSIONS	
May	1,531,984
June	3,577,834
July	3,977,502
August	4,687,708
September	5,808,942
October	7,955,551

Complimentary Passes Issued:	6,059,380
Paid Admission:	21,480,141
TOTAL	27,539,521

KEY DAILY ADMISSIONS	
May 1 (Opening Day)	137,557
July 4 (America Day)	330,542
October 9 (Chicago Day)	761,942
October 30 (Closing Day)	252,696

Source: [Harlow Higinbotham], *Report of the President to the Board of Directors of the World's Columbia Exposition* (Chicago, 1898), pp. 339–54, 402–9.

bibing the Exposition's commemorative and patriotic agendas, three quarters of a million people participated in Jackson Park's celebration of the host city. Chicago Day's paid admissions were three times greater than those of the busiest day at the 1876 Centennial Exhibition, and it surpassed by fifty percent the largest crowd at the 1889 Paris Universal Exposition. The only blemish on the otherwise ebullient occasion was the report that four people had been killed in the crush of the crowd at the Alley L station near Jackson Park. But ignoring the tragedy, the self-congratulatory rhetoric remained to the end. "Chicago Day," declared the *Daily Columbian,* "will pass into history as the greatest peace festival known to the annalists of the world's civilization."[51]

The last days of the Exposition season were played out against Congress's spirited debate on the repeal of the 1890 Silver Purchase Act, internecine feuding in city politics, and the close of the last sessions of the Congress

Auxiliary. Women attending the WCTU conference created headlines when they took their campaign for reform into Chicago's nefarious Levee and retreated to the fairgrounds, professing to be "shocked" by the pervasive misery and sin in the Exposition's backyard. On Saturday, October 28, the newspapers announced that Marshall Field had pledged one million dollars to create a permanent Columbian Museum in the Palace of Fine Arts after the Exposition closed. That same day, Mayor Carter Harrison hosted a gathering of the nation's mayors for "Mayors Day" at Jackson Park.[52]

On Sunday, October 29, the *Tribune* printed a larger than usual edition, with a special supplement chronicling the events of the Exposition season. Chicago had already appropriated as her own Charles Dana's mocking tribute of 1890—"Windy City"—and the supplement was meant to show that the city had lived up to its large promises and great expectation. Themes of national exceptionalism, patriotism, and civic pride informed the articles, as they had the event it summarized. One page carried a series of sketches highlighting the special days of the season, with a poem entitled "Uncle Sam Talks It Over":

> We're comin' to an end of it. The fellers want to go.
> We've had a grand old frolic, but its time to close the show.
> My western boys have beat the world, ther' ain't no sort of doubt,
> But I'm gittin' purty tired, and I swan I'm tuckered out. . . .
> So put your things on, Columby. It's nearly time to go,
> We'll have the blaze of glory now, and then we'll close the show.
> The boys is gittin' tired and we're all in need of rest,
> But the world has learned a lesson from Chicago and the West.[53]

The Exposition, however, ended with anything but a "blaze of glory." That same issue of the *Chicago Sunday Tribune* carried the news that Mayor Carter Harrison had been assassinated at his home on Saturday evening, shortly upon his return from the fairgrounds. After being granted admission to the mayor's home on Ashland Boulevard, a disgruntled office seeker named Eugene Patrick Prendergast had argued with Harrison and then shot him three times. The assailant fled the scene but later turned himself in at the local precinct house. Attended by a neighborhood physician and his two grown children, Harrison died within twenty minutes of being shot, before his beloved fiancée Annie Howard could reach his side. As a measure of his devotion, Harrison seemed to those around him to be concerned only for his betrothed; his last word before death was "Annie!" "It was thought best not to move the remains," the *Tribune* explained in a somber tone, "and there on the study floor he who closed his door to none lay dead last night with her who was to have been his bride weeping passionately by his side."[54]

This was hardly the note on which to launch the "new era" so identified with the fair. Monday, October 30, had been designated "Columbus Day" at Jackson Park, with festive ceremonies planned to bring the world's fair full circle. But in deference to mourning rituals around the city, Exposition management canceled the program in favor of a more subdued memorial service. There was no joy that day, and a "frigid character" pervaded Music Hall. Clarence Eddy played Chopin's "Funeral March" on the great organ, and Chicago's political and financial leaders, many of whom had played a role in the fair, eulogized Carter Harrison and expressed their sorrow in his passing.[55] Social and civic organizations around Chicago passed resolutions honoring the mayor and expressing deep regret for his family's and the city's loss.

Tragedy was not the note on which Exposition directors hoped to conclude their festival of progress. Rather, they hoped for some fitting ceremony to rival the pomp and circumstance of opening day, when they had launched the Exposition upon a sea of uncertainty. But news of Carter Harrison's death temporarily eclipsed what had been accomplished in Chicago in the summer of 1893.

If readers of the Monday—Columbus Day—issue of the *Tribune* had managed to turn to page seven, they would have found a summation fitting to the occasion, one that Edgar Lee Masters and Hilda Satt would echo years later in their separate remembrances. In his assessment of the achievement at Jackson Park, one of the country's leading custodians of culture offered a reverential testament to the "wonders" of the Columbian Exposition. His words foreshadowed the judgment his Altrurian Traveller would give to the season of renewal on the shoreline of Lake Michigan.

"It is the greatest thing that ever came into my life," William Dean Howells told a reporter of the Chicago world's fair. "It gives verity and value to everything. . . . There never was and may never be again anything so beautiful."[56] Despite the incongruities, contrasts, and controversies that informed this season of renewal, few visitors dissented from Howells's remembrance of that summer by the lake.

Notes

1. Edgar Lee Masters, *A Tale of Chicago* (New York, 1933), p. 251.

2. Edgar Lee Masters, *Across Spoon River: An Autobiography* (New York, 1936; reprint edition, 1969), pp. 168–71.

3. Hilda Satt Polacheck, *I Came a Stranger: The Story of a Hull-House Girl*, ed. by Dena J. Polacheck Epstein (Urbana, 1991), p. 40.

4. *Chicago Daily Tribune* (hereafter *CDT*), 5–16 June 1893; Rossiter Johnson, ed., *A History of the World's Columbian Exposition*, 4 vols. (New York, 1897), 1:409–10.

5. "Lilly Finds a Pail of Beer," *Chicago Record*, 8 May 1893.

6. *CDT* and *Chicago Record*, 14–28 June 1893.

7. In Daniel H. Burnham, "Final Report of the Director of Works," 8 vols. (Chicago, 1894), 7:1–42, 72–74, Daniel Hudson Burnham Papers, Art Institute of Chicago.

8. "Report of the Columbian Fire Company," in Burnham, "Final Report of the Director of Works," 8:53–62.

9. *Chicago Sunday Tribune* (hereafter *CST*), 13 August 1893; *CDT*, 11 July 1893; *NewYork Times*, 4 August 1893; Benjamin Truman, *History of the World's Fair* (Chicago, 1893), pp. 80–81.

10. "Report of the Engineer of Water Supply, Sewerage and Fire Protection," in Burnham, "Final Report of the Director of Works," 2:71–73; Michael P. McCarthy, "Should We Drink the Water?: Typhoid Fever Worries at the Columbian Exposition," *Illinois Historical Journal* 86 (Spring 1993): 2–14.

11. See Robert W. Rydell, "A Cultural Frankenstein?: The Chicago World's Columbian Exposition of 1893," in Neil Harris et al., *Grand Illusions: Chicago's World's Fair of 1893* (Chicago, 1993), pp. 166–69.

12. *CDT*, 3 May 1893, 10 May 1893.

13. "Wall Street in Panic," *CDT*, 5 May 1893; "Object to Bloomers," *CDT*, 5 May 1893.

14. *Chicago Herald*, 29 May 1893.

15. "Suspends the Writ," *CST*, 11 June 1893; "Gates Will Be Open," *CST*, 18 June 1893.

16. William Ackerman to James Ellsworth, Memorandum entitled "Total Cost of Music," 7 October 1893, Special Collections Division, Chicago Public Library; George Wilson to Ellsworth, 27 July 1893, CPL. Wilson, "Final Report, Bureau of Music" (Chicago, 1894), Special Collections Division, Chicago Public Library. On Thomas's career, see Theodore Thomas, *A Musical Autobiography*, 2 vols., ed. by George Upton (Chicago, 1905); Ezra Schabas, *Theodore Thomas: America's Conductor and Builder of Orchestras, 1835–1905* (Urbana, 1989); Lawrence W. Levine, *Highbrow/ Lowbrow: The Emergence of Cultural Hierarchy in America* (Cambridge, Mass., 1988), esp. pp.85–242.

17. Craig H. Roell, *The Piano in America, 1890–1940* (Chapel Hill, 1989), p. 7; *CDT*, 3 May 1893.

18. The caricature is reproduced in Richard Samuel West, *Satire On Stone: The Political Cartoons of Joseph Keppler* (Urbana, 1988), pp. 420–21.

19. George H. Wilson to James W. Ellsworth, 29 June 1893; Wilson to George Davis, 20 July 1893, James Ellsworth Papers, Special Collections Division, Chicago Public Library; Schabas, *Theodore Thomas*, pp. 209–12; Theodore Thomas, *A Musical Autobiography*, ed. by George Upton, 2 vols. (Chicago, 1905), 1:195; *Minutes of the Board of Directors, World's Columbian Exposition*, 6 June 1893, Chicago Historical Society.

20. Theodore Thomas to James W. Ellsworth, 24 September 1893, James W. Ellsworth Papers.

21. Charles Follen McKim to Daniel Burnham, 18 May 1893, Charles Follen McKim Papers, Library of Congress.

22. George H. Wilson, "Final Report, Bureau of Music" (Chicago, 1894), Special Collections Division, Chicago Public Library.

23. John Philip Sousa, *Marching Along!: Recollections of Men, Women and Music* (Boston, 1941), pp. 129–38.

24. *Chicago Herald*, 28 June 1893.

25. "Dvorak Has Arrived," *CDT*, 12 August 1893.

26. "Bohemia at the Fair," *CST*, 13 August 1893.

27. "For National Music," *CST*, 13 August 1893.

28. *CDT*, 8 October 1893; Johnson, 1:452–53.

29. "Red Letter Days," *CDT*, 13 October 1893; Truman, *History of the World's Fair*, p. 609; *CDT*, 10 October 1893; Johnson, 1:453.

30. Johnson, 1:440–42,;432; *The Columbian Exposition and World's Fair Illustrated* (Philadelphia, 1893), p. 2.

31. Ida B. Wells, *The Reason Why the Colored American Is Not in the World's Columbian Exposition* (Chicago, 1893). Douglass's Introduction was reprinted in Philip S. Foner, *The Life and Writings of Frederick Douglass*, 4 vols. (New York, 1955), pp. 409–77.

32. Wells, *The Reasons Why*, pp. 12, 63–79.

33. Elliot M. Rudwick and August Meier, "Black Man in the 'White City': Negroes and the Columbian Exposition, 1893," *Phylon* 26 (1965): 354–61.

34. "Appeal of Douglass," *CDT*, 26 August 1893; Rossiter Johnson, *A History of the World's Columbian Exposition*, 4 vols. (New York, 1897), 1:430.

35. "Appeal of Douglass," *CDT*, 26 August 1893. Douglass's involvement in the Columbian Exposition is also touched on in William S. McFeely's *Frederick Douglass* (New York, 1991), pp. 370–72.

36. *Chicago Herald*, 5 August 1893; *CDT*, 5 August 1893; *New York Times*, 5 August 1893.

37. Marietta Holley, *Samantha at the World's Fair* (New York, 1893), p. 622; Clara Louise Burnham, *Sweet Clover: A Romance of the World's Fair* (Boston, 1894), p. 200.

38. *Chicago Herald*, 5 August 1893.

39. T. A. Faulkner, *The Lure of the Dance* (Los Angeles, 1913).

40. [Harlow Higinbotham], *Report of the President to the Board of Directors of the World's Columbian Exposition* (Chicago, 1898), pp. 482–91.

41. Holley, *Samantha*, p. 620.

42. *Sweet Clover*, pp. 26–27. Several popular portrait books of Midway residents sold during and after the Exposition season. Two of the more comprehensive collections were *Portrait Types of the Midway Plaisance* (St. Louis, 1894), and *Chicago Times Portfolio of the Midway Types* (Chicago, 1893).

43. *Chicago Herald*, 4 August 1893.

44. For a brief account of Train's life and exploits, see Dennis B. Downey, "George Francis Train: The Great American Humbug," *Journal of Popular Culture* 14 (Fall 1980): 251–61.

45. *CST*, 27 August 1893; *New York Times*, 16 August 1893.

46. *CDT*, 11 August 1893.

47. *Chicago Times*, 17 August 1893; *CDT*, 17 August 1893.

48. *CST*, 13 August 1893.

49. [Harlow Higinbotham], *Report of the President* (Chicago, 1898), pp. 339–54, 402–9.

50. *CDT*, 26 October 1893. The agreement with the Commission and the City of Chicago required that the Exposition corporation return use of Jackson Park on or before January 1, 1894.

51. *Chicago Herald*, 12 October 1893; *Daily Columbian*, 11 October 1893; *Chicago Record*, 10 October 1893.

52. *CDT*, 23–28 October 1893. The museum became known as the Field Museum of Natural History, which later relocated to a new building at the south end of the Loop. The Fine Arts Building, the only Exposition structure to survive, then became home for the Museum of Science and Industry.

53. *CST*, 29 October 1893.

54. *CST*, 29 October 1893.

55. *CDT*, 30–31 October 1893.

56. *CDT*, 30 October 1893. Howells's comments were given to the *New York Sun* and reprinted in the Chicago paper.

Epilogue

"It seemed to me," Edgar Lee Masters wrote in his autobiography, *Across Spoon River*, "that there were wild wails in the air when the White City burned one night just as the gates were closed for good. It was late fall and cold; and in the parks the leaves were drifting down. A kind of autumn was in my feelings, for at last the carnival time was over; and a new and rather unhappy time was setting in."[1] Actually it was January that Masters remembered, but though he got his months confused, the poet's personal feelings bore more than an incidental resemblance to the cultural mood of America in the years following the Columbian Exposition.

The World's Columbian Exposition concluded in an atmosphere not characteristic of world's fairs. Carter Harrison's death and the worsening economic depression cast an ominous shadow over the celebration of progress at Jackson Park, and the brilliance of the White City seemed suddenly clouded by the darkening realities of the times. What was conceived originally to be a celebration of the four hundredth anniversary of Christopher Columbus's discovery of the New World had been refashioned into a summary statement of the range of material and cultural progress in America *since* that first encounter. That it should end on such a somber note was not what the managers had in mind. As the failing economy sobered their loftier expectations, plans to keep the Court of Honor and the major exhibition halls intact as a great civic center were abandoned. The Palace of Fine Arts would alone be preserved as a permanent museum, and the remainder of the structures at Jackson Park were to be sold for their scrap value. But with credit conscripted, the buildings sat idle and abandoned for months.

On the evening of January 8, 1894, a fire broke out in the Casino at the eastern end of the Court of Honor, and before it was extinguished the conflagration had engulfed the Peristyle and the Music Hall. Flames leapt across the promenade to the Manufactures and Liberal Arts Building, destroying a large portion of the roof and the foreign exhibits still within its walls.[2] In late February, as the economic depression descended on Chicago, a second fire erupted in the Court of Honor, destroying the colonnade between the Palace of Mechanic Arts and the Agriculture Building.

Five months afterward, on the evening of July 5, 1894, a third conflagration erupted, destroying what remained of the once majestic Court of Honor. Although it was never proven, some officials speculated that disgruntled workers angry with the city's tactics in the Pullman Strike had intentionally set the blaze. The Chicago Wrecking and Salvage Company, which had purchased the salvage rights for $100,000, suffered an enormous loss. Within a year, the White City, which had inspired a sense of wonder and had come to symbolize a generation's hopes for the future, lay in ashes, a charred victim of the times.

The winter of 1893–94 was a particularly difficult period for Chicago and the nation. Declining productivity and rising unemployment exacerbated conditions in the city, and without the buffer of the fair, Chicago slid full-force into depression. Many of the social problems illuminated by the reform congresses took on a striking immediacy, with depleted relief stations and legions of the unemployed and homeless wandering city streets. William Stead, the English journalist and reformer who had contributed the "Civic Church" paper to the Parliament of Religions, arrived in Chicago after the fair closed and roamed its streets for months. Stead strolled the Levee interviewing inhabitants and promoting his campaign for civic regeneration, and he made a copious study of city property and tax records. In March 1894, Stead published the results of his investigation into Chicago's moral character in a sensational book entitled *If Christ Came to Chicago*. Detailing the extent of social impurity and political corruption, Stead's tome foreshadowed the emerging genre of muckraking literature that would become popular in years to come. A source of scandal and embarrassment within the city, *If Christ Came to Chicago* offered a view of Chicago quite contrary to the image promoted in the Columbian Exposition.[3]

Perhaps the best indication of how dramatically the mood in Chicago had changed since the fair came in the form of labor violence during the summer of 1894. The Pullman Strike in July pitted Eugene Debs and the American Railway Union against the power of George Pullman and the nation's railroad executives. The Pullman Strike, which brought federal troops into Chicago to protect the property of the Pullman Palace Car Company, ignited emotions for and against the interests of workers and gave startling testimony to the explosive character of the Labor Question debated a year earlier in the Congress on Labor.

For all of the contentiousness and turmoil that engulfed the city after the close of the Columbian season, few doubted the positive effects of the world's fair. In celebrating the material, industrial, and artistic accomplishments of Chicagoans and other Americans, the 1893 world's fair became a great comparative laboratory—a "College of Democracy"—by which to judge the present aspect of national life. Furthermore, in its range of material and human "encounters" the Exposition brought Europe to America and America to Europe on a scale never before realized. More than a sideshow melting pot or simplistic expression of capitalist hegemony in the industrial age, the Chicago's world's fair was a symbol—a cultural moment, if you will—that embraced the main currents and conflicting tendencies of the age. It also set a standard by which all subsequent international exhibitions would be judged.

The Exposition not only mirrored the culture of its time; it impelled into being the commonplaces of a "new era." From the Ferris Wheel to electricity, and from a model kitchen with instant breakfast cereals to the ordnance of modern war, the 1893 world's fair offered intimations of a world being born. The intellectual reform congresses reflected the currency of traditional values, while revealing new forms of expression that would shape public discourse and private values in the years ahead. Temples of technology and palaces of pleasure coexisted that summer by the lake, and their collective impression would linger for generations to come.

For Daniel Burnham and the consulting artists and architects, the Columbian Exposition secured lifelong friendships and added immeasurably to their collective effort to fashion a new vision for urban-industrial America. "You gave me a beautiful time," Charles Follen McKim wrote Daniel Burnham in late October 1893, "and the last days of the Fair will always remain in my mind, as were the first, especially identified with yourself. It will be pleasant for the rest of our natural lives to be able to look back to it and talk it over and over and over again, and it goes without saying that you can depend on me in everyway [sic] as often hereafter as you may have need of me." Like any people who have struggled through a great cause together, the experience created a strong emotional bond among the designers. McKim, who initially had declined Burnham's invitation to join the effort, ended his letter of friendship with an unexpected expression of gratitude for Frank Millet: "Give my love to Frank Millet," he asked of Burnham.[4]

Such gestures of fraternal devotion were not uncommon among the consultants, and in the years to come several of them collaborated on important civic projects, though none as extravagant as the Chicago world's fair. Burnham went on to become the preeminent city planner of the early twentieth century. He traveled the world developing plans for municipal growth for cities as different as San Francisco and Manila. His 1909 Plan of Chicago (with Edward Bennett) remains the archetypical example of modern urban planning, the embodiment of the City Beautiful Movement and Progressive Architecture. In the years following the Exposition, before encountering personal and professional misfortune, Louis Sullivan emerged as the prophet of modernism to a younger generation of architects like Frank Lloyd Wright and Walter Gropius and theorists like Sigfried Giedion and Lewis Mumford.

The Chicago industrialists and financiers who invested in the Columbian Exposition were not disappointed, financially or professionally. The fair managed a profit of almost a half-million dollars, a rarity among international exhibitions; simply to have broken even would have been an accomplishment. Many of the officers of the Exposition Corporation went on to distinguished careers in banking, finance, and corporate development. Lyman Gage assumed an important role in national affairs, serving as William McKinley's Secretary of the Treasury, and James Ellsworth, like others, succeeded in diverse ventures. The names Armour, Field, Palmer, Higinbotham, and Wacker have become synonymous with Chicago's commercial and cultural ascendancy.

Chicago artists and literary figures also found a measure of advantage, or at least creative encouragement, in the Columbian Exposition. The laurels earned in 1893 blossomed into what Sherwood Anderson called a "Robin's Egg Renaissance," which later critics would judge, if not an American Renaissance, then certainly a Chicago Renaissance in arts and letters. Shortly after the fair closed, Hamlin Garland and other writers formed a club, "The Cliff Dwellers," which promoted literary and artistic sensibilities in the city. Although each would leave Chicago eventually, Hamlin Garland, Edgar Lee Masters, Ben Hecht, Charles McArthur, Floyd Dell, and Theodore Dreiser stayed long enough to participate in the cultural awakening that was fueled by the Exposition. Harriet Monroe started *Poetry Magazine* and helped to introduce the world to the talents of Vachel Lindsay, Ezra Pound, and T. S. Eliot.[5] Chicago became an artistic mecca in the decades after the Exposition, attracting pensive writers and poets, aspiring painters, and practitioners of innovative musical sounds from the Deep South. Although Dwight L. Moody's career came to an end shortly after the Exposition season, his apprentice Billy Sunday went on to take his mentor's place as the foremost evangelist of his generation.

In the years following the 1893 Chicago world's fair, it was as if the world moved into a different season. By 1933, when Chicago hosted another international exhibition, the Century of Progress, "a kind of autumn" had settled over the landscape. Not only was the nation in the midst of the worst economic decline in its history, the anticipated "new era" so confidently awaited in 1893 had not arrived, at least not in the manner or form expected. In the four decades that separated the Columbian Exposition and the Century of Progress—White City and the Rainbow City—much of the technological wizardry of 1893 became commonplace. Electricity, the automobile, the telephone, the motion picture projector, and an array of machines had been adapted to the most basic of human tasks. A burgeoning middle class and its consumer comforts became a more representative feature of American society, and new avenues of leisure and recreation hinted at on the Midway were now regular features of urban culture. But the new technology also facilitated a startling acceleration in the pace of life, much as Henry Adams anticipated in his ruminations on the dynamo. The wondrous machines not only allowed for expanding possibilities and comforts, they seemed in their own way to accelerate the fragmentation of community that Adams had glimpsed that summer by the lake.[6]

In the years following the Columbian Exposition, public discourse—a cultural conversation—betrayed a fascination with what might be called the vogue of the "New." One heard much talk of the "New Woman," the "New Negro," and the like to complement changes in other spheres of life and learning. Modernist sensibilities challenged traditional notions of gender, race, and even sexuality, sometimes with disconcerting consequences.[7] Old conventions and stereotypes could prove remarkably resilient in the facing notions of equality and citizenship.[8]

In architecture and the arts, in an understanding of human psychology and behavior, in historical writing and in literary and biblical criticism, critics revealed an affinity for novel approaches and new modes of expression. The impact of scientific methodology and terminology provided a sense of immediacy and relativism to enlightened discourse on human nature and social reform issues. In the realm of science, the New Physics broke fresh ground in an understanding of the time-space continuum. Perhaps the most dramatic example of the vogue of the New was Sigmund Freud's disquisitions on the subconscious. Like Freud's speculative inquiry, the architecture of Frank Lloyd Wright, the Pragmatism of William James, and Albert Einstein's theory of relativity each in its own way reflected the subtle yet substantial departure from older forms and habits.

If one were to examine the features of public discourse in the "new era" between Chicago's fairs, one would find, too, a significant shift in sensibilities. The "autumn" of which Edgar Lee Masters wrote was reflected in the character of social thought, as it was in the features of social life. With the advent of Modernist forms and beliefs, the cultural conversation took on a more somber and deterministic tone than that of the 1890s. A younger generation of social critics and novelists spoke more often of the "discontinuities" of mass culture, and they talked more often of the need for "social reconstruction." In their preoccupation with themes of "crisis" and "authenticity" and in their rejection of the certainty of established authority (paternal and institutional), these same critics were attempting to secure some new principle on which to base personal and social relationships. In their world, as numerous writers have pointed out, personal experience became the point of departure for a social critique profoundly at odds with traditional conventions and forms. Less apparent in the postwar era was the optimism that had informed the harbingers of progress in 1893, replaced by an embrace of a "tragic view of life." The hopeful confidence of Edward Bellamy's

Looking Backward or even William Dean Howells's Altrurian civic life, was now cast into doubt by a younger and less certain generation. "Here was a new generation . . . ," F. Scott Fitzgerald wrote of his contemporaries in *This Side of Paradise*, "dedicated more than the last to the fear of poverty and the worship of success; grown up to find all Gods dead, all wars fought, all faiths in man shaken." Indicative of the mood, in 1919 Henry Adams's *The Education of Henry Adams* was awarded the Pulitzer Prize.[9]

Literary and artistic expression in the postwar era demonstrated the extent to which the "darker side of modernity" now challenged themes of exceptionalism and progress. It is perhaps revealing that in 1933, the year Chicago hosted the Century of Progress, American critics were rediscovering *The Education of Henry Adams* and its author's gloomy foreboding about mass society. Even if critics failed to discern the depth of Adams's reservations about the coming society, they nonetheless found it fashionable to invoke the pessimism they associated with his lament on the Virgin and the Dynamo.

"The First World War," John Dewey explained of the new sensibility,

was a decided shock to the earlier period of optimism, in which there prevailed widespread belief in continued progress toward mutual understanding among peoples and classes, and hence a sure movement to harmony and peace. Today, the shock is almost incredibly greater. Insecurity and strife are so general that the prevailing attitude is one of anxious and pessimistic uncertainty. Uncertainty as to what the future has in store casts its heavy and black shadow over all aspects of the present.[10]

Dewey's contemporary and fellow critic Lewis Mumford evoked similar imagery of a center that no longer held. "The period through which we are living presents itself as one of unmitigated confusion and disintegration . . . a period whose evil fulfillments have betrayed all its beneficent promises," Mumford wrote in *The Condition of Man*. "Behind all these phenomena of physical destruction," he continued, "we can detect an earlier and perhaps more fundamental series of changes: a loss of communion between classes and peoples, a breakdown in stable behavior, a loss of form and purpose in the arts, with a growing emphasis on the accidental and the trivial . . . and a break up of the over-all pattern of meaning."[11] Although social thought continued to embrace themes of renewal and regeneration, one can scarcely imagine a more startling contrast to the public speculations about a "new era" surrounding the Columbian season.

As the designers of the Columbian Exposition forged the appearance of unity in the common ensemble at Jackson Park, the designers of the Century of Progress reflected the theme of diversity in the eclectic assemblage of structures clustered along the lake. Perhaps unintentionally they also exhibited a greater sense of discontinuity in their architecture. Whereas some saw the exhibition's eclecticism reflecting cultural diversity, Henry Adams might have found this a measure of the triumph of multiplicity over unity.

For all of the differences of appearance, the Century of Progress had much in common with the Columbian Exposition. Traveling down the central boulevard and coursing through the exhibition halls, visitors were able to escape, if only for a day, the humdrum and hardship of Depression-era America. There was the innovative technology and the accustomed attractions to inspire people's fantasies and lift their spirits. Sally Rand, fan in hand, excited the imagination as Fatima as her companions had so many summers before, and the twin-towered Sky Ride with its miniature zeppelins connected to high-tension wires was an obvious bow to the Ferris Wheel. Where the giant locomotive engines had dominated the 1893 transportation exhibits, in 1933 Buckminster Fuller's Dymaxion car suggested interesting possibilities for future automobile engineering. Where the Columbian Exposition had dazzled visitors with its display of electricity, the Century of Progress offered an innovative display of the possibilities of atomic energy. In the spirit of previous international exhibitions, the Century of Progress cast its eyes to the future.

On the five hundredth anniversary of Christopher Columbus's encounter with the New World, few reminders of the World's Columbian Exposition remained. Across the nation and in Chicago a forceful and contentious civic debate did ensue, however, on whether a suitable remembrance was appropriate in 1992. One indication of how far Columbus's star had fallen and how much the cultural mood had shifted in a century was the city's decision not to host another commemorative exposition. Few civic leaders could be persuaded that the potential benefits of another world's fair would outweigh the great costs involved in such an undertaking. Furthermore, the very mention of Columbus could elicit impassioned denunciations of the contested meaning of his maiden voyage.

Though one of the four stars on the flag of the City of Chicago honors the 1893 fair, few citizens are aware of the fact. Jackson Park has been re-landscaped, and the grounds do not resemble the manicured lawns of a century ago. The Palace of Fine Arts still stands at the north end as the Museum of Science and Industry, but most visitors are unaware of its original purpose. The Ho-o-den Temple (a gift of the Japanese government) stood on the Wooded Island until vandals destroyed it in the early 1940s; all of the other buildings and statuary were destroyed or removed to other locations.

A smaller facsimile of the *Republic* stands on an isolated path on the edge of Jackson Park. The statue is badly neglected and in need of a fresh coat of gold leaf. Motorists who do not stop to read the memorial plaque would not know that the tarnished figure was once a part of the greatest cultural event in the city's history.

The aged *Republic*'s facsimile stands as a fitting commentary on an event and an age now left to memory. Once it symbolized the dreams and expectations of a generation of Americans who confidently awaited the golden age of a "new era." As the potent symbol of renewal, this gilded image of maternal strength and national purpose was the centerpiece in an artistic ensemble meant to reconcile the conflicting tendencies that informed the cultural landscape. Now the *Republic* stands alone by the lake, its arms uplifted and its eyes cast across the sprawling city and the prairie beyond. But the force of the statue's symbolic meaning is lost, as the world of the Columbian Exposition has passed from the scene. The Exposition's memory lingers, however, as does the hope of renewal it sought to capture so many seasons ago.

Notes

1. Edgar Lee Masters, *Across Spoon River: An Autobiography* (1936; New York, 1969), p. 172.

2. France was among the nations whose exhibits were damaged in the January fire; over a year passed before the Exposition management and the exhibitors reached a financial settlement.

3. William T. Stead, *If Christ Came to Chicago* (Chicago, 1894). For a consideration of Stead's campaign and the reaction within Chicago, see Dennis B. Downey, "William Stead and Chicago: A Victorian Jeremiah in the Windy City," *Mid-America* 68 (October 1987): 153–66.

4. Charles Follen McKim to Daniel H. Burnham, 23 October 1893.

5. For an overview of the so-called Chicago Renaissance, see Bernard Duffey, *The Chicago Renaissance in American Letters: A Critical History* (Westport, 1972). On the flight of midwesterners to the cultural mecca of Greenwich Village, see Christine Stansell, *American Moderns: Bohemian New York and the Creation of a New Century* (New York, 2000), esp. pp. 11–72.

6. See William D. Miller, *Pretty Bubbles in the Air: America in 1919* (Urbana, 1991), esp. pp. 209–18.

7. Nancy F. Cott, *The Grounding of Modern Feminism* (New Haven, 1987); Stansell, *American Moderns*, pp. 225–310; Leila Rupp, *Worlds of Women: The Making of an International Women's Movement* (Princeton, 1997).

8. Matthew Frye Jacobson, *Whiteness of a Different Color* (Cambridge, Mass., 1998); Leon F. Litwack, *Trouble in Mind: Black Southerners in the Age of Jim Crow* (New York, 1998).

9. An important new book on the cultural criticism of the postwar generation is Casey Nelson Blake's, *Beloved Community: The Cultural Criticism of Randolph Bourne, Van Wyck Brooks, Waldo Frank, and Lewis Mumford* (Chapel Hill, 1990). See also Malcolm Cowley's *Exile's Return* (New York, 1934) and *A Second Flowering* (New York, 1956). On the theme of "authenticity," see T. J. Jackson Lears, *No Place of Grace: Antimodernism and the Transformation of American Culture, 1880–1920* (New York, 1981); on "discontinuities" in modernity, see Anthony Giddens, *The Consequences of Modernity* (Stanford, 1990), pp. 3–7.

10. Dewey wrote these words in 1948 in the way of an introduction to a new edition of his *Reconstruction in Philosophy*, originally published in 1920. See John Dewey, *Reconstruction in Philosophy* (1920; Boston, 1957), p. vi.

11. Lewis Mumford, *The Condition of Man* (1944; New York, 1973), p. 14. Writing in a new "Preface" to the 1973 edition, Mumford began with the observation, "Since 'The Condition of Man' appeared in 1944, the condition of man has worsened. What were once only local demoralizations or disasters now threaten to turn into planetary calamities" (p. v). Like Dewey before him, Mumford makes it clear that the "condition" to which he is responding is not merely the product of wartime exigencies.

Bibliographical Essay

Henry Adams, in his imaginative autobiography, *The Education of Henry Adams*, made the offhand comment that with respect to cathedrals and other cultural forms "one sees what one brings." A master of the understatement, Adams's observation is as applicable to those who have written of the World's Columbian Exposition as it is to those who visited the fair in 1893. In a general sense, historians like visitors have tended to find in the Chicago world's fair what they were looking for. Or put another way, the vast literature on the Columbian Exposition can be read to reveal as much about the investigators as it does about the object of their investigation.

What follows is not a comprehensive bibliographical essay. Rather, its purpose is to suggest the secondary sources that have most influenced my understanding of the Columbian Exposition and its relationship to America's cultural landscape at the end of the nineteenth century. The chapter notes give a fuller accounting of the manuscript and archival sources I have consulted, as well as the wealth of newspaper, magazine, and other contemporary and more recent publications on the fair. For reasons of brevity I have not included subtitles in works referenced here. A statement regarding archival collections is included at the end of this essay.

My approach to "culture as conversation" has been shaped by R. W. B. Lewis's *The American Adam* (1955), a brief but essential work on nineteenth-century culture and the controversial notion of American exceptionalism. Readers will also note my interest in the history of American religious thought and expression. On the subject of American civil religion, and the place of religion in American life, the following are invaluable: Robert Bellah, *The Broken Covenant* (1975); Robert Bellah, et al., *Habits of the Heart*

(1985); Catherine Albanese, *Sons of the Father* (1976); Ernest L. Tuveson, *Redeemer Nation* (1968); and Ruth Bloch, *Visionary Republic* (1985). Leigh Eric Schmidt's *Holy Fairs* (1989) has important insights into popular religion in the eighteenth and nineteenth centuries.

On American exceptionalism and its critics, see Michael Kammen, "The Problem of American Exceptionalism: A Reconsideration," *American Quarterly* 45 (March 1993): 1–43; Ian Tyrrell, "American Exceptionalism in an Age of International History," *American Historical Review* 96 (October 1991): 912–19; Dorothy Ross, "Historical Consciousness in Nineteenth Century America," *American Historical Review* 89 (October 1984): 1031–55; and Byron E. Shafer, ed., *Is America Different?* (1991).

Michael Kammen's *Mystic Chords of Memory* (1991) is a magisterial interpretation of cultural history and tradition in the emergence of "modern America." I have also benefited from and been influenced by T. J. Jackson Lears' *No Place of Grace* (1981); Sacvan Bercovitch's *Rites of Assent* (1993); Peter Conn's *The Divided Mind* (1983); Robert M. Crunden's *Ministers of Reform* (1982); Alan Trachtenberg's *The Incorporation of America* (1982); and Robert C. Allen's *Horrible Prettyness* (1991). Works that provide an introduction to consumer culture and popular taste include John A. Kouwenhoven's *Made in America* (1962); Miles Orvell's *The Real Thing* (1989); and Thomas Schlereth's *Victorian America* (1991).

Kermit Vanderbil's *Charles Eliot Norton, Apostle of Culture in a Democracy* (1959); Russell Lynes's *Taste-Makers* (1954); and Russell B. Nye's *This Almost Chosen People* (1966) are important but often neglected studies of late-nineteenth-century culture and ideas. On social and cultural politics, see John L. Thomas, *Alternative America* (1983); Casey Nelson Blake, *Beloved Community* (1990); Alan Dawley, *Struggles for Justice* (1991); and Daniel Rodgers, *Atlantic Crossings* (1998). Matthew Frye Jacobson's *Barbarian Virtues* (2000) is an enchanting introduction to American attitudes toward foreign peoples.

Several important works emphasize a fundamental tension or bifurcation of values in modern American culture. In addition to Lears and Conn, see Lawrence W. Levine, *Highbrow/Lowbrow* (1988), and Joan Shelley Rubin, *The Making of Middlebrow Culture* (1991). Levine also wrote an important essay that appeared as "Progress and Nostalgia: The Self Image in the Nineteen Twenties," *The Unpredictable Past* (1993).

In a perceptive review essay entitled "Shaping America's Dreams in Chicago," *New York Times Book Review* (September 22, 1991), Alan Trachtenberg observed that the Columbian Exposition has carried a "freight of implication." A cottage industry of sorts flourishes around scholarly and popular interest in the Exposition, and the fair's one hundredth anniversary in 1892–93 accelerated an ongoing enthusiasm for the event. In its own time the Columbian Exposition generated an abundance of publications, and in the intervening years scholars have continued to look to the fair to chart the contours of a national society in the late nineteenth century.

In 1892–93, Christopher Columbus was extolled as an agent of progress, and the Columbian Exposition functioned as a benediction to four centuries of American progress. A century later one is more likely to hear terms of "invasion," "conquest," "hegemony," or "holocaust" in public assessments of the Columbian legacy, and these same issues have been associated with the Columbian Exposition. An excellent starting point for a consideration of the fair and its relationship to the Columbian legacy is Thomas J. Schlereth's "Columbia, Columbus, and Columbianism," *Journal of American History* 79 (December 1992): 951–68.

In the past three decades there have been three published monographs that provide a general overview of the Columbian Exposition. Resting entirely on secondary sources, each drew attention to the Exposition but neglected the extensive archival materials that bear on the subject. David Burg's *Chicago's White City of 1893* (1976) was the first published monograph that attempted to summarize the entirety of the Exposition in a thematic format. R. Reid Badger's *The Great American Fair* (1979) offers an interpretive analysis of its "institutional" character and the fair's "illusion of promise" for a society in transition. Robert Muccigrosso's *Celebrating the New World* (1993) is a general overview of the Exposition's multifaceted character. Also of note is Stanley Applebaum's *The Chicago World's Fair of 1893: A Photographic Record* (New York, 1980). The most useful bibliography of Exposition sources is David J. Bertuca, et al., eds., *The World's Columbian Exposition* (1996). Another useful, but now somewhat dated, reference work is John E. Findling, ed., *Historical Dictionary of World's Fairs and Expositions, 1851–1988* (1990).

Two important essays have served to redirect scholars' interest in world's fair studies and in the Columbian Exposition. In the title essay to *The Anthropology of World's Fairs* (1983), Burton Benedict presents an elaborate account of the development of turn-of-the-century international exhibitions, with special attention to San Francisco's 1915 Panama Pacific Exposition. Benedict points out the importance of fairs to the emergence of a "new middle class" of city dwellers increasingly disposed to new patterns of consumption and recreation. He concludes these new enterprises "serve[d] to rearrange status hierarchies and to validate the rise of a middle class." Neil Harris offers a complementary assessment in "The Great American Fairs and American Cities: The Role of Chicago's Columbian Exposition," in *Cultural Excursions: Market Appetites and Cultural Tastes in Modern America* (1990). By 1893, international exhibitions had evolved from images of the fair as a "warehouse" to the fair as an "extravaganza," from "instruments of exchange" to more elaborate festivals "tied to dreams of metropolitan expansion."

Shaped by prevailing notions of class and cultural conflict—the notion of a "contested terrain"—recent scholarship has provided a critical assessment of the Exposition's *dubious* legacy. The Chicago Historical Society's commemorative volume *Grand Illusions: Chicago's World's Fair of 1893* (1993) embraced the skepticism many scholars associated with the Columbian legacy and the 1893 world's fair. "The overall character of the World's Columbian Exposition," Wim de Wit declared in one of the volume's essays, "emerged out of attitudes of cultural inferiority with which Americans in general, and Chicagoans in particular, were struggling during the last quarter of the nineteenth century." Such harsh judgment tended to overshadow the complexity and diversity of the Exposition, and the manner in which it perhaps unwittingly reflected the cultural tendencies of the era. The overall tone of the volume also muted insightful essays by other contributors, among them James Gilbert, Robert Rydell, and Neil Harris.

Following a path laid down by Burton Benedict, and Alan Trachtenberg's influential *The Incorporation of America* (1982), Robert Rydell has been the most imaginative advocate of international expositions as instruments of class and cultural hegemony. "These events were triumphs of hegemony," Rydell wrote in *All the World's a Fair* (1984), "as well as symbolic edifices." "World's fairs performed a hegemonic function precisely because they propagated the ideas and values of the country's political, financial, corporate, and intellectual leaders and offered these ideas as the proper interpretation of social and political reality." Perhaps the most succinct expression of this analysis is found in Rydell's provocative essay "A Cultural Frankenstein? The Chicago World's Columbian Exposition of 1893," in *Grand Illusions* (1993). This argument is carried forward in Rydell's subsequent publications, including *World of Fairs: The Century-of-Progress Expositions* (1993), and Rydell, et al., *Fair America: World's Fairs in the United States* (2000). On marketing the Midway displays, see Curtis M. Hinsley, "The World as Marketplace: Commodification of the Exotic at the World's Columbian Exposition," in Ivan Karp and Steven D. Lavine, eds., *Exhibiting Cultures: The Poetics and Politics of Museum Display* (1991).

Ellen Litwicki's doctoral dissertation, "Visions of America: Public Holidays and American Cultures, 1776–1900" (1992), expands on this theme of public ceremonies as contested terrain among competing social groups. Although she devotes little attention to the Columbian Exposition per se, Litwicki's study raises discussions of hegemony to a more sophisticated level, with important implications for culture studies in general. See also Michael Robertson, "Cultural Hegemony Goes to the Fair," *American Studies* 33 (1992): 31–34. A useful critique of "cultural hegemony" as an analytical tool is found in Jackson Lears's "The Concept of Cultural Hegemony: Problems and Possibilities," *American Historical Review* 90 (June 1985): 567–93.

The Columbian Exposition has long been associated with the history of its host city. Numerous works have drawn a reflective eye to the relationship between Chicago and the fair, judging the latter as an expression of the former's spirit. James Gilbert's *Perfect Cities* (1991) offers an important discussion of the fair in relationship to other aspects of Chicago's civic culture in 1893. In this vein, Helen Lefkowitz Horowitz's *Culture and the City* (1976) provides an insightful assessment of cultural philanthropy in Chicago in the late nineteenth and early twentieth centuries. Kathleen D. McCarthy's *Noblesse Oblige* (1982) covers some of the same ground but takes a broader chronological perspective on charity and philanthropy in the city.

The study of Chicago's growth in the nineteenth century continues to captivate scholars. William Cronon, *Nature's Metropolis* (1991), and Donald Miller, *City of the Century* (1996), treat the fair within the larger context of Chicago's nineteenth-century development. Ross Miller's *American Apocalypse* (1990) is concerned with the 1871 Great Fire but draws a parallel to the fair in the city's rebuilding efforts. On the social scene in Chicago between Fire and Fair, see Carl Smith, *Urban Disorder and the Shape of Belief* (1995). Susan E. Hirsch and Robert I. Goler's *A City Comes of Age* (1990) is an attractively illustrated overview of Chicago in the 1890s.

Indispensable older studies of Chicago include Harold W. Mayer and Richard C. Wade's *Chicago, Growth of the Metropolis* (1973) and Perry Duis's *Chicago, Creating a Tradition* (1976). Hugh Danziel Duncan's *Culture and Democracy* (1965) provides an important Midwest perspective on Chicago's cultural development. From the perspective of the so-called Chicago Renaissance in literature and culture, see Carl Smith, *Chicago and the American Literary Imagination, 1880–1920* (1984), and Bernard Duffey, *The Chicago Renaissance in American Letters* (1972).

Urban historians have associated the 1893 fair with a wave of municipal planning and reform summed up in the City Beautiful Movement. Perhaps the most succinct study of the fair as a model city is Thomas Hines's *Burnham of Chicago, Architect and Planner* (1979), which treats the fair as instrumental to Burnham's career as an urban planner. Two other studies of urban planning that bear on the Exposition's cultural importance are William H. Wilson's *The City Beautiful Movement* (1989) and David Schuyler's *The New Urban Landscape* (1987). Still valuable for its insights on landscape architecture is Norman T. Newton's *The Design of the Land* (1971). Witold Rybczynski's biography of Frederick Law Olmsted, *A Clearing in the Distance* (1999), which appeared as this study was being completed, offers important insights into the Exposition's relationship to other commissions late in Olmsted's career. Rybczynski's work provides an important complement to Laura Wood Roper's older biography of Olmsted, *FLO* (1973).

There is a wealth of source material on the architectural character and controversy of the Exposition plan. Inevitably, this discussion revolves around Louis Sullivan and his modernist attack on the fair's Beaux Arts design. Sullivan's critique is found in two separate tomes: *Kindergarten Chats* (1918) and *Autobiography of an Idea* (c.1924). Virtually every popular periodical of note published some commentary on Exposition architecture before or during the season, and these publications reflect important impressions from the period. Perhaps most important are Henry Van Brunt's commentaries in *Century Magazine* (1892) and the *Atlantic Monthly* (1893), and Montgomery Schuyler's "Last Words About the World's Fair," which originally appeared in *Architectural Record* (1894). Carl Condit's *The Chicago School of Architecture* (1975) remains the classic study of Chicago's contribution to modern architecture and its contrast with the Exposition. The reaction of foreign visitors to Loop commercial architecture and to the Exposition they came to see is chronicled in Arnold Lewis, *An Early Encounter with Tomorrow* (1997).

Several doctoral dissertations assess the significance of the fair's design plan: David H. Crook, "Louis Sullivan, the World's Columbian Exposition, and American Life" (1963) is especially good; Titus M. Karlowicz, "The Architecture of the World's Columbian Exposition" (1965); Maurice F. Neufeld, "The Contribution of the World's Columbian Exposition of 1893 to the Idea of a Planned Society in the United States" (1935).

Important critiques of Sullivan's involvement are found in Robert Twombley, *Louis Sullivan* (1986), and especially David S. Andrew's insightful *Louis Sullivan and the Polemics of Modern Architecture* (1985). As previously mentioned, Thomas Hines's *Burnham of Chicago* (1979) contains several excellent chapters on the fair's architecture. See also Donald Hoffman, *The Architecture of John Wellborn Root* (1973), and Paul Baker, *Richard Morris Hunt* (1980).

Sigfried Giedion's, *Space, Time and Architecture* (1941) and *Mechanization Takes Command* (1948) are essential reading on the rise of modern forms and structures, as is William H. Jordy's *American Buildings and Their Architects* (1972) for architectural trends in the late nineteenth century. Among Lewis Mumford's voluminous library of cultural studies, *The Brown Decades* (1971) and *Sticks and Stones* (1955) provide useful commentaries on Gilded Age architectural trends. Readers should also take note of Wim de Wit's critical appraisal in "Building and Illusion," in *Grand Illusions* (1993). Also of note regarding architecture and decorative arts is Richard Guy Wilson, et al., *The American Renaissance, 1876–1917* (1979).

Interest in the Exposition as a public ceremony has been strengthened by investigations into the construction of memory and acts of commemoration. John Bodnar's *Remaking America* (1992) is an excellent study of public memory and national identity. A more recent and in some respects companion volume that assesses memory and civic rituals of patriotism is Cecilia Elizabeth O'Leary's *To Die For* (1999). Michael Frisch's "American History and the Structures of Memory," *Journal of American History* 75 (March 1989): 1130–55 provides a perceptive commentary on history and memory, as do the other essays in the journal's special edition volume devoted to "Memory and American History." On ritual, memory, and tradition, see Michael Kammen, *The Mystic Chords of Memory* (1991), and David Glassberg, *American Historical Pageantry* (1990). Although it appeared after this study went to press, David Blight's deeply nuanced narrative of memory and the American Civil War, *Race and Reunion* (2001), assesses in helpful ways the state of "memory studies."

More attention has been paid to the relationship of African Americans to the Columbian Exposition than to any other social group. Ida Wells's influential pamphlet, *The Reason Why the Colored American Is Not in the Columbian Exposition* (1893), has survived as an important critique of the marginalization of black Americans in the fair and the larger culture. For a recent edition with commentary, see Robert Rydell, ed., *The Reason Why the Colored American Is Not in the Columbian Exposition* (1999). Rydell presents a provocative overview of racial practices in "A Cultural Frankenstein?" in *Grand Illusions* (1993). Elliott Rudwick and August Meier's "Black Man in the 'White City': Negroes and the Columbian Exposition, 1893," *Phylon* 26 (1965): 354–61 rekindled interest in the issue of race in the Exposition program. The most comprehensive study of African and African-American participation in the Exposition is Christopher Robert Reid's *"All the World Is Here!"* (2000). Anna R. Paddon and Sally Turner's "African Americans and the Columbian Exposition," *Illinois Historical Journal* 88 (1995): 19–36 provides a more limited discussion of the issue; a more impressionistic account is found in Barbara J. Ballard's "A People Without a Nation," *Chicago History* (Summer 1999): 27–43.

Although the role of women in the Exposition program has received notice, there is still much room for interpreting the clash of ideals in the Congress of Representative Women and its ancillary sessions. More an encyclopedic effort than an interpretive assessment, Jeanne Madeline Weimann's *Fair Women* (1981) is the most complete account of the involvement of women in the enterprise. A brief synopsis of the larger study is found in Jeanne Madeline Weimann's "A Temple to Women's Genius: The Women's Building, 1893," *Chicago History* (Summer 1977). Doctoral dissertations by Virginia Grant Darney and Mary Frances Cordato have built a stronger analytical framework around the issues Weimann defined. See Mary Frances Cordato, "Representing the Expansion of Women's Sphere: Women's Work and Culture at the World's Fairs of 1876, 1893, and 1904" (1989), and Virginia Grant Darney, "Women and World's Fairs: American International Expositions, 1876–1904" (1982). On the international dimensions of women's culture see Leila J. Rupp, *Worlds of Women* (1997). Ian Tyrrell emphasizes the influence of evangelical Protestantism on the international women's movement in *Women's World, Women's Empire* (1991). Nancy Cott's *The Grounding of Modern Feminism* (1987) offers an informed consideration of the changing ideology behind women's political and social activism. Anne Firor Scott's *Natural Allies* (1991) is good on the growth of women's voluntary associations. Though it does not directly address the Exposition, Joanne J. Meyerowitz's *Women Adrift* (1988) has important things to say about single wage-earning women in turn-of-the-century Chicago.

There are several useful studies of photography at the World's Columbian Exposition. James Gilbert's "Fixing the Image: Photography at the World's Columbian Exposition," in *Grand Illusions* (1993) provides an interpretive overview of C. D. Arnold's work in relation to controlling the public representation of the experience. See also Julie K. Brown, *Contesting Images: Photography and the World's Columbian Exposition* (1994). On the relationship between the Exposition, urban culture, and the rise of professional photography in the nineteenth century, see Peter Hales, *Silver Cities* (1984). In this context, see Miles Orvell, *The Real Thing* (1989).

The reform congresses sponsored by the World Congress Auxiliary deserve greater attention. Precious little has been written on the wealth of social, political, and economic perspectives offered through the thousands of sessions during the Exposition season. If any aspect of the Exposition deserves greater scrutiny it is the World's Congress Auxiliary and its relationship to cultural attitudes at the turn of the century. Of all the meetings, only the World's Parliament of Religions has remained of interest to scholars. For a valuable, but not comprehensive, overview of the Parliament and its relationship to religious circles, see Richard Hughes Seager, *The World's Parliament of Religions* (1993). On Catholicism and the Americanist controversy, see Gerald Fogarty, *The Vatican and the Americanist Crisis* (1974). Other works that establish a context for discussing religion include Martin E. Marty, *Modern American Religion* (1986), which deals chiefly with Protestant denominationalism; George Marsden, *Understanding Fundamentalism and Evangelicalism* (1991); and T. J. Jackson Lears, *No Place of Grace* (1981).

Manuscript Sources

Daniel H. Burnham Papers. Daniel H. Burnham Library. Art Institute of Chicago. Burnham's private and official correspondence for the period 1890–94 are found in twenty-one bound copybooks that cover the longer period of 1890–1912. Burnham's own "Final Report of the Director of Works of the World's Columbian Exposition" (8 folio volumes), now available on microfilm, is invaluable. A third division of the collection is the six-part "Materials by and about Daniel Burnham"; parts three and four pertain to his Exposition work. There are also unpublished manuscripts and notes from interviews (perhaps belonging to biographer Charles Moore) and other ephemera. A multivolume scrapbook contains clippings of newspaper and magazine articles, artists' sketches, and so forth. The Art Institute also possesses C. D. Arnold's glass plate negatives of views of the buildings and grounds. Finally, an unpublished "Copybook of Letters of McKim, Mead, and White" chronicles the firm's relationship with Burnham and the other principals.

World's Columbian Exposition Collection. Chicago Historical Society. The Chicago Historical Society has the most extensive collection of published and unpublished materials on the Columbian Exposition. The society also has a voluminous photographic collection, as well as other Exposition ephemera. The two-volume set entitled "Minutes of the Board of Directors, World's Columbian Exposition of 1893" covers the years 1890–95. A companion to these records are the several folders entitled "Minutes of the Executive Committee, World's Columbian Exposition of 1893." On the role of women, see the multivolume "Minutes of the Board of Lady Managers, World's Columbian Exposition, November 24, 1890–October 31, 1893." Equally important for the years 1890–94 is the nine-volume "Official Correspondence of Bertha Palmer." The society's archives contain a complete original set of the *Daily Columbian* newspaper.

World's Columbian Exposition Collection. Special Collections Division. Chicago Public Library. The Library's collection is divided into several parts and sheds light on various aspects of the Exposition. Chief among its holdings are the Papers of James Ellsworth. Ellsworth was the Chicago banker, industrialist, and art collector who served on the Exposition's Board of Directors. His papers contain private and official correspondence beginning in 1889 and four volumes of miscellaneous materials related to the Exposition. Notes, programs, corporate records, and in some instances copies of rules and regulations for the exhibiting departments are contained therein. Portions of Daniel Burnham's "Final Report" and George Wilson's "Final Report of the Department of Music" are found in the Ellsworth Papers.

The Library's Pamphlet File contains over one hundred pamphlets, brochures, clippings, and announcements about Exposition events. The five-volume "World's Congress Auxiliary Organization" contains a near-complete set of programs and schedules for the summer congresses.

Frederick Law Olmsted Papers. Library of Congress. The Olmsted Papers, now available on microfilm, details the involvement of FLO & Co. in the Exposition. The entire collection consists of seventy-three containers (sixty reels of microfilm) covering the years 1777–1928. Containers 23 and 24 (reels 21–23) contain the private and official correspondence of Olmsted, Henry Sargent Codman, and Frederick Law Olmsted, Jr. that are pertinent to the world's fair. Containers 68–71 (reels 57–59) contain notes, reports, and printed matter bearing on the landscape design. The Olmsted-Codman correspondence is a natural complement to the letters in the Burnham Papers at the Art Institute. Between the two collections a full picture of the artistic and personal relationship can be deciphered. Also contained in the Olmsted Papers are the several auditor reports and the "Official Minutes of the World's Columbian Commission" (1890).

William James Onahan Papers. Archives of the University of Notre Dame. For students of American Catholicism, the Onahan Papers are invaluable. The collection contains nineteen boxes of materials pertaining to the

World's Parliament of Religions and the Columbian Catholic Congress. Onahan's private and official correspondence for the years 1889–93 are supplemented by programs and announcements, magazine and newspaper clippings, and copies of most of the presentations to the Catholic Congress. Also found in the Onahan collection is the unpublished dissertation by Sister M. Sevina Pahorezki, O.S.F., "The Social and Political Activities of William James Onahan" (1942). Related materials can be found in the Papers of Daniel Hudson, editor of the Catholic magazine *Ave Maria*.

Index

About the Author

DENNIS B. DOWNEY is Professor of History at Millersville University. The author of two books and more than two dozen articles, Downey is a specialist in American social and cultural history in the period 1870–1930.